DAVIS H. WAITE

The Ideology of a Western Populist

John R. Morris

UNIVERSITY
PRESS OF
AMERICA

Library of Congress Catalog Card Number: 82-40106

To

the memory

of my mother and my father

TABLE OF CONTENTS

PREFACE

In recent years, a number of new books on Populism have appeared, including state histories, ideological studies, biographies, and a new general history. These have added to our knowledge of Populism as well as further seeking to clarify and define what Populism was. Few, if any, however, have been in-depth ideological studies of a particular Populist leader. This book attempts that chore, insofar as the research materials available allowed.

In Populist history, Davis H. Waite has remained relatively obscure, and in Colorado history, as governor, his image has been negative. He has deserved neither fate.

Waite was a social pioneer of his time, a courageous fighter for the rights of the people against powerful private interests, one of the best friends labor has ever had in any state governor's office, and a more genuine Western hero than the outlaw types and the lucky strike-it-rich millionaire types who have figured all too prominently in presentations of Western and Colorado history.

While I have been helped and influenced by many people, I would especially like to acknowledge my debt to the following: Mr. Walter Gerash, with whom I had the earliest discussions about Waite; Dr. Norman Pollack, whose writings especially enabled me to clarify my thoughts about Populism; Dr. Philip S. Foner, whose writings on labor Populism and the evolution of Populist Party politics I found quite helpful; Dr. Hal Bridges, Dr. Robert Athearn, and Dr. Carl Ubbelohde, for their aid at the dissertation level; the late Mr. Wayne Mueller, Mr. Eugene Deikman, Dr. Herbert Aptheker, Dr. Pollack, and Mr. Gerash, for making suggestions and for encouraging me to publish; the staffs, at the time of my research, at the Colorado State Archives, the Colorado State Historical Society, the Western Collections division of the Denver Public Library, and the University of Colorado library; Mrs. Frank Waite, daughter-in-law of Governor Waite, with whom I had helpful visits; the late Dr. John E. Eggleton, for introducing me to University Press; Mr. James Lyon and Ms. Helen Hudson of University Press, for their continual help; and Mrs. Elsie Shirley and Ms. Jennella Crouch, for their typing of the manuscript.

I would also like to pay special tribute to the following: Miss Letitia A. Brace and the late Mrs. Beatrice Thompson, teachers especially responsible for my early intellectual development and stimulation; Dr. Jeremiah Stamler, who encouraged me in the right direction at a difficult period; Mr. Anthony Ellis, from whom I learned much about the Black experience; and Dr. Hal Bridges, from whose lectures and seminars, especially in social and intellectual history, I received much knowledge and inspiration.

My thanks are also due to my wife and to my late parents. My father, the Reverend Leon E. Morris, took his Christian social ethics seriously and was more of a latter day Populist than he realized.

John R. Morris

Portales, New Mexico
January 6, 1982

DAVIS H. WAITE

CHAPTER I

THE POPULIST PARTY

Populism is a term that has acquired such a broad meaning in recent times as to render it almost meaningless. To some writers, populism has become practically synonymous with agrarianism. Politicians with widely differing views who pose as champions of the people against special privilege have been called populistic. In this study, however, the term populism will refer to the new political party movement, the Populist or Peoples' Party of the eighteen-nineties in the United States.

Born in Cincinnati in May, 1891, the Populist Party achieved its greatest success at the polls in 1892 and 1894. Its presidential candidate in 1892, James B. Weaver, polled over one million votes and gained twenty-two electoral votes, winning in Colorado, Kansas, Idaho and Nevada. In the congressional election year of 1894, the Populists increased their vote to nearly a million and a half. In both 1892 and 1894, the Populists elected several men to Congress and filled hundreds of state and local offices. The Populists fused with the Democrats in support of William Jennings Bryan for President in 1896. From this fusion the Populist Party never recovered its independent political identity. Die-hard elements continued to hold national Populist Party conventions and nominate presidential candidates through the election of 1908.

The drama of Populism unfolded in the turbulent decade of the nineties which may have been gay to some, but were troubled and tragic times to many others. In the three decades since the Civil War, industrial capitalism had emerged fully triumphant and grown to maturity. The industrialist and financier were firmly in the saddle. With far more similarities than differences, the Republicans and Democrats were both clearly under big business dominance. The embattled farmer, especially in the Midwest and the South, and the growing labor force of the cities both began to organize in these decades to defend their interests. The Grange, the Greenbackers, the Northern, Southern and Colored Alliances, the Knights of Labor, the American Federation of Labor, the Western Federation of Miners, the United Mine Workers and the Socialist Labor Party were some of the results.

Industrial strife became especially bitter in the nineties, fostered by the worst depression of the century during the middle years of the decade. The bottom completely dropped out of the silver mining industry upon which the prosperity of the Rocky Mountain West rested.

Proponents of money and land panaceas or more radical socialist and anarchist solutions became more numerous.

The Populist movement was in a very real sense the culmination and a fusion of many of these earlier developments during the previous quarter of a century.

The platform of the 1892 national Populist nominating convention at Omaha is considered the most representative statement of Populist Party principles. This document will be referred to throughout this work as the Omaha Platform. The preamble, radical in tone throughout, spoke of "a nation brought to the verge of moral, political and material ruin." Corruption dominated the voting process and the legislative chamber. Business was "prostrate" and labor "impoverished." "The fruits of the toil of millions are boldly stolen to build up colossal fortunes for a few, unprecedented in the history of mankind; and the possessors of these, in turn, despise the republic and endanger liberty." The press was said to be controlled by these same few. American society was fast dividing into two classes: "tramps and millionaires." A vast money conspiracy was thought to have been organized on two continents. The two major political parties, the Republicans and the Democrats, struggled "for power and plunder," while neglecting the needs of the people, the preamble continued.

The proposed remedies were actually much less radical than the tone of the preamble. The major planks of the platform dealt with money, transportation, and land. In the money plank, the platform called for a government-issued national currency to be distributed directly to the people without the use of private banks; free and unlimited coinage of silver; a graduated income tax; governmental economy; and a system of postal savings banks. The transportation plank advocated public ownership of the railroads, the telegraph, and the telephone. The land plank rested on the principle of land use by the actual

2

settler. Land "should not be monopolized for speculative purposes." The government should reclaim all
land held by aliens and excessive land held by the
railroads and other corporations beyond their needs.

A series of ten resolutions concluded the platform. Several of these appealed directly to labor: a
shorter work day, enforcement of the eight-hour day in
government work, condemnation of the Pinkerton system
of private armies of hired mercenaries employed by
corporations, condemnation of the contract labor system, "further restriction on undesirable immigration,"
and sympathy with a clothing industry strike led by
the Knights of Labor. The resolutions called for
several political reforms designed to return political
power more closely to the people — the Australian
ballot, the initiative and the referendum, direct election of U. S. Senators, and one term for the offices
of President and Vice-President of the United States.
The resolutions also voiced opposition to "any subsidy
or national aid to any private corporation — for any
purpose."

The Populist movement consisted of four main
elements: agrarian, silver, labor, and middle-class
social reformers. Heirs of the agrarian protest tradition of the Grangers, Greenbackers, and Farmers'
Alliances, the Populists had a strong base in the
Great Plains and the southern states. Much of the
Omaha Platform was similar to the platforms of the
Farmers' Alliances.[1] However, the Populist Party was
a complex movement composed of many diverse elements.
These included members of the Knights of Labor, Alli-
ancemen, silverites of the Rocky Mountain West,
Single-Taxers, Grangers, Greenbackers, members of
local trade union assemblies and state labor federa-
tions, socialists of various types, and individual
reformers interested in woman suffrage, prohibition,
and other political and social reforms.

The Populist Party did not produce any dominant
leader. Rather, there were a number of spokesmen with
varying backgrounds, personalities and ideas. These
spokesmen were mainly from white-collar, "middle-class"
backgrounds, especially law, politics, and journalism.
Few, if any, were actual farmers or laborers.

Populism has become identified with eccentricism
in the eyes of some because of the colorful nicknames
and individual traits of some of its leaders but, in
the main, the leadership was distinguished chiefly by

3

a deep concern over the future of American society and a belief that a program of reform was needed to remedy the deficiencies and to meet the challenges of that society.

Among the known Populist names were James B. Weaver of Iowa and James G. Field of Virginia, Populist presidential and vice-presidential standard bearers in 1892; Ignatius Donnelly of Minnesota, who had been associated with the Grange, Greenbackers, and the Alliance, and who authored books on Atlantis, on the Shakespeare-Bacon controversy, and a utopian horror fantasy on the degradation of American civilization entitled Caesar's Column, which was a kind of precursor of Jack London's The Iron Heel on a fascist America; Henry Demarest Lloyd of Illinois, a leading spokesman of urban Populism and author of Wealth Against Commonwealth, a muckraking expose of the Standard Oil trust; fiery women orators from Kansas, Annie L. Diggs and Mary Elizabeth Lease, who urged the farmers to raise less corn and more hell; Texas Populist leader James H. "Cyclone" Davis; Eugene V. Debs, organizer of the American Railway Union and future Socialist Party leader; the famous lawyer and defender of the underdog, Clarence Darrow; Jacob Coxey of Ohio, leader of Coxey's march of the unemployed to Washington during the depression of the nineties; Governors Lorenzo D. Lewelling of Kansas and Davis H. "Bloody Bridles" Waite of Colorado; Congressman "Sockless" Jerry Simpson of Kansas; agrarian Great Plains Senators William A. Peffer of Kansas, James H. Kyle of South Dakota, and William V. Allen of Nebraska; millionaire silverite Senators from Nevada, William M. Stewart and John P. Jones, whose only real association with the Populists was on the silver issue; leader of the Southern Populists, who worked courageously for racial cooperation, Congressman Tom Watson of Georgia; Herman E. Taubeneck of Illinois, national chairman of the Populist Party and a spokesman for the more moderate, silver-oriented Populists in the mid-nineties; George F. Washburn of Massachusetts, eastern division chairman of the Populist Party; W. S. Morgan, author, journalist, and an organizer of the Arkansas Wheel, which later affiliated with the Southern Alliance; Robert Schilling of Wisconsin; Leonidas L. Polk and Marion Butler of North Carolina; M. C. Rankin of Indiana; and Paul Van Dervoort of Nebraska. Other Populist Congressmen included Lafe Pence and John C. Bell of Colorado, O. M. Kern and W. A. McKeighan of Nebraska, H. E. Boen of Minnesota, and John Davis, William Baker, T. J. Hudson, and W. A. Harris of Kansas.

4

The present work is an ideological study of one of these Populist spokesmen, Davis H. Waite, the Populist governor of Colorado. Waite was one of the most colorful and controversial Populist figures. His name is connected with three of the most dramatic episodes in Colorado history: the Mexican silver dollar plan, the Cripple Creek strike of 1894, and the Denver City Hall War. Nationally, he achieved a reputation as one of the leading radical reformers among the Populists. Similar to Franklin D. Roosevelt, he had an intense group of followers who almost worshipped him, while, on the other hand, there were those who saw him as a dangerous threat to law and order. Part of this sharply divided attitude towards Waite was no doubt due to the crisis situations which confronted him while governor.

CHAPTER II

THE LIFE AND CAREER OF DAVIS H. WAITE

At an age when most modern citizens of the United States are retired and collecting social security, Davis H. Waite emerged from obscurity as a mining town newspaper editor to become the Populist governor of Colorado and a controversial national figure. Before coming to Colorado, Waite, a native New Yorker, spent a long career pursuing several occupations and jumping from state to state as though the United States were a giant chessboard on which he hoped to make the right moves to achieve his version of the "American dream." Twice in pursuit of his dream he obeyed Horace Greeley's famous dictum to go West; once, like the busted Pike's Peakers, he went the other way. Indeed, Waite seemed to personify what Thomas Wolfe later described as the wanderer on the lonely earth, driven onward in an endless quest of what he may have only faintly understood.

Born in Jamestown, New York, on April 9, 1825, Waite was a "representative of Pilgrim stock touching English Commonwealth days and those of Colonial and Revolutionary fervor."[1] In 1660, the Waite family ancestry, three sturdy Welsh brothers, landed on New England shores. Davis Waite was a descendent of Joseph Waite, the brother who eventually settled in New York. He was educated in the Jamestown, New York public schools and studied law in his father's office. He was five feet, ten inches in height, and of light complexion. In his later years as governor, he wore a well-developed white beard which matched his white head of hair. Firm but kindly gray eyes peered through his frameless spectacles.

His appearance, beliefs, and utterances earned him such appellations as "Old Hickory," "Andrew Jackson of the West," the "Rocky Mountain Eagle," and "Abraham Lincoln of the Rockies," and the famous "Bloody Bridles."

He was married twice. His first wife was Frances Russell, by whom he had four children: John, Arthur, Belle, and May Josephine. Frances Russell Waite died in 1880, and in 1885 he married Celia Crane Maltby, a cousin of his first wife. Celia Waite bore him one child, Frank.

In the years following his legal studies he practiced law, took up newspaper work, and entered the
mercantile business. Politically, in these early
years Waite considered himself a Jeffersonian-Jacksonian Democrat, and he cast his first vote for the Democratic Party. Ideologically, he was to think of himself as a Jeffersonian-Jacksonian all his life. He
early manifested political independence when he voted
for Martin Van Buren for President on the Free Soil
ticket of 1848.

In 1850, Waite moved to Wisconsin and engaged in
the mercantile business in Fond du Lac. He voted for
Franklin Pierce, the Democratic candidate for President, in 1852, but, like James B. Weaver of Iowa and
Ignatius Donnelly of Minnesota, he early joined the
new Republican Party. Waite won election to the Wisconsin state legislature in 1856 as a Republican
representing Marquette County. He served one term.
In 1856, Waite cast his vote for the first Republican
Presidential candidate, John C. Fremont. Moving to
Missouri in 1857, he taught in a small high school
near St. Louis. With the outbreak of the Civil War
he was forced to resign because of his anti-slavery
sympathies. In the crucial 1860 election, he voted
for Stephen Douglas because there was no Lincoln ticket in Missouri. Each Presidential election thereafter
from 1864 until 1892, he voted for the Republican nominee except in 1876, when he was ineligible to vote
because of residency requirements.

In 1861 Waite returned East to become principal
of Warren High School in Warren, Pennsylvania, but
soon left this position to return to Jamestown and
practice law. Newspaper endeavors engaged his attention again, and he edited the Chautauqua Democrat, a
Republican paper, and became the proprietor of the
Jamestown Journal. After fifteen years in the East,
he again looked westward, moving in 1876 to Larned,
Kansas, where he took up ranching and then entered
law practice. His health was a factor in his westward
moves. In 1878 he was elected to the Kansas state
legislature for one term on the Republican ticket.[2]

In 1879, the silver boom lured Waite to Leadville,
Colorado, where he prospected and practiced law for
two years. He then followed the silver boom across
the Continental Divide to Aspen where he lived the
last twenty years of his life except for the two years
while he was governor. In Aspen, he again practiced
law while prospecting, but soon entered other fields

8

of endeavor as well. He served as a justice of the peace and became the first superintendent of schools for Pitkin County. Waite also was associated with both the Aspen Times and the Aspen Chronicle in an editorial capacity during the eighties.

In 1891, Waite launched the Aspen Union Era, a weekly newspaper which championed reform and Populist ideas. He served as co-editor with George C. Rohde from August, 1891 to March, 1892; from March to August, 1892, he was sole editor. It was this role that helped him to become known to the statewide forces which formed the Populist movement in Colorado.

Davis H. Waite was elected the governor of Colorado on the Populist ticket in 1892. He served one term of two years. His program and actions established him as probably the most militant reform-minded governor in the history of Colorado. In 1894, he was defeated in his bid for re-election.

Waite did not abandon the political wars following his defeat. During the next four years, the former governor made several national lecture tours espousing the cause of Populism. He also engaged in two short-lived publishing attempts, Our Nation's Crisis and Waite's Magazine. Both were political magazines. Waite fought against the Populist forces favoring fusion with the Democrats on the basis of the single issue of silver. In 1896, he supported the Bryan-Watson ticket, believing it to be a true reform ticket. During this election, he also ran as a "middle-of-the-road" Populist gubernatorial candidate. Many ardent supporters urged him to withdraw from the hopeless race in favor of Bert L. Bailey, the Populist fusionist candidate.[3] Waite stayed in, and received a very small vote.

In 1897, he continued his lecture tours and with the first (and apparently the last) publication of Waite's Magazine in October, 1898, his public activities apparently came to an end. He became ill and died of paralysis while preparing Thanksgiving dinner at his home in Aspen, on November 27, 1901.[4]

CHAPTER III

POPULISM IN COLORADO: THE WAITE ADMINISTRATION

Reformist and third-party activity in Colorado did not begin with the Populists in 1892. In the seventies, the Greenbackers became the first minor party on the ballot in Colorado, and had state tickets for four consecutive elections from 1878 through 1884. The hotbed of Colorado Greenbackism was Boulder County where the Greenbackers polled twenty-five per cent of the vote in 1877. In the Boulder municipal elections a year later, the Greenbackers elected most of their ticket with the aid of temperance elements. In 1882 the Prohibition Party first appeared on the ballot in Colorado.[1] The Farmers' Alliance was organized in 1885 and numbered five thousand by 1890. The Knights of Labor was quite active in the eighties and early nineties, especially in Denver and the mining towns.[2] Reform-minded third parties were active in the elections of 1886, 1888, and 1890. The Union Labor Party was organized in 1888.[3]

In 1890, an Independent Party composed of Alliance and Union Labor Party elements was formed in Denver. It held a state convention attended by delegates from twenty-five counties. State and congressional tickets were nominated and a platform was developed. The party polled only five thousand votes.[4] In the off-year local elections of 1891 the Alliance ticket was victorious in four counties and made good showings in others.[5]

Though Waite had previous experience with political innovations, he apparently developed new reformist tendencies in Aspen, and altered certain Republican ideas such as his belief in a protective tariff. He joined the Knights of Labor, which was strong in Aspen in the late eighties and early nineties. This group probably influenced Waite greatly. He served as secretary of the local assembly of the Knights, which met every Friday.[6] He also joined the Workingmen's Party which was formed in Aspen in 1887. This party entered its own candidate for some offices in the local election in the spring of 1888. Workingmen's-Democratic coalition candidates won the races for city treasurer and third ward alderman. Two hundred out of fourteen hundred votes for mayor went to the labor party candidate.[7]

11

A Populist Party organization was formed in
Denver in September, 1891. In the same month, a convention of Pitkin County Populists elected Waite
chairman of the Pitkin County Central Committee and
chose him as one of its four delegates to the Populist
state convention.[8] Waite also became a member of the
state central committee of the Colorado Populist
Party.[9] In November, 1891, the elections yielded no
victories for the Populists.[10] Yet there were some
encouraging signs; in Pitkin County the new party
drew 481 votes.[11]

Waite was a delegate to both the St. Louis reform
convention of February 22, 1892 and the national nominating convention of the Populist Party in Omaha,
on July 4, 1892. From the latter convention came the
famous Omaha Platform to which Waite constantly referred thereafter as the basis of his beliefs. He
was instrumental in getting the silver plank written
into the platform at the St. Louis convention, and he
also assisted in developing the Omaha Platform.[12]

The Populist Party of Colorado, meeting the last
week of July, 1892 in Pueblo, agreed to support the
Omaha Platform, and nominated a complete slate of
state and congressional candidates. The party was a
combination of agricultural, silver, labor, and middle-
class reform elements. However, the silver issue was
dominant and was the chief reason for the success of
the Colorado Populists in 1892. A state silver league
had been formed, based on local silver clubs which
were organized in every county in the state, beginning
with Aspen in Pitkin County.[13] The league's goal was
to unite all parties on the silver issue. Both Republicans and Democrats at their national conventions
failed to nominate candidates or to write a silver
plank satisfactory to the silver interests. The
Colorado State Silver League, meeting in convention
at the same time as the Populist Party, endorsed the
entire state Populist slate by a margin of nearly
three to one.[14]

On September 12, 1892, the state Democratic
Convention met in Pueblo and endorsed the national
Populist ticket of James B. Weaver and James G. Field.
It did not nominate a state ticket, leaving individual
Democrats free to support the state Populist ticket.[15]
The Democratic Convention adopted an address to the
people of Colorado, which was based entirely on the
silver theme and which blamed all social ills on the
lack of free coinage. A small faction bolted the

Democratic Convention, nominated a state Democratic ticket, and agreed to support Grover Cleveland for President.[16]

Waite was chosen by the Populists to run for governor. He was opposed for the nomination by Julius Thompson of Rico who was considered a moderate, recently converted from the Republican Party.[17] Waite won the nomination over Thompson by a vote of 174½ to 144½.[18] His running mate was D. H. Nichols of Boulder. Referring to the Populist nominations, the Denver Republican said: "The ticket is a weak one and will secure no recognition outside of the purely People's Party ranks. The candidates are of the calamity howler order and fitted to follow the Weaver obsequies."[19]

The Rocky Mountain News, edited by the influential veteran Democrat turned Populist, Thomas M. Patterson, favored the Populist national ticket and the entire state ticket except Waite. It termed the Waite nomination a disappointment, and said, "The nomination is considered particularly weak and it is fairly probable the large contingent of bolters will now go ahead and hoist the name of Julius Thompson of Rico as gubernatorial candidate who will lead the silver forces on to an inning at the November election." The News further commented: "The office (of governor) is one that requires dignity, self-restraint, wisdom, business tact, and force of character in the occupant. Mr. Waite does not possess these qualities in such combination as to make him a safe governor of the state should he be elected. For these reasons the News cannot support him, and it says so frankly and pointedly at the outset, that no man rest in doubt as to its opinions."[20]

Yet in October, the News changed its mind about Waite, supporting him for governor and predicting his triumph. It editorialized: "No speaker in Colorado has shown more comprehensive knowledge of the dangerous drift of public affairs, because of the domination of wealth unjustly bolstered by class legislation, and none have evinced higher powers of analysis and more incisive logic in exposing the iniquitous conditions that are perverting our industrial system and in pointing out the way to relief."[21]

Waite waged a vigorous statewide campaign, visiting forty-nine out of fifty-six counties.[22] Many did not take Waite's campaign seriously until near elec-

tion time. Typical were the comments of the Trinidad
Chronicle and the Fort Collins Courier. The Chronicle
said the Populists were really the old Greenbackers
whose following had dwindled to the "farmers' alliance
contingent." The Courier cautioned the Democrats
about joining the Populists, since the latter would
"shortly explode."[23]

In winning the governor's race, Waite received
over forty-four thousand votes and a five-thousand
vote majority. He felt that his vote was composed of
five thousand genuine Populist votes, twenty-six
thousand Democrats who supported the Populists and
thirteen thousand Republicans who did the same. The
majority of the vote represented concern over silver
and not the Omaha Platform, according to Waite.[24] He
contended that, "though elected by over five thousand
majority, he had no political organization at his
back." He commented that "he was elected by the non-
partisan action of the state silver league, which
endorsed his nomination after he had been nominated by
the People's Party state convention, and also by his
thorough and judicious canvass of the state, more complete than had ever been made in Colorado up to that
time."[25] Along with many others, Waite remarked that
the opposition had underestimated the Populist strength
until it was too late. The governor thought that the
Republicans had depended on the "usual election frauds"
in Arapahoe, El Paso, and Pueblo Counties to see them
through.[26]

The party composition of the Colorado state
legislature from 1893-1895 (Ninth General Assembly)
was as follows:[27]

	Republicans	Democrats	Populists	Total
Senate	15	8	12	35
House	33	5	27	65

The House was thus under clear Republican control.
The Senate was under Populist-Democratic control.
However, no fruitful cooperation occurred on legislation in the Senate. Waite was not averse to Democratic Party cooperation on the basis of the Omaha Platform. The Populists in the assembly lacked unity and
had no real leaders. Consequently, although a number
of distinctive Populist measures were introduced in
the assembly, no integrated and coherent legislative
program was presented or developed by any party. The
Republicans, as defenders of the status quo, played

the role of obstructionists. The Ninth General Assembly, like preceding ones, was under strong external pressures from the railroads and corporate and utility groups. A number of Populists were not immune to these pressures despite the professed program of the Populist Party. The whole situation was well-suited to a defense of the status quo. "In an assembly where party lines had been obliterated and where factions fought for petty advantage, the corporate interest had little difficulty in safeguarding its privileges and thwarting 'pernicious' legislation."[28]

Governor Waite had campaigned on the Omaha Platform. He continued this stand as governor, and fought it out with the legislature and the opposition in general on this basis.

His inaugural address was moderate and conciliatory in tone. The Rocky Mountain News remarked, "Governor Waite was listened to with an intensity of attention that was striking. Like a practiced orator he began in easy, well-modulated tones which soon swelled out into fullness with a clearness of articulation that made every syllable distinctly audible . . . His utterances were esteemed to be the clear cut pronouncement of a statesman easily rising to the level of an important occasion."[29]

The railroad question received top priority in Waite's inaugural address, being discussed first, and in greater detail than any other question. He asked for an end to rebates and discriminatory rates, an end to the pass system and to pooling arrangements. He recommended a railroad commission with power to fix rates and to hear complaints without recourse to the courts.

Governor Waite asked for an end to the "criminal waste" of public lands and a wiser land policy which would favor the actual settler. Public lands should be leased rather than sold. The United States should relinquish control of arid lands in Colorado by ceding them to the state.

In the field of labor, Waite recommended compulsory arbitration; a general eight-hour day law; an amended mechanics lien law, sufficient to secure wages; an employers' liability law; a stringent anti-child labor law; and an anti-Pinkerton law. Other recommendations included: abolition of capital punishment; women suffrage in municipal elections; a salary system

15

rather than a fee system for the payment of county officials; an Australian ballot to be locally administered; lower priced school textbooks through a system of bidding; laws favoring the debtor and weakening the position of the creditor; government economy; a general revision of the Colorado Constitution; direct election of United States senators; and payment of United States pensions and salaries in silver dollars or silver certificates.

The governor ended with a special plea for the free coinage of silver at the ratio of sixteen to one. "This was the prime issue in this state at the last election," he remarked. The silver question was both a national and a state one. However, "the free coinage of silver is an absolute necessity in this state, although in consequence of our unparalleled resources we may prosper to some extent without free coinage."

Waite concluded his inaugural message dramatically with a typical resort to historical and Biblical references: "When the thirteen colonies rebelled against the British government there was to the human eye or understanding, not the least hope of success. So now the hosts of monopoly are pressing the people into a Red Sea, but the same God, who through many ages and in many climes, opened a way of escape for the oppressed of so many races, still rules the destinies of nations, and He will so order it that this last, greatest and best of free governments shall never perish from the earth."[30]

The Ninth General Assembly in its regular session in 1893 enacted very little of the governor's program. Among the positive accomplishments of the assembly were: Dairy inspection provisions, regulation of oleo manufacture, establishment of state boards of health, pharmacy, and pardons; setting up statewide system of local boards of health and providing a detailed description of their functions; a start in free kindergartens; an eight-hour day for state and local government employees; a reform charter for Denver; provisions for handling contested elections for presidential electors and supreme, district, and county judges; and woman suffrage. The last named achievement was generally regarded as the most significant one.[31]

Waite strongly criticized the assembly for its failure to act on his program and charged it was subservient to corporate influence. Some legislators moved for a resolution of censure against the governor.

This did not pass, but the estrangement of the executive and the legislative branches of government grew.[32]
Waite later remarked that "he did not expect, without
a Populist majority in either house of the general
assembly, to accomplish much in the line of reform,
but with the constitutional veto power and with more
than one-third Populist vote in each branch of the
legislature, he did hope at least to check the tide of
class legislation which for so many years had run
against the debtors of the state."[33]

As governor, Waite used the veto power freely.
He voted forty bills in a thirty-day period after the
end of the session.[34] In describing the assembly session, Waite said, "For the remainder of the regular
session and one month after, the governor was kept
busy vetoing class legislation passed by the Ninth
General Assembly . . . in the interest of creditors and
for the oppression of the debtor class. These vetoes
of the governor would have been of little account, if
the Populist traitors could have got at them, but the
session was so far advanced (within ten days of its
close) that by retaining the bills till the close of
the session, the governor had an additional thirty days
for their consideration, and his veto could not be set
aside. In the interest of justice and for the protection of the rights of the people the governor freely
used this power."[35]

In mid-1892 through 1894, Colorado suffered from
economic distress and mass unemployment resulting from
the twin blows of the depression of 1893 and the repeal of the Sherman Silver Purchase Act. Governor
Waite called a special session of the legislature to
meet in January, 1894 to deal with the problems brought
about by the crisis. This call was warmly supported
by the rank-and-file Populists and strongly opposed by
the Republican Party and conservative interests in
general who feared the upsetting of the status quo and
the possibility of additional taxes. Waite not only
sought means to aid the poor and unemployed, but he
"looked for reforms to be compelled, for which under
ordinary circumstances there was no hope."[36] In this
respect, he anticipated the New Deal by forty years.

In his message to the special session, Waite
emphasized the money question as the way out of the
dilemma. This was in line with Populist thinking that
the solution of the money question was the key to
economic prosperity. Since the national government
was not going to take action to gain free coinage of

17

silver or provide a more ample money supply, it was
assumed that the state would have to act. Several
plans were proposed. The chief one was the Mexican
dollar plan under which Colorado silver was to be
shipped to Mexico, coined into Mexican dollars, returned and made legal tender in Colorado by act of the
legislature. This plan and others had the twin aims
of restoring silver production through providing a
market outlet and gaining a more ample money supply.
This question is discussed at greater length in the
chapter on money.[37]

The other chief concern of Waite in his special
message was the plight of the debtor. He advocated
changes in the trust deed and attachment laws to provide relief for the debtor groups, charging that the
present laws entirely favored the creditor classes.
However, Waite did not plan to interfere with existing
contracts.[38] He also asked for a reduction of penalties and interest on delinquent taxes to aid the
debtor.

Seventy-eight bills were introduced in the
special session, but only eleven were enacted. Most
of the governor's program was not given serious attention. Funds were scarce even to help pay for the
extra session. The same lobbying activity was in
evidence as during the regular session.

The special session lasted two months. At first,
the Senate refused to act at all, but finally submitted
to the governor and public pressure, though never
initiating any bills. A bill proposing the initiative
and the referendum lost in the House by two votes.[40]
The assembly amended the attachment and trust deed
laws and diminished the penalties for delinquent taxes.
Waite listed these as the real accomplishments of the
special session, and declared that it had done more
than the regular sessions of the Seventh, Eighth, and
Ninth General Assemblies combined.[41] Acts furthering
refining the Australian ballot system in Colorado were
also passed. These acts defined registration and
voting procedures and methods of ballot preparation.[42]

The personnel of the Waite Administration were
drawn mainly from business, professional, political,
and journalistic circles. Michel Lorentz, Governor
Waite's private secretary, was a native of New York
City. He had been a school teacher in the East, and a
miner in Aspen.[43] Lieutenant Governor David H. Nichols
had a long political background as speaker of the House

18

in the territorial legislature, Colorado state legis-
lator, Boulder County sheriff, and member of the State
Board of Penitentiary Commissioners. Nichols was
mainly responsible for the state university being
situated in Boulder in the seventies.

Secretary of State Nelson O. McClees, only thirty-
two, was a Pueblo realtor; Attorney General Eugene
Engley was a southern Colorado lawyer, journalist, and
politician; State Auditor Floyd M. Goodykoontz was a
southwestern Colorado businessman; State Treasurer
Albert Nance was a Denver realtor.[44] Engley was an
especially militant-minded Populist reformer, but he
and Waite had personal squabbles while in office.

The three appointees of the Denver Board of Public
Works, Thomas B. Buchanan, Arthur C. Harris, and L. H.
Flanders, a Republican, came from business backgrounds.
Buchanan, a former leading Greenbacker and Indianapolis journalist turned Denver realtor, and Harris,
former banker and grocer, were among the staunchest
supporters of the administration program and philoso-
phy. The original members of the Denver Fire and
Police Board, George Phelps, C. B. Stone, and D. V.
Martin, a Democrat, likewise had business backgrounds.
Israel G. Berry, an ardent Populist appointed warden
of the state reformatory at Buena Vista, was a Montrose
journalist and publisher.[45] Albert Frost was a Denver
attorney who was appointed to a judgeship. Henry C.
Childs, Land Board Register, and R. A. Southworth,
Deputy State Engineer, were officials of the Colorado
Farmers' Alliance.

Dr. T. D. Baird, a leading Walsenburg Populist,
was appointed a member of the State Board of Medical
Examiners. The Rev. Myron W. Reed, Denver Protestant
minister and an ardent Populist, was the male member
of the three-member board of control of the State Home
and Industrial School for Girls at Denver. Mrs. Emma
G. Curtis of Canon City was the leading woman Populist
in the state administration as a member of the Board
of the State Industrial School at Golden. She was one
of Waite's most regular correspondents, discussing in
detail not only administrative problems, but the general Populist program and philosophy.

Other leading correspondents, not holding official state positions, included: John W. Sanborn,
Greeley realtor; A. J. Overholt, Salida physician;
Quitman Brown, Yuma rancher; G. C. Rohde, Gunnison
journalist; A. C. Fish and B. L. Bailey, Denver

19

journalists; and Giles Otis Pearce, Cripple Creek metallurgist.[46]

Several Populists in the administration used their position to good effect to advance the Populist cause in words and deeds. Judge Albert Frost of Denver made a practice of defending the rights of the poor in court, and would not jail the vagrant unemployed. The Populist State Superintendent of Public Instruction advocated a general state tax to equalize educational opportunities, night school for workers, an end to child labor, and free textbooks.

Attorney General Eugene Engley, in his 1893-1894 report, advocated far-reaching political reforms: a new and more democratic constitution; revision and codification of Colorado statutory law; a one-house legislature; the initiative and referendum; proportional representation in legislative bodies; fewer elections; abolition of the grand jury and retention of the petit jury only in criminal cases; elimination of the office of coroner as "dead wood from Saxon feudalism"; and abolition of capital punishment. Engley also presented the thesis that crime should be treated as a disease.[47]

All was not happiness and unity in the Populist administration, however. This was to be expected from the uneasy coalition of forces that made up the Populist administration and the violent opposition to Populist reform measures. Governor Waite had more than his share of woes with personnel. Dr. T. A. Hughes of the State Medical Board was dismissed from his post for allegedly disposing of funds without due authority. Two members of the State Agricultural Board were dismissed for poor selection of public lands to be purchased for development of educational funds.[49] In July, 1893, the State Inspector of Coal Mines, John McNeil, was dismissed on charges of neglect of duty in providing for the safety of the mines.[50] In May, 1894, all three penitentiary commissioners were removed on charges that they had illegally appointed a detective and that they were engaged in illegal paroling practices.[51]

Waite's main appointment problem involved the Denver Fire and Police Board. Twice the governor dismissed two of the three members of the board on the grounds they were not enforcing the anti-gambling laws. Three of the four dismissed were Populists. The second case nearly led to the disaster of a civil war in

Denver and the complete breakdown of civil government. This issue is treated at greater length in a later chapter.

The troubles in the gold-mining area of Cripple Creek, treated in the labor chapter, also occurred in 1894. These events made the year 1894 a truly turbulent one in the history of Colorado politics.

The Populist administration, defeated on the legislative floor, scored signal victories in social struggles at Denver and Cripple Creek before bowing out in electoral defeat in the fall of 1894. Waite's bid for re-election as governor failed as the conservatives, especially alarmed by the turn of events during 1894, launched a vigorous and successful counter-offensive with all the plentiful financial, journalistic, and political forces at their command.

With their support of the Bryan candidacy in 1896, the Populists in Colorado as elsewhere practically ceased to exist as an independent political force. The Populists, however, did continue to run candidates and to survive in a greatly weakened form until the turn of the century.

CHAPTER IV

MONEY

In 1896, Francis A. Walker, noted economist and onetime president of the American Economic Association, wrote an essay in which he expressed concern about the relationship between the volume of money and prosperity. This fittingly symbolized the great emphasis on the money question among U. S. citizens in the late nineteenth century. Being a defender of the status quo and an apostle of laissez-faire competition, Walker's views were far removed from those of Waite and other Populists.[1] Yet each was obsessed with the money issue in a way which is difficult for people in the late twentieth century to understand. Reformers with various monetary theories were to be found in abundance. Categories clearly discernible in the maze of monetary theorists were the gold standard advocates, the silver advocates, and the paper money advocates.

The argument over money was no mere academic exercise in economic theory. It mirrored the social struggles of the times. Gold was identified with the rights of the creditor, the preservation of social order and stability, and the defense of propertied interests. Silver and greenbacks were identified with the rights of the debtor and the preservation and extension of liberty and opportunity. Many people were deeply in debt, especially farmers in the West and the South. They sought monetary inflation in order to more easily pay off their mortgages and other encumbrances. Silver mine owners and miners naturally joined forces with the agricultural debtors at the point of espousing government purchase of silver and silver coinage to encourage monetary inflation.

The Populists stressed the money issue above everything else. The Populist Party platform was based on the trinity of land, transportation, and money. But the greatest of these in the eyes of many, including Davis H. Waite, was money. "Money is the issue and don't you fail to remember it. Money, MONEY, M-O-N-E-Y. The politicians can fool the people no longer," proclaimed editor Waite early in 1892.[2] While espousing other measures to improve the social order, he believed that those who placed other issues first such as the tariff, the single-tax, prohibition, socialism, or woman suffrage were wasting their time

23

and creating division among reformers.[3]

Waite shared with other money advocates a philosophy of history which ascribed the rise and fall of civilizations to the monetary situation. An abundance of money brought prosperity and liberty, a scarcity of money brought economic and cultural decline.[4]

His speeches and writings spiced with plentiful Biblical allusions typical of the times, Waite delved into various periods in world and U. S. history to argue his point: the Medieval period was associated with a long continued fall in the general range of prices; the prosperity of the age of European exploration was linked to the gold and silver discoveries in the Americas; the Currency Act nullifying paper money was responsible foremost for the revolt of the British North American colonies in 1775;[5] gold discoveries in California heightened economic activity; issuance of Greenbacks during the Civil War played a key role in the victory of the Union side; deflation policies since the Civil War had brought grave economic problems.

Discoveries of gold could aid monetary inflation and economic prosperity; silver, however, being more plentiful and cheaper, was more likely to do so. Paper money had even more enticing possiblities to the monetary inflationists, especially if there were no requirements that the paper currency be backed by gold reserves. All that was necessary was for the government to turn loose the printing presses and print the money that was needed. This was the appeal of the paper money called "greenbacks" which were printed during the Civil War without regard to metallic reserves. The Union got the money it needed during wartime, money became plentiful, and prices rose.[6] Thus the "greenback", to the Populist mind, referred to paper money which was backed only by government decree as opposed to the usual currency notes which are considered to be represented by at least a certain amount of gold or silver reserves held by the government and the banks.

Waite As A Greenbacker

Greenback defenders argued that post-war prosperity depended on a continuance of war-time policies. However, a clamor to increase the value of the greenbacks through a contraction of the volume of the currency occurred soon after the war. Those favoring greenbacks naturally opposed it. In 1868, they obtained a temporary victory with the reissue of $44,000,000 in greenbacks which had been retired, and the prohibition of further retirement of greenbacks.

Then, in 1875, a Resumption Act was passed which fixed January 1, 1879 as the date when greenbacks would be on a par with gold. Also, part of the greenbacks were to be retired. This act infuriated greenback advocates but, in 1879, resumption occurred and green-backs, like other paper currency notes, were worth their full value in gold.[7]

Farmer and labor support for greenbackism developed shortly after the Civil War. In 1868, Midwest farmers supported the so-called "Ohio Idea" which was the suggestion that the principal of government bonds due be paid in greenbacks rather than in gold. The Democratic Party sought votes in 1868 by defending this greenback motion.

Early organized political support for the green-back came from labor in the East through the National Labor Union.[8] The National Labor Party adopted a greenback platform in 1872.[9] The Knights of Labor, chief labor organization in the United States during the seventies and eighties, early turned its attention to greenbackism.

The depression of the mid-seventies increased agitation for monetary reform. The Greenback Party emerged in 1875, spurred by farmers demanding independent political action. In the late seventies, labor and Greenback forces cooperated and in several states their organizations fused. The national greenbackers are sometimes referred to as the Greenback Labor Party during the 1878-1879 period. As one labor historian has noted, "In several states, workingmen's associations became Greenback clubs, and trade unions joined in recruiting members for the new movement. Wherever a local assembly of the Knights of Labor existed there was certain to be a number of Greenback clubs."[10]

The Greenback Party espoused the cause of green-backism in three presidential elections, nominating Peter Cooper in 1876, James B. Weaver, later the Populist standard bearer, in 1880, and Benjamin G. Butler in 1884. The vote was small in each presidential election, but in the 1878 Congressional elections Greenback Party candidates polled about a million votes and elected fifteen Congressmen, six each from the Midwest and the East and three from the South. James B. Weaver was the leading spokesman for the greenback viewpoint in Congress.

In the eighties the Greenback Party died out. Yet the ideas associated with greenbackism were to live on in the minds of a number of people in the last years of the nineteenth century. Especially was this true of reform elements connected with such movements as the Farmers' Alliances, the Knights of Labor, and the Populists. Leading Populists such as Ignatius Donnelly, James B. Weaver, Jerry Simpson, Robert Schilling, and Jacob Coxey had been active in the Greenback movement, and continued to support greenback ideas in the Populist Party.

Lacking much knowledge about Waite during the seventies, one can only conjecture. In moving from New York to Kansas in 1876, he jumped over the storm center of midwest agrarian greenbackism. He left New York before the height of Greenback Labor activity in the East. As mentioned earlier, it is known that Waite was elected to the Kansas state legislature as a Republican in 1878. He left for Colorado the next year. When and where Waite was attracted to green-backism remains an intriguing question. There is nothing to indicate he was associated with the Green-back movement. It is clear that he emerges to full view a few years later as a greenbacker.

From the earliest issues of the _Aspen Union Era_ in 1891, Waite printed articles and editorials favoring greenbackism. The root cause of the economic difficulties of the seventies, he claimed, could be traced back to 1866 when the policy of the contraction of the currency by the withdrawal of greenbacks began. Prosperity and credit were good at the time, so the effects were not felt immediately. What the silverites later referred to as the "Crime of '73", eliminating the silver dollar, was belittled as a cause of the depression on the basis that the amount of silver minted at the time was too insignificant to have any effect.

Although editor Waite resided in the silver mining town of Aspen, Colorado, he proclaimed that the free coinage of silver was not the answer. Silver would help add to the amount of money in circulation, but Wall Street would make up for this by withdrawing an equal amount of national bank currency. The only

26

remedy was to increase the currency in greenbacks to at
least fifty-five dollars per capita. Only greenbacks
could supply the plentiful monetary inflation which was
needed. The bankers would not be able to control the
issue of greenbacks which would be produced directly by
the government.[11] So ran the pro-greenback argument on
the pages of the Aspen Union Era.

The issuance of greenbacks would also solve all
the problems of government expenses and taxation,
editor Waite averred.[12] This was, of course, a proposal for a simple one-shot approach to curing the
problems of government financing similar to the one-
shot approach of Henry George's single tax.

In typical Greenbacker fashion Waite felt that
money itself had no intrinsic value; it was only a
creation of the government and of law. Money to him
was not a natural product or a product of human labor.[13]
No individual could make any kind of money except
counterfeit money, he said. Waite had flatly contradicted himself at this point for, if money was not a
product mined by human labor but only a creation of the
law, why then had the discoveries of gold and silver
in Peru and Mexico and later in California and Australia
made such a difference to ecnomic prosperity, as he
maintained?

Waite and other money advocates seemed to confuse
the ultimate value of the metal with its utilitarian
forms. For purposes of expediency the metal is cut
into certain sizes and stamped. Governments fix certain standards and establish the weight and fineness
of each coin. These standards and measurements may
change.

Opponents of greenbacks were fond of invoking
Gresham's law that cheaper money invariably drives
dearer money out of circulation. The Aspen Union Era
contended that Gresham's law was not applicable — as
an example it cited the results of the passage of the
Bland Act which called for the government to purchase
at least two million dollars of silver each month.
Gold actually increased later, it said. Furthermore,
the question was irrelevant, the newspaper maintained,
since gold and silver could supply only a small per
cent of the money needed.[14]

Waite was never opposed to silver per se. However, during his period as governor and later, when
the silver issue became more prominent, he continued

to defend the greenback position against those who felt
silver was the ultimate monetary answer. He clashed
with William H. Harvey, the apostle of silver, after
his influential Coin's Financial School appeared.
Harvey, quite an admirer of Waite, had sent him a copy
of his book with the inscription on the inside cover:
"To Governor Waite, the Jackson — the Andrew Jackson
of the present age — from the Author."

The governor thoroughly perused his copy of Coin
as is indicated by the frequent comments to be found
along the margins throughout the book. He objected to
Harvey's distinction between primary money — gold and
silver — and secondary or credit money which included
national bank notes, greenbacks, and all other forms
of paper money.[15] This downgraded greenbacks which
Waite felt should be primary money as much as gold and
silver.[16]

In 1895, one year before the famous election
between Bryan and McKinley over the silver issue, the
ex-governor wrote to E. D. Benson of Seattle: "We can
issue greenbacks as full legal tender for the payment
of all debts, public and private without exception."[17]

Even during the election year of 1896 when the
tendency was to throw everything overboard in favor of
silver, Waite insisted upon the whole financial plank
of the Omaha Platform, not just silver. The main solution of the money problem, he still maintained, was a
government issuance of paper money to secure the necessary monetary inflation. Silver could be an important first step in this direction but, nonetheless,
only a first step.[18]

It may be a surprising thing to many that, in the
silver state of Colorado where Populism is usually
equated with silver, its Populist governor was a greenbacker. However, popular myths to the contrary,
Waite's position was hardly unique among Populists.
The Omaha Platform of 1892 — the ideological bible
of the Populists — emphasized a thorough revamping
of the whole financial structure. A government banking
system with a government issuance of paper money was
featured. The silver plank was separate, distinct, and
subordinate. When the silver issue rose to greater
prominence many Populists thought the issue to be
tangential and only one step towards the major goal.
The St. Louis conference of the Populist Party in late
1894 reasserted its Omaha Platform position on the
money issue despite the growing silver sentiment.

28

Recent research has suggested that the rank-and-file Populists of Kansas and Nebraska were far more interested in thorough-going financial reform than in silver. Indeed, they even feared that silver would become a predominant issue.[19]

Important national Populist leaders held greenback views including Ignatius Donnelly, chief spokesman of agrarian Midwest Populism and main author of the Omaha Platform;[20] Thomas Watson, the major Populist figure in the South;[21] Robert Schilling, a Populist leader from Wisconsin and a former Knights of Labor organizer;[22] Mary E. Lease of Kansas;[23] George F. Washburn of Massachusetts;[24] and James B. Weaver, former Greenbacker and Populist presidential standard bearer. The latter, however, was a leader in the move to a silver platform in 1896.[25] Henry Demarest Lloyd remarked that most Populists received their money education from the Greenback Party.[26]

Governor Lorenzo Lewelling of Kansas once wrote Governor Waite: "Ours may be called a silver party but we will not have silver alone, and indeed the philosophy of populism is the philosophy of greenbackism, and there is in fact, as you yourself know and believe, no reason whatever for the existence of metallic money of any kind."[27]

THE BANKING SYSTEM

Governor Waite believed that a government owned and operated banking organization was essential to put monetary controls in the hands of the people. It was the other major leg of a democratic system besides a workable greenback plan. He charged that "there is no monopoly which has been so grasping and so utterly useless as our national banks. They have created an aristocracy of wealth, and in a career of robbery of only thirty years have filched from the people more riches than the dynasties of Europe possess as the result of their own and their ancestors' robberies for a thousand years."[28]

State banks were little better. "Both the old state bank idea and the national bank idea are essentially dishonest, and give, and are designed to give to the banker an opportunity to collect interest upon what he owes."[29]

Writing to the national Populist leader, Ignatius Donnelly, the Governor lamented, "If we can't abolish banks of issue, the country is lost."[30]

There was a strong Jacksonian flavor in these sentiments.

High interest rates which burdened many people in the agrarian West and South were, of course, a chief cause of the agitation against the banks. "In the nature of things," Waite said, "there can be no permanent financial prosperity until the country is relieved of the necessity of making immense loans either from the banks or from the government."[31] He tended to see the issue rather strangely in terms of cash versus credit. Thus business should be put on a cash basis to get away from the ruinous credit system. While realizing that the credit system could not be completely eliminated, the Governor thought it could be minimized to an extent which today seems bizarre. At this point the Greenbacks would come to the rescue: a vast expansion of the currency would provide the needed cash and eliminate for good the enormous debt load including the interest payments which so many keenly felt.

Waite was correct in asserting the dangers of banking monopoly. He was correct in demanding a publicly controlled and more flexible financial system which would meet the needs of a rapidly expanding economy. But he was not very realistic in demanding a cash basis for an increasingly complex industrial system. In view of the increasing power of a rising industrial oligarchy, he was also naive in thinking that a wad of greenbacks and more control over the banks would by themselves place the economic system on a more democratic basis.

As a partial answer to the banking problem, Waite advocated postal savings banks as a safe means of deposit. It should be remembered that the 1890's was long before the days of the FDIC. The proposal for a postal savings system was a Populist plank which became a reality in the early 20th century. Waite asserted, "In Europe and in Canada they have postal savings banks, where people can deposit their money, and the government is responsible for its safety and repayment. Sometime the people will insist on a safe place of deposit for their savings."[32]

Silver

Although Waite was a greenbacker, he was forced
as Governor of Colorado to turn his attention to the
silver issue. Not only was Colorado a major silver
state, but silver became a prominent political issue
in the early nineties.

Silver production in the United States jumped
from 116,015 ounces in 1860 to 54,500,000 ounches in
1890.[33] Most of this output was concentrated in a few
western states. The value of the silver produced in
Colorado in 1877 was about $4,500,000; by 1889 it had
risen to over $20,000,000.[34] Silver mining had become
Colorado's leading industry. From the late seventies
silver predominated over gold until the difficult times
of the nineties when Cripple Creek gold came partially
to the rescue. Leadville, the leader in the silver
boom, was by 1880 the second largest city in Colorado.
Lake County, including Leadville, continued to be the
top silver producer in 1890 with the Aspen area in
which Waite resided running a close second.[35] Silver
was also found extensively in such widely scattered
areas as the San Juan basin of southwestern Colorado
and the Georgetown area west of Denver. The arrival
of the railroads in the silver mining towns greatly
reduced the transportation costs, resulting in sky-
rocketing silver production. Finding a market for
silver produced in Colorado and other western mining
states was another story.

The general price trend during the last several
decades of the 19th century in the United States was
downward. Greatly increased silver production without
adequate demand was bound to further depress the price
of silver. Added to this was the fact that there had
been a large increase in the world supply of silver.
Silver had been demonetized in many parts of Europe.
The silver price fell steadily after 1873 and took a
sharp turn downward in 1876. Silver producers now
discovered the bullion value of the silver dollar to
be below the face value of the coin, so it was profit-
able to coin silver. Congress, however, had passed
the 1873 Coinage Act demonetizing silver.

Two silver acts — the Bland-Allison Act of 1878
and the Sherman Silver Purchase Act of 1890 — had been
passed by Congress at the behest of silver and agrarian
forces. The Bland-Allison Act called for the government to purchase from two to four million dollars of

silver each month. Silverites charged that this was always kept to the minimum. Limited coinage did occur under the act.[36] The Sherman Act provided for the purchase of 4,500,000 ounces of silver bullion every month. While allowing the purchase of large amounts of silver, it did not provide for an even limited amount of silver coinage. Both acts fell far short of the goal of free coinage of silver. Neither act brought about the desired monetary inflation which agrarian debtors and reformers desired. As the price of silver fell, the government was even able to buy the required amount of silver under the Sherman Act for fewer dollars, greatly disturbing the silver mine owners.[37]

In Colorado, Governor Waite could not avoid the fact that the silver issue was of paramount political importance. He freely acknowledged that the silver sentiment was largely responsible for his gubernatorial triumph in 1892. However, while sympathizing with the silverites, he was not primarily interested in the silver question. He was a genuine reformer, and in monetary matters was a greenbacker as we have seen. Yet he did espouse the cause of the free coinage of silver. His reasons fell into three categories:

1. Free coinage of silver would naturally help the silver-producing states including Colorado.

2. Free coinage of silver would be a small step toward a more abundant money supply and would help bring about the needed price increase or inflationary tendency.

3. Free coinage of silver would be a means of educating the people on the money question. They would learn that the free coinage of silver was not the final answer, but they would realize the beneficial results to be gained through an increase in the money supply.[38]

Scores of silver clubs were organized in Colorado during the 1891-92 period. There were 220 active silver clubs in Colorado in 1892.[39] Waite was active in the Aspen group and served as a delegate to the Colorado Silver Convention in April, 1892, where he was a member of the resolutions committee.[40]

As governor, Waite became more vigorous in defense of silver than he had been as a newspaper editor. In his inaugural address the governor stated that "the free coinage of silver, at the ratio of sixteen to one, is one of the first importance to Colorado."[41] He maintained that the silver question was also a national one related to the "welfare of every farmer and laboring man North and South." He suggested that the pensions of the United States and the salaries of U. S. officials be paid in silver dollars or silver certificates. Despite his silver emphasis, his more basic greenback views subtly crept into the inaugural address when he spoke of the free coinage of silver relieving the "money famine" to "some degree" and when he attacked the financial policies of the "past twenty-five years," evidently referring to the late sixties as the starting point of monetary woes.[42]

Governor Waite gained national recognition when he authored an article on silver which appeared in Harper's Weekly in the summer of 1893. He declared that the steady decline in the price of silver was felt more acutely in the Colorado mining camps than anywhere else in the country, since Colorado produced forty per cent of the national total. The silver decline combined with the deepening economic depression led to the formation of relief committees in a number of Colorado towns.

During the hectic and crisis-ridden summer of 1893, Governor Waite made the famous speech for which he ever after received the appellation of "Bloody Bridles." This speech on silver was addressed first to a throng of two thousand at the Colorado State Silver Convention on July 11, 1893, and then in August, 1893, to the National Silver Convention meeting in Chicago. With the economic crisis deepening into the worst depression the United States had known, the clash of political forces became aggravated and emotions became taut. Faced with the additional prospect of the repeal of the Sherman Silver Purchase Act at the special session of Congress called by President Cleveland in the late summer, Waite became militant. He equated the fight for the free and unlimited coinage of silver at sixteen to one with patriotism, national independence, and the preservation of liberty.

The stirring ending contained the famous "bloody bridles" phrase:

"The war has begun. It is the same war which must always be waged against oppression and tyranny to preserve the liberties of man —

that eternal warfare of monarchy and monopoly
against the right of the people to self government and which, during the last century has so
conquered the masses as to reduce to pauperism
the "common people" of almost every nation under
Heaven except the United States. Our weapons
are argument and the ballot — 'a free ballot
and a fair count.' And if the money power shall
attempt to sustain its usurpation by the stronghold we will meet that issue when it is forced
upon us, for it is better, infinitely better,
that blood should flow to the horses' bridles,
rather than our national liberties should be
destroyed."[44]

In a typical Waiteian manner, the speech contained
patriotic, Biblical, and historical allusions. Abraham
Lincoln was quoted to the effect that it was a crime
for government to contract the money supply while debts
were outstanding. The governor likened the knifing of
the silver interests to what "the devil proposed to
Jesus Christ on the mountain."

Both the Cleveland Administration and the English
"money power" came in for bitter attack in the speech.
With prophetic accuracy, he proclaimed that Cleveland's
silver policy "will shut up the mines, destroy the
mining towns and cities, and drive the miners of the
Rocky Mountain region bankrupt upon a cold and unfeel-
ing world," and noted that "a cry of agony does arise
from the mountains and the valleys of Colorado, in
bitter protest against a policy the most atrocious
since Louis XIV revoked the edict of Nantes in 1685,
and banished from France 500,000 of her people."

Waite spoke darkly of the possible need for another
American Revolution of 1776 if foreign powers dictated
our monetary policies. He especially had in mind
British financiers. His opposition to international
monetary conferences was based on fear of their dominance.

The speech was heartily condemned in leading
eastern newspapers, being presented as evidence that
the West was indeed on the verge of anarchy under the
leadership of such "wild radicals" as Davis Waite.
The supposedly objective and non-sensational New York
Times headlined a front page story the following day:
"BLOOD TO THE HORSES' BRIDLES — Gov. Waite Talks War
in the Denver Silver Convention — Proposes to Meet the
Usurpations of the Money Power with Revolution if

Necessary."[44] This was a wild distortion, of course, since the governor had advocated peaceful change through "argument and the ballot" and saw force only as an ultimate consequence imposed, it should be noted, by the oppressor. One of the few eastern Congressmen sympathetic to silver, J. C. Sibley of Pennsylvania, saw Waite's speech, on the other hand, as an indication that the people were prepared to preserve their liberties.

Monetary theories in the late nineteenth century were often accompanied by simplified conspiracy explanations for the existing conditions. Waite seemed to take seriously the idea of the "Crime of '73" (demonetization of the silver dollar) and the conspiracy explanation of it. In his speeches he accused Senator Sherman and others of engineering the 1873 Act by bringing to the United States one Ernest Seyd, an English banker, with $500,000 in cash supplied by English financiers, especially the Rothschilds, in order to bribe Congressmen.

The Governor became personally involved in the Seyd case through contact with a Fredrick A. Luckenbach in Denver. Luckenbach had at one time presented himself to Waite as the author of an affidavit on Ernest Seyd in which the latter presumably confessed to the plot ascribed to him. He claimed his business had been boycotted and ruined due to his "truthful affidavit."[45]

Writing to Ignatius Donnelly who was interested in documenting the Seyd case, Waite stated that a sister of Luckenbach's, a Mrs. M. Matteron, who resided in Denver, was a respectable and well-known woman, and had been a Populist candidate for the Colorado General Assembly in 1894. According to Mrs. Matteron, Luckenbach had invented and patented several ore machines which made him financially prosperous. In the silver crisis of the nineties he had sustained great losses. "As to the truth of the affidavit there can be no question," Mrs. Matteron asserted.

According to Waite's testimony to Donnelly, Mrs. Matteron showed Waite a letter from Mr. Luckenbach, then in New York (1895), in which the latter reaffirmed the truth of the affidavit. Luckenbach was becoming exceedingly suspicious and fearful, asking his sister to refrain from doing anything to draw him out on the affidavit matter. He said he could not publicize the case until Seyd's death. While Luckenbach's coyness would be sufficient to make the reader suspicious, Waite hoped the affidavit could be sustained as a major blow against the gold camp. "I think on the whole I have made out a pretty strong case for Mr. Luckenbach," he concluded to Donnelly. What the exact facts are in this bizarre case no one seems to know even today.

Waite's Mexican Dollar Proposal

The price of silver plummeted from eighty to sixty-two cents per ounce in early June of 1893. Later in the summer, the repeal of the Silver Purchase Act was the final blow. The bottom had dropped out of Colorado's number one industry. Silver mine owners agreed to close down production. Every mine in the Leadville district closed. Smelters shut down at Leadville, Aspen and Pueblo.

The general national depression of the nineties thus hit Colorado especially hard. Many banks closed, including twelve in Denver within a period of three days. Railroads suffered, several lines being forced into receivership. Many workers faced cuts in wages or the loss of a job altogether. Thousands were unemployed. Many poured into Denver where a relief camp was set up. Several thousands left the state as the railroads offered low fares to the Missouri River.

Clearly the time seemed ripe for drastic action to help relieve the distress. It was against this background that Governor Waite and others proposed various state monetary remedies. There seemed to be no hope for action on monetary problems from Washington. The conviction grew that Colorado must either work out its salvation alone or in cooperation with allies from the West and South.

More money in circulation and an outlet for silver were felt to be the two chief needs. The general situation would have been a perfect opportunity for Governor Waite to set forth his greenback ideas except for the fact that he was deep in the heart of a silver area. The influence of silver and the silver mine owners was so great that all monetary proposals turned upon silver.

Some advocated a state silver bullion depository with certificates of the deposits to be accepted as a currency in Colorado. A bill was introduced in the

36

state assembly to this effect. Others suggested such measures as state bank notes, the issue of "souvenir silver coins" and the coinage of a composite dollar of gold and silver.

In an article appearing in the North American Review the governor implied that under certain conditions the states still had coinage rights. The states had the power of coinage until 1789, he argued, but the right of Congress to coin money had been conceded under the new Constitution and the "right is exclusive so long as the right is exercised."[46]

However, in his message of the special session of the state legislature in January, 1894, Waite stated his belief that the various state schemes suggested for the creation of money were illegal.[47] He had another alternative in mind. On September 19, 1893, the governor had addressed the following message to President Porfirio Diaz of Mexico:

Your Excellency:

It is not impossible that the silver producing states may avail themselves of that clause in our Constitution which provides that states may make gold and silver coin a tender in payment of debts. In as much as when the United States Constitution was adopted and went into operation (1789) the only gold and silver coins in existence, so far as the United States were concerned, were foreign coins, it seems clear that the states have a right to make the Mexican dollar a legal tender in Colorado for the payment of all state dues and all debts collected in our state. It is quite probable that other states will follow Colorado if we lead off in this matter. I am anxious to know upon what terms the mints of Mexico would receive and coin for us our bullion silver.

Will you please answer at your earliest convenience?

With sentiments of the highest of yourself, personally, and for a more intimate and extensive interchange of commerce between Mexico and our nation,

I am,

Very respectfully yours,

Davis H. Waite[48]
Gov. Colorado

Diaz replied as follows:

City of Mexico
October 11, 1893

Davis H. Waite, Governor of Colorado, U. S. A.

Esteemed Sir — From the Governor General Don Pedro Rincon Gelardo, your esteemed letter of the nineteenth of last month is received. I have not answered until now owing to absence from the city.

The subject to which you refer is really of the very first importance to the commercial relations of both nations, and I hope you will inform me of the results reached in your country in an effort to get legal status to the Mexican dollar in the territories of the various states of the American Union.

In obedience to your wish, I have the pleasure to manifest or make known the tribunals of the laws of Mexico. The amounts of silver imported from the United States are subject to the same formalities and to pay the same fees and duties for coinage as the silver produced in the republic. These fees and duties are: 4.41 per cent for coinage, ½ per cent for coat of arms, and besides this there would be the expense of assaying.

I take this occasion to offer you my infinite services and attentions.

Porfirio Diaz

Thus had Waite initiated his fantastic and daring idea that Colorado silver be shipped to Mexico, coined into Mexican dollars, and made legal tender in Colorado through authorization by the state assembly. The Mexican dollar scheme was placed at the top of the

agenda for the special session which met to deal with
the economic crisis facing Coloradoans.

In his message to the session Waite attempted to
meet certain objections to the plan. He answered the
objection that Mexican and South American dollars would
be plentiful in Colorado by saying that indeed he hoped
this would be true in order to furnish the needed
inflation. To the objection that gold, U. S. silver
dollars, and greenbacks would leave the state, he
countered that this had essentially already happened.
To the charge that a single silver standard would result Waite replied that he did not think so, but that
a single silver standard would be preferable to a single
gold standard.

Critics argued that it would make "a foreign dollar
— a Mexican dollar, a dishonest dollar, a 57 cent dollar, legal tender." The governor answered that it gave
Colorado, just so far as it is possible without congressional action, all the results of the free coinage
of silver. Critics suggested that it was dishonest to
pay a debt in a dollar of less value than in the dollar
borrowed. Waite replied that the original dishonesty
occurred many years earlier, and his plan only rec-
tified matters.[49]

Opinion in both houses of the Colorado legislature
was strongly opposed to the Mexican dollar plan. It
was unconstitutional, it would flood the state with
depreciated currency, and it would bring disrepute to
Colorado, said the critics.[50] One member of the state
assembly called for immediate adjournment of the special session, saying the Mexican dollar plan was
ridiculous and unconstitutional, and might bring bimetallism into disrepute.[51]

It has sometimes been asserted that Waite must
have been a crackpot to have put forth such a scheme.
The governor apparently intended to use the plan to
dramatize the monetary issue. Writing to the national
Populist leader Ignatius Donnelly, he said, "I hardly
expect that our General Assembly will adopt my silver
policy. So far as the proposition to make domestic
and foreign dollars containing not less than 371½ grains
fine silver is concerned, the only result will be to
force the issue before the public and compel its discussion." He told Donnelly that ideas similar to his
Mexican dollar plan were being discussed in Kansas,
North Dakota, and Texas. What Waite probably hoped

for was a combined threat of a number of western and
southern states which would force Washington to act
favorably on the silver issue.[52]   Indeed, he indicated
this in his letter to Diaz.

Fired with enthusiasm by Waite's imaginative plan,
other political leaders began to sense the potential
of combination. Senator William M. Stewart of the
silver state of Nevada visualized a common approach to
the Mexican dollar plan by a number of states.[53]   Governor Sylvester Pennoyer of Oregon thought other states
would follow Colorado's lead, and the Colorado coin
would come into common circulation.[54]

Politicians and monetary enthusiasts hotly debated
the proposition. Discussions centered around several
points: constitutionality, economic consequences, and
moral rights. B. L. Bailey, publisher of The Bi-
Metallist, approved the governor's plan.[55]   Governor
L. D. Lewelling of Kansas supported Waite's position,
but feared the reaction of Congress.[56]   Herman Taubeneck, national executive secretary of the Populist
Party, said he was not a lawyer, but he supported
Waite's plan "from a standpoint of justice and right."[57]
Ignatius Donnelly also sympathized, but warned Governor
Waite not to move too fast, urging him not to sacrifice
himself for the silver mine owners as they were not all
for him anyway.[58]

Others Waite consulted were more skeptical.
Charles S. Thomas, influential Denver Democrat and
silver advocate, cautioned that federal authority on
financial matters was exclusive.[59]   Thomas B. Buchanan,
a Waite appointee to the Denver Department of Public
Works and an old-time Greenbacker and a staunch Populist, forecast that the Mexican dollar plan would
"produce a total dislocation in the monetary relations
of Colorado."[60]

Meantime, Colorado's two U. S. Senators, Henry M.
Teller and Edward O. Wolcott, were pushing their own
scheme to have the Mexican dollar coined at the Carson
and San Francisco mints, using Colorado bullion. Governor Waite doubted that Mexico would grant coinage
authority to U. S. mints.[61]

Though not accepted in Colorado, Governor Waite's
Mexican dollar idea continued to live elsewhere. In
1896, the Populist Senator Marion Butler of North
Carolina introduced a bill in the Senate making the

Mexican silver dollar and the Japanese yen full legal
tender in the United States. He wrote to Waite, "I
consider your argument with reference to the power of
the states . . . to make foreign coins containing more
than 371½ grams of pure silver a legal tender, con-
clusive and unanswerable." State action was also
promised.[62]

Following the election of 1896, interest in plans
similar to Waite's seems to have died out. The discovery of gold in Alaska, South Africa, and Australia
at the end of the century and the return of economic
prosperity weakened interest in the silver cause and
in various state and national plans for monetary
inflation including greenbackism.

CHAPTER V

THE THEME OF ANTI-MONOPOLY

The crucial decades of the late nineteenth century witnessed the triumph of industrial capitalism in the United States. The simpler, smaller, and predominately agrarian society known throughout most of the American history was gone.

Rapid technological developments and mass production techniques led to the new industrial order. Some of the features of this new order were the large corporation, the factory system, urbanization, massive immigration, and a more ruthless exploitation of the new land and natural resources. Two new classes, the industrialist and the factory worker, rose to prominence in American society. The resulting impact on all areas and institutions of American society — political, social, religious, cultural — was profound.

The corporate giant became the dominant structure in American economic life. A vast centralization and concentration of capital wealth occurred. By the end of the century one or a few corporations were in control of many areas of production. Trusts, holding companies, and pooling agreements became familiar terms in describing economic integration. Further concentration of wealth was accelerated with the increasing merger of banking and industrial capital, especially in such industries as the railroads, during the economic depression of the nineties. Reform groups, labor groups, and farmer groups protested that this concentration of wealth and power presented a basic threat to the traditional American democratic ideal.[1]

The Populist Party was a part of this protest movement which may be called the anti-monopoly movement. The preamble to the 1892 Omaha Platform of the Populists charged that "the fruits of the toil of millions are boldly stolen to build up colossal fortunes for a few, unprecedented in the history of mankind; and the possessors of these, in turn, despise the republic and endanger liberty. From the same prolific womb of governmental injustice we breed the two great classes — tramps and millionaires."[2] Further on, the preamble assailed the Democrats and the Republicans for "proposing to drown the outcries of

43

a plundered people with the uproar of a sham battle over the tariff, so that capitalists, corporations, national banks, rings, trusts, watered stock, the demonetization of silver, and the oppressions of the usurers may be lost sight of."[3] Later, there was reference to "the formation of combines and rings," and the assertion that "we seek to restore the government of the Republic to the hands of the 'plain people.'"[4]

In the spirit of the Omaha Platform, Waite was against the growth of monopoly power. He believed that the United States was moving from a republic to a "plutocratic oligarchy," and that equality of opportunity was being destroyed by the forces of special privilege. Referring to a study of wealth based on the 1890 census, Waite noted the estimate that nine per cent of the American people owned seventy-one per cent of the wealth. The study further indicated that 4047 millionaire families owned twenty per cent of the nation's wealth. It also showed that from 1880 to 1890, population in the United States had risen only 25.75 per cent while mortgages had risen by 90.49 per cent and the gross sum of indebtedness by 156.04 per cent.[5] Waite asserted that, "it is impossible that the present condition of affairs can long continue. To all who stop to think it is evident that the opportunities to rise to wealth out of the mud of servitude are becoming less and less."[6]

Statistical studies conducted in Waite's own time period amply bear out his contentions. In referring to these analyses Harold U. Faulkner, in his Politics, Reform, and Expansion — 1890-1900, says that "the distribution of wealth in 1900 was shockingly unequal. . . . It is safe to conclude that 80 percent of Americans lived in 1900 on the margin of subsistence while the remaining 20 percent controlled almost the entire wealth of the country."[7]

Waite contended that monopoly existed in many economic areas. In one attack on monopoly, he referred to "land monopoly, money monopoly, transportation monopoly, trade monopoly, patent monopoly, liquor monopoly, and any or all other monopolies."[8] Calling attention to ownership of coal and iron ore lands by a few corporations, he described the dangers of monopoly controls over natural resources. The most important resources in Colorado, for example, were in the hands of a few corporations, he said. An example was the Colorado coal monopoly.

In 1892, there were 3,771,234 tons of coal mined in Colorado. One company, the Colorado Fuel and Iron Company, produced 1,912,703 tons, over half of the total. The C. F. & I. was either the dominant or nearly sole producer in every coal mining area except the northern Colorado fields. It dominated the rich coal fields of Las Animas and Huerfano Counties in southern Colorado, which produced nearly half of the coal mined in the state. Five companies produced 83 per cent of the total coal mined, or 3,136,487 tons. Besides the C. F. & I., these companies were the Trinidad Coke and Coal Co., the Canon City Coal Co., the United Coal Co., and the Victor Coal Co.[9]

Governor Waite might have referred to other industries in Colorado to buttress his point.

In 1882, the Colorado Coal and Iron Company began producing steel in Pueblo. In October, 1892, this company merged with the Colorado Fuel and Iron Co. This one company dominated both coal and steel production in Colorado. The management of the Colorado Coal and Iron Co. and Colorado's leading railroad, the Denver and Rio Grande, had been "closely related" and the two companies had "parallel developments."[10]

Other areas of Colorado industry manifested the same tendency towards greater economic concentration. A few companies such as the Omaha and Grant Smelting Company, the Globe Smelting and Refining Company, and the Pueblo Smelting Company dominated the smelting industry.[11] In 1899, the merger of most of Colorado's smelters resulted in the formation of the smelter trust, the American Smelting and Refining Company. In the same year, the sugar beet industry began in Colorado, and by 1905, several factories combined to form the Great Western Sugar Company.[12]

The concentration of economic and political power in Colorado in the late nineteenth century and early twentieth century could well be indicated by reference to some of Colorado's leading names which included Jerome B. Chaffee, Nathaniel P. Hill, Thomas M. Patterson, Horace A. W. Tabor, Henry M. Teller, Edward O. Wolcott, William J. Palmer, Charles Boettcher, David H. Moffat, J. J. Hagerman, William S. Stratton, Alva Adams, John and William Evans, John F. Shafroth, Charles S. Thomas, and Casimero Barela. Many of these people got their start in mining or in mining law. Several of these people represented an integration of political and economic power.

Waite was also concerned with the monopoly of the press. The press, he asserted, was controlled "by an Associated Press monopoly, which alters or suppresses all items of news as supposed best for the interests of the monopoly." He believed that newspaper editorials often "misquoted law" and "misrepresented facts."[13] Since the regular commercial press was largely hostile to his reforming zeal, he spoke from bitter experience on this point.

Waite's newspaper, the Union Era, attacked the growing concentration of wealth and power in the steel industry and ridiculed Andrew Carnegie and his Gospel of Wealth:

> The gall of this man Carnegie is monumental. He speaks of "wealth going more and more from the hands of the few into the hands of the many!" He must mean the many millionaires. "The wages of labor rise!" And this very man Carnegie within the last six months has reduced the wages of laboring men at the steel works at Allegheny City and other points in which he is interested over thirty percent. He lies like a goldbug. Carnegie suggests a taxation of the estates of millionaires after their death of fifty percent. There is some sense in this suggestion, but we have far more faith that the millionaires will get justice after death, than while they are living.[14]

The economics of special privilege produced their ill effects on other parts of the social organism, Waite asserted. There was a noticeable growth of "a host of social evils such as crime, gambling, prostitution, blackmailing, bribery, deception and perjury."[15] A century ago, Waite believed, "education, science, and philosophy" were on the side of freedom. This was no longer true. Now, "theological and scientific universities are founded by millionaires whose professors teach that the axioms of political economy and the truths of the Declaration of Independence are lies."[16]

Historically, Waite probed the question of special privilege and wealth held by ruling elites. Ancient times had its share of woes and troubles with the Pharaohs, Herods, Caligulas, and Caesars. Jesus had

46

his difficulties with the ruling forces of his society. He had "pronounced that terrible Phillipic 'O ye generation of serpents, how can ye escape the damnation of Hell,'" as "he knitted a whip of small cords and drove the money changers from the temple."[17] In modern times, the British ruling class or money power had become the force which dominated the world.[18] Through exploitation by the new industrial and financial forces of the Western European powers, the great mass of people in Europe, Asia, and Africa were pauperized by the end of the nineteenth century. Even in England, Waite remarked, one-third of the people were dependent on charity for support. In Belgium, the average wage was seven cents a day. The same concentration of wealth and increase in poverty were to be seen in Russia, Turkey, France, and many other countries, he continued.

Pauperization in America had not reached the same stage, Waite believed, due to the vast tracts of public land. "But we are fast treading the same path, and without a change in the present system or policy must soon accomplish the same result so clearly manifest in the old world." In 1800, there were no millionaires in the United States, and the very poor were scarce, Waite asserted. During the War of 1812, the first great fortunes were amassed. John Jacob Astor and others had accumulated profits through commerce. Wealth was widely diffused, however, during the early decades of the nineteenth century. "The aristocracy of birth, to which wealth was simply accessory, had viewed with contempt the efforts of the French philosophers, and of Franklin, Paine, Jefferson, and other patriotic reformers of the new world, who laid broad and deep the foundations of liberty, and reared a temple which was to be a refuge and strong rock of defense for the oppressed of all nations and climes."[19]

With the triumph of industrialism in the United States, a new aristocracy of wealth had risen and was bent on destroying the democracy of the pre-Civil War era, the governor asserted. In the last thirty years, both old parties, the Democrats and the Republicans, had become the instruments of the "tyranny of oppression" of the money power. Waite warned that "the monopolists are organizing their forces to defend their robber system and we must unite and fight or surrender completely to their power."[20]

As governor, several of Waite's vetoes reflected an anti-monopoly viewpoint. One bill which he vetoed extended the life of corporations. The governor commented: "I am opposed in general principle to increase the powers or diminish the liabilities of corporations without good cause shown."[21] The governor opposed a bonding bill on the grounds it gave special privileges to corporations.[22] He opposed insurance company legislation because he believed that it protected an insurance company monopoly which already charged double the rates to be found east of the Mississippi.[23]

Governor Waite supported the national anti-trust convention which was held in Chicago in 1893. He wrote to Ignatius Donnelly that he could not attend, but would send a delegation "to fight monopoly."[24] Waite dismissed the Sherman Anti-Trust Act as ineffective and largely meaningless. Senator William Stewart of Nevada had written to Waite that he was opposed to the Sherman Anti-Trust Act because it would only be used against labor organizations. Waite replied, "As to the Sherman Trust bill you were a true prophet, but possibly the very tyranny practiced under that law will arouse the people and compel an amendment or repeal."[25] He was referring to the use of the Sherman Act to break the Pullman railroad strike in 1894.

Many writers on Populism have argued or simply assumed that the Populists looked backward to an earlier, simpler golden agrarian age and wanted a return of laissez-faire competition. Waite does not fit into this view. The return of competition was not the answer to monopoly for Waite. He observed, "Competition grows sharper and more unscrupulous. Shrewdness and hustling enterprise supplant honesty and ability. Business in its mad rush for existence descends to lower and lower depths and how must it end?"[26]

Waite was not anti-industrial. Rather he insisted on a remolding of the industrial order to serve the many rather than the privileged few. Monopoly had to be reorganized to serve the public welfare. Addressing the graduating class of the agricultural college at Fort Collins, he said:

> Monopoly of a public nature organized in the interest of caste, but which derives every chartered privilege from the people, is sucking the life blood of the prosperity and liberty of the nation. It has been supposed, and some may now think, that such results are inseparable from monopoly. But this is not the case. It all depends upon whether the monopoly is

organized in the interest of a privileged class or in the interest of the people. The United States post office is a proof that a monopoly organization in the interest of the people is a blessing and not a cure. The remedy for all monopolies, of every kind and nature, is found in their reorganization in the public interest (italics supplied).[27]

This statement is apparently as close as Waite ever came to espousing socialism. Actually, it revealed the characteristic pragmatic approach of Waite. Whether public ownership or some form of public regulation would be best would depend on the individual case.

In demanding the reorganization of monopoly in the public interest Waite was not at variance with the Omaha Platform. Students who connect Populism with rugged individualism, limited government, states' rights, and the return to a simpler era of laissez-faire competition would do well to ponder the following statement in the platform:

We believe that the powers of government — in other words, of the people — should be expanded (as in the case of the postal service) as rapidly and as far as the good sense of an intelligent people and the teachings of experience shall justify, to the end that oppression, injustice, and poverty shall eventually cease in the land.[28]

Waite forecast dire consequences for the country if the forces of monopoly were not defeated. He believed that victory would come through some kind of radical but peaceful change via the ballot box:

It must end in the common ruin that overwhelmed all earlier republics and civilizations, or the wisdom, learning, and experience of the Past and Present must point out a way of escape from the Red Sea which threatens us - - - - I believe that the end will come with a change so radical that no trace of the old disease will remain - - - so sudden that no black scorial of war, famine, and crime will mark the transition - - - - a peaceful victory by the ballot.[29]

While advocating public regulation of large scale corporate enterprise, there is nothing to indicate he did not continue to believe in competitive small business enterprise. After all, Waite himself had been mercantilist, newspaper proprietor, rancher, lawyer, land owner, and mining prospector.

Davis Waite and the Socialists

To assume that Populism was almost entirely an agrarian movement as Hicks and others have done is very misleading. Populism was a complex movement of varied forces and often conflicting ideas and tendencies. The socialists were a vital component of the Populist movement. Indeed, the Populist leader Henry D. Lloyd was moved to say after the 1894 elections that the socialists were "the most intelligent, most energetic, most reliable workers we have."[30] More conservative Populist leaders did not like the socialists and did not agree with Lloyd. The socialist orientation with its call for a planned economy and the public ownership of the means of production and distribution represented, of course, the most radical and thorough-going application of Waite's call for a reorganization of monopoly to serve the public welfare.

Waite became identified with the more reform-minded elements of the Populist movement, which included the socialists. On questions of reform, Waite usually was in agreement with the socialists. Though radical in his criticisms of monopoly, Waite's approach was essentially pragmatic, leaving little room for theoretical analysis or thorough long-term solutions. Humorously, but not very logically, Waite suggested that since he was getting old only short-term solutions could concern him. He said:

> Being a man somewhat advanced in years.
> I am inclined to take what might be called a
> practical view of matters. I pay but little
> heed to any proposed reform if the system is
> not practical and as particularly applicable
> to practicality I inquire is the problem con-
> stitutional? That is, can the citizen with
> the undoubted rights the constitution gives
> elect a Congress or legislature which has the
> authority to grant the relief sought?[31]

Waite subscribed to the New Nation edited by the utopian socialist Edward Bellamy, and may have been influenced to some extent by it.[32] However, Waite considered the Bellamy movement itself little more than a devisive nuisance similar to the Single Taxers and the Prohibitionists.

Until the late nineties the main Marxian socialist group in the United States was the Socialist Labor Party. Its leader, Daniel De Leon, wanted nothing to do with the Populist Party, but in spite of De Leon, many members of the Socialist Labor Party worked with the Populists.[33] There is nothing on record to indicate that Waite ever commented about the S. L. P., or took cognizance of its existence. However, Waite's relationship with several individual Marxian socialists is of interest. Waite had acquired a national reputation as a friend of labor. Some socialists felt Waite was ripe for conversion to the socialist cause. F. G. R. Gordon wrote to him:

> I recently noticed an article from you in a Texas Populist Party paper which shows that you know free silver will not do much for the working class in America. I organized the first P. P. club and was the first State Secretary of the party in this state. I have left the party disgusted at the way we progressed backwards. I am a member of the Socialist Labor Party which I regard today as the only party standing for the true interests of the working class. I have no doubt there are at least 500,000 socialists in America and could we once unite them and organize 10 per cent into Socialist sections we would inside of ten years convert this country to socialism. The issue is not money or tariff — it is socialism vs. capitalism.

> I believe you are a socialist and if you are you can do a power of good by joining hands with the only political party in America that means a real change — with such men as you, Debs, Lloyd, and others we can go forward to a real victory. The machinery of the party is placed in the hands of the people by means of the initiative and referendum and no other party in this country does that; therefore, it follows that every other party will be owned by a set of political bosses just as soon as they are large enough to be worth controlling. I certainly believe it is your duty to investigate

51

this movement and if you find it is right your
duty is to help it on; if you find it is not
right your duty is to point out such wrong to
such as me. The radical populists have nowhere
to go except into a radical party such as the
Socialist Labor Party. With best wishes for your
future success and the hope that you will one day
be with us - - -.[34]

William Riley of Massachusetts wrote to the
governor as "an old-time Socialist, once on the Council of the International, with Karl Marx, with whom I
was well acquainted." However, his main present interest seemed to be in typical Populist financial and
political reforms. An obvious admirer of Davis Waite,
he remarked, "You are known and respected by many
thousands of people, outside of Denver — by hundreds
of thousands who don't know the names of the big little
blusterers, who bawl and sweat for pelf and place, like
hogs scrambling for swill. Take courage. Not only in
Denver, and in Colorado, but throughout the world,
there are many thousands of people looking to you as
a leader."[35]

Norman Lermond of Maine suggested to Waite that
socialism would develop in the western states, especially California, Oregon, Washington, Texas, and
Colorado, where natural resources were plentiful and
the radical sentiment strong. Socialism would then
march triumphantly eastward.[36]

Eugene V. Debs was Waite's most famous socialist
correspondent. Debs and Waite corresponded occasionally over a period of several years from 1894 to 1899.
During the earlier part of the period, Debs was still
only a reformer and a Populist.[37] They also met from
time to time at various rallies and national gatherings after Waite ceased to be governor. Their interest in each other undoubtedly stemmed from the Cripple
Creek and Pullman strikes of 1894. Debs had been
sentenced to six months in jail for his role in the
Pullman strike. (See chapter on labor.)

When Debs was released from jail in Woodstock,
Illinois on November 22, 1895, Waite spoke at the wel-
coming rally in Chicago where he lashed out at the
government's use of the injunction to break strikes.[38]

Topics discussed by Debs and Waite in their
correspondence included labor, Populism, woman suffrage, the election of 1896, and socialism. Writing

from McHenry County Jail at Woodstock in July, 1895, Debs, referring to a Populist gathering in Fort Worth which Waite would attend, stated:

> The platform you outline meets with my hearty approval and I know I shall be able to enthusiastically approve each sentiment you express at the Fort Worth meeting. The disintegrating forces are at work in both the old parties. They will not be able to harmonize on the money issue as we will get the full benefit of the disruption which is inevitable. Everything now depends upon how the People's Party shall handle itself in the coming months. If present councils prevail and the leaders of the movement are true to themselves and to the principles of the party, there is no question but that the People's Party will triumph over the Goldbugs and their henchmen, tools, and parasites, and inaugurate all the great reforms to which they are pledged.[39]

Debs received Waite's 1895 periodical publication in the jail. "We read <u>Our Nation's Crisis</u> with genuine satisfaction, but suggest that one copy will serve the purpose as we pass it from hand to hand until we have read it.[40] Mere palliatives will not answer the demand. We must, as you say, strike at the root of the evil, and we must strike with united force and persistence until the evil shall be extirpated. I am with the People's Party and see no reason why all reformers cannot unite upon their platform. It may not be just what any of us wish but it affords common ground upon which we can muster our forces."[41]

Writing two weeks later in answer to Waite's emphasis on the need for political action by labor, Debs remarked:

> I am satisfied that the great body of organized laborers will insist upon political action notwithstanding any restraining influence that may be exercised upon them by their leaders. Organized labor never can accomplish anything until it unites for active, political work and this is so self-evident that a man who cannot clearly see it must be obtuse indeed. But there are leaders whose mission it is to keep labor divided and at cross purposes and these will of course do what they can to prevent anything like political action. But the men are

beginning to comprehend the drift and I am greatly
mistaken if they do not break away from the old
programme and follow their instincts in the
application of the one possible remedy for the
evils of which they are the victims.[42]

In a letter in 1899, Debs stated clearly to Waite
his conversion to socialism and the reasons for it.
He said:

> I have an enormous mass of correspondence
> before me, but as soon as I can enforce a little
> leisure I will read your article on the Rights
> of Labor which appears in the American of the 3rd
> ult. I have with pleasure noticed the very flat-
> tering editorial comment of the article, and
> glancing over it I am satisfied I shall find in
> it much of interest and value. The history of
> the Cripple Creek affair will be of special
> interest to me. In answer to your inquiry I have
> to say that I am giving my time to the advocacy
> of straight out socialism, I am devoting my
> present time largely to lecturing on that subject,
> and have but just returned from a three weeks
> course in the West as far as Omaha where I had a
> fine audience. I care little about the money
> question. It will never be settled under the
> present system. It is the question of the pri-
> vate ownership of the earth. I am after the whole
> Capitalistic animal and care little about the
> fleas that are rotting in its hide. As long as
> the means of production are privately owned and
> industry is operated for private profit, working-
> men will be slaves, no matter what kind of a
> monetary system we may have. Socialism furnishes
> the complete remedy and I have no time to waste
> on any of the make-shifts this side of it. Our
> movement is spreading rapidly and I am full of
> hope. Before 1910 is written Socialism will have
> swept this country.[43]

It is not known what Waite's reaction was to this
last message from Debs. However, there is no evidence
that Waite changed his own views in the less than three
years he had to live. With the strong growth of
socialist sentiment in the early years of the twentieth
century in the United States, a number of radical
Populists did reach the conclusion that socialism was
the only answer to monopoly and entered the ranks of
the new Socialist Party. One Populist leader, Henry

D. Lloyd, already a socialist in his views, was on the verge of joining the Socialist Party at the time of his death in 1903.[44]

CHAPTER VI

TRANSPORTATION AND LAND

Transportation and land were the two major sections, in addition to money, in the Omaha Platform. The question of the railroads was a relatively new one; the issue of land ownership was an old one dating back to the early days of the republic. As with the issue of money, the problem of monopoly was the central concern in both the transportation and land planks of the platform. At one key point, the circumstance of land monopoly and transportation monopoly interlocked because of the large grants of land which had been made to the railroads.

The Railroads

In the decades following the Civil War, a system of railroads pushed across the vast stretches of the western half of the United States and completed a transcontinental system. These railroads greatly accelerated the settlement of the central and western portions of this country. They played an important role in the development of a nationwide economy, and helped greatly to lay the foundations for modern American industrial society.

However, the railroads were not an unmitigated blessing. Unlike the East, a few railroad lines dominated the West almost from the beginning, and they were powerful and influential. The individual citizen, whether farmer, businessman, or otherwise, had little chance of bargaining favorably with these corporate giants. The railroads brought about problems and engaged in practices which resulted in vigorous protests by various groups, especially the farmers. The railroad companies asserted that their affairs were private, and that no national, state, or local authority had any right to interfere.[1]

Nonetheless, William Larrabee, ex-governor of Iowa, expressed a common view when he said that the railroad had assumed the character of an international highway and was quite public in nature, though under private ownership.[2] If the railroads were public in nature, it was argued, they should come under public scrutiny.

Protests against the railroads arose over poor railroad construction, numerous accidents, discourtesies to travelers and shippers, waste, corruption involving many governmental officials, pooling arrangements, high rates, discrimination in rates, rebates to favored customers, the railroad pass system, unwise management, ownership of large amounts of land by the railroads, and eastern and foreign control of railroads.[3]

During the late nineteenth century many attempts were made to bring the railroads under greater public control through state and national government action. The earliest and most vigorous efforts were by farm groups intent on curbing the power of the railroads. The early leader was the Patrons of Husbandry, commonly known as the Grange. The state Granges' opposition to the railroads centered in the mid-western Great Lakes area during the seventies.[4] Laws regulating the railroads were passed in Illinois, Minnesota, Iowa, and Wisconsin. These laws were upheld in the case of Munn vs. Illinois in 1877. From 1876 to 1880 the United States Supreme Court sustained several other state "Granger" laws regulating the railroads. In 1886 in the Wabash vs. Illinois case the Supreme Court reversed itself, making state regulation difficult. In the case of Minnesota vs. Chicago, Milwaukee, and St. Paul Railway Company in 1890, the position of the states was made even more difficult when a Minnesota "Granger" law was declared unconstitutional because it had not allowed a judicial review of rates.[5]

It soon became more logical in any event to regulate the railroads at the national rather than the state level, as giant integrated railroad systems crisscrossed state lines.

The Interstate Commerce Act, the first national attempt to regulate the railroads, was passed in 1887. This law, which set up the Interstate Commerce Commission, was ineffective during the remaining years of the nineteenth century.

The Farmer's Alliance, which became a powerful agrarian protest movement in the eighties, continued the Granger tradition of opposition to various railroad practices. From 1889-1892, the Alliances cooperated with the Knights of Labor and other reform groups in working out a common program of action at several conventions. The platform invariably called for either stringent public control or public ownership of the railroads. At a meeting in St. Louis in December, 1889,

58

the Southern Alliance and the Knights of Labor demanded
that "The means of communication and transportation
shall be owned by and operated in the interest of the
people as is the United States postal system." Meeting
at the same time, the Northern Alliance pressed the
same demand and added "that the government take steps
to secure the payment of the debt of the Union and Central Pacific railroads and their branches by foreclosure
and sale, and any attempt to extend the time again for
the payment of the same beyond the present limit will
meet with our most emphatic condemnation."[6]

Reform conventions at Ocala, Florida in 1890, and
at Cincinnati in 1891, wrote platforms containing a
compromise plank on the railroads in order to obtain
broader support. The Cincinnati plank read, "We demand
the most rigid, honest, and just national control and
supervision of the means of public communication and
transportation." The stronger demand was restored to
the St. Louis convention of February 22, 1892, which
laid the groundwork for the Populist national nominating
convention in July at Omaha. The demand for public
ownership of the railroads was incorporated into the
Omaha Platform.

The first trains connected Colorado with the
outside world in 1870. The Denver Pacific connected
Cheyenne and Denver; the Kansas Pacific connected Kansas and Denver.[7] Both out-of-state railroads and local
railroad companies built in Colorado in the seventies.
Chief of the latter was the Denver and Rio Grande which
connected the important north-south artery from Denver
to Trinidad. Highlighting Colorado railroad history
during the seventies was the railroad war between the
Atchison, Topeka and Santa Fe and the Denver and Rio
Grande railroads.[8] Railroad development in Colorado
was especially significant in the eighties. Not only
was the mileage more than tripled, but the rails pene-
trated deep into the mountains to reach important
mining centers. The daily newspaper of Aspen noted
that the most important event in 1887 to this booming
silver mining town was the coming of the railroad.[9]
Ore could now be shipped cheaply to market. The railroads also played an increasingly important role in
linking such commercial centers as Denver with the East.

Railroads in Colorado by the early nineties
included the Denver and Rio Grande; Chicago, Rock
Island, and Pacific; Chicago, Burlington and Quincy;
Atchison, Topeka, and Santa Fe; Union Pacific; Rio

Grande Southern; Pueblo and State Line; Manitou and
Pike's Peak; Gilpin Tramway; Colorado Eastern; Rio
Grande Junction; Missouri Pacific; Colorado Midland;
and Denver, Texas and Gulf. The Denver and Rio Grande
had 1017 miles of track in 1892, the most mileage in
the state.

     With the development of the railroads in Colorado
came the usual criticisms. Rates, rebates, pooling
agreements, and the pass system were the chief issues.
Also involved were such questions as the general efficiency of railroad management, land owned by the railroads, proper public knowledge of railroad operations,
management-labor disputes, safety measures for the
rugged mountain terrain, and eastern-foreign controls.[10]
When Colorado entered the Union in 1876, the new state
constitution provided that the legislature could alter
or repeal railroad charters and forbid "unreasonable"
discrimination in rates. These provisions were a
reflection of the "Granger" laws in midwestern states.[11]
The constitution also forbade local aid to railroads
in Colorado.[12] There was no further restrictive railroad legislation in Colorado until the mid-eighties.
In 1885, the Colorado House of Representatives formed
a special railroad committee to investigate discrimination in rates, which, it was alleged, was blocking the
development of manufacturing in Colorado. As a result
of this investigation, the office of railroad commissioner was established on April 6, 1885. William B.
Felker was named the first commissioner. Thereafter,
matters remained in a quiescent state until W. A. Hamill
was appointed railroad commissioner by Governor John L.
Routt in 1891. Despite the reiteration by both major
political parties of the need for adequate railroad
regulations, little was done between 1885-1892, and
the powers and finances of the railroad commissioner
were limited.[13] No reports were issued between Felker's
in 1885 and Hamill's in 1892.

     The report of W. A. Hamill at the end of 1892 is
very instructive in analyzing the Colorado railroad
situation on the advent of the Waite administration to
power. Hamill's outlook was in the militant reform
tradition shared by Waite, and helped to set the stage
ideologically for Waite's recommendations to the state
legislature concerning the railroad question. Hamill
assailed the railroads for combating any public control
or regulation:

There has been for the last ten years an earnest desire on the part of the people of Colorado for general railroad legislation. Commencing with the legislative session of 1881 there has been a determined opposition by the railroad corporations of the state to the enacting of any railroad legislation whatever, and they have measurably succeeded in carrying out their wishes in opposition to the people of the state.

The act of 1885, under which this department is now operating, was passed by the Fifth General Assembly in the face of the most bitter opposition that could be offered to any measure that looked towards the common good.[14]

What was needed was a railroad commission which had real power to regulate freight and passenger rates, Hamill asserted. Thirty-two states had enacted laws regulating railroad companies, and "many of them went so far as to give the railroad commissioners the absolute power to fix rates of freight and passengers, and to publish a schedule of such rates, by which the railroad companies must be governed."[15] Railroads in other states had fought regulation, too, Hamill noted, but the railroads had not been hurt by the rules and regulations that had been put into effect.

The last Colorado legislature had failed to make an appropriation for the railroad commissioner. Therefore, Hamill had not even been able to publish the facts and statistics that he had gathered about railroad operations in Colorado. No funds were available to investigate accidents, although there had been an increase in railroad accidents throughout the country. In Colorado 68 people were killed and 198 were injured between July 1, 1891 and December 31, 1892.[16]

Davis Waite constantly pledged his full adherence to the Omaha Platform and thus to public ownership of the railroads. He reaffirmed his belief in this principle specifically on a number of occasions. In August, 1892, the following editorial comments appeared in the Aspen Union Era. "Public ownership of the railroads would reduce rates to one-fifth of the present rate. This would greatly increase the traffic. This would require many thousand more railroad men. Can the boys see it? Private ownership of the railroads is a charter from the government to rob without fear of any laws."[17]

However, as governor of a state, his main concern was of necessity the regulation of the railroads.

Governor Waite gave top priority to the railroad question in his inaugural address. It was the first topic discussed, and it was discussed in greater detail than any other. He said, "There is nothing of greater importance to the people of Colorado than the railroad question. There is no issue that for a longer period has engaged the attention of the citizens of the state, or upon which the public sentiment has been so united, and none in which fewer practical concessions have been made to the sentiment."[18]

In attacking railroad abuses, Waite focused upon rate discrimination: "The right to make tariffs and enforce their collection is inherent in any railway system, but the right, directly or indirectly, for any railway to rebate a portion of its tariff, and thus discriminate between its customers in the collection of its revenues, is a right which no civilized government claims and no sovereign has dared to exercise for centuries."

Waite especially accused the railroads of discriminating against the Colorado silver mining industry. A freight charge of $8.00 per ton was levied on silver ore shipped to Denver from Aspen, Leadville, and other Colorado silver mining camps. On the other hand, coal, which was owned by the rail company, was shipped from Trinidad, Canon City, and other coal mining areas to Denver for $5.00 per ton. Furthermore, "there are many mineral deposits unworked, and some entire counties in Colorado, possessed of abundant, varied, and valuable mineral resources, and undeveloped simply because the rates of railroad transportation are prohibitory."

Railways did not properly recognize that they had a greater public responsibility than the ordinary business, the governor charged. No state rail commission ever made an unfair demand; yet the companies opposed the commissions in every way possible and acted as though they were being ruined. Pooling arrangements often brought long hauls at lower rates than any ever commanded by a state commission. The railroads acceded to the "absurd and extortionate demands" of the "monopolies, trusts, and combines," but never protested against them. Instead they made up for it by impositions on "local traffic and non-

62

competing points." The people of Colorado, Waite continued, had no intention of hurting the rail companies. The railroads, however, showed no intention of changing their policies.

Waite made four recommendations to the state legislature:

First — The repeal of the present law providing for a railway commission.

Second — A new act for a railway commission, with three commissioners, empowered to hear and determine complaints without recourse to the courts, and to revise the rates of the carriage of passengers and freight.

Third — That the system of pooling, as now in force among the railways of the state be made illegal; and

Fourth — That the issuing by any railway company of any pass or free ticket to, or the acceptance of or traveling upon such pass or free ticket by any state, district, or municipal official be made a penal offense.[19]

Unfortunately, from the standpoint of adequate railroad regulation, the state assembly acted only on the governor's first point. The 1885 railroad commission law was repealed, and the state of Colorado was left without a railroad regulatory act. What had happened was reminiscent of the repeal earlier of the state "Granger" railroad laws in several midwestern states.[20] When the bill to repeal the 1885 law was passed, Governor Waite vetoed the bill on the grounds that the 1885 act was better than nothing. The bill was repassed over the veto by the necessary two-thirds vote. The veto could not have been overridden without considerable Populist support. Seven out of thirteen Populists opposed Governor Waite in the Senate; in the House, nine Populists joined thirty Republicans and five Democrats to override the veto. The governor charged that the railroad act had been repealed so that his Populist administration could not put teeth into it.[21]

In his disavowal of the railroad pass system, Waite set a personal example. He received passes from the Denver and Rio Grande, the Santa Fe, and the Union

Pacific, but he returned them.[22] Waite thus indicated that he intended to remain free of pressures stemming from favoritism in order to pursue a policy of railroad reform.

Supporters praised Waite for his actions. William Garner of Trinidad hoped other Populists would follow his example.[23]

Even during the troubled days of the Cripple Creek strike in 1894 when special trains were supplied to state officials, Governor Waite refused to become entangled in any position where favors might be owed. President E. T. Jeffrey of the Denver and Rio Grande furnished a special train to Cripple Creek to aid the governor in settling the dispute. Jeffrey said the company would make no charge, but Waite charged the state for the train.[24]

Waite continued to remain firm on the railroad question despite his setback at the hands of the state legislature. He belittled the Populists for backing down on the problem at a time when he thought action could be taken due to the increased difficulties experienced by the railroads during the economic crisis of the nineties. Public ownership became more and more the theme in his speeches and correspondence.

The governor disagreed with those who maintained nothing could be done about the railroads:

> The monopolists say "there is no remedy for these railroad extortions. The people must grin and stand it for the United States can't possibly buy up the railroads. They cost too much." My friend, you mistake the remedy. The way is to confiscate the Pennsylvania Railroad and all others which unjustly discriminate . . . They say government cannot make the railroad business pay. Well, that is no objection. It ought not to pay anything but construction, expenses, and repairs. Government could run the roads at much less expense than private enterprise; it could dispense with simply competing lines. Hardly a railroad in the country now is run up to its capacity. It could dispense with ticket scalpers and runners, with the vast and demoralizing pass system under which those the most able to pay now ride free, but most of all it would dispense with unjust discrimination.[25]

Other nations had similar railroad difficulties, Waite averred, and they had found the answer in public ownership. In Germany, for instance, the fares and freights were less than half those of the United States.[26] In California, all political parties demanded that the government foreclose on the Union Pacific, Waite noted. The Denver Board of Trade, "not a Populist on it," called for the same action. The railroads were going into the hands of U. S. receivers during the depression of the mid-nineties. Overspeculation and railroad mismanagement had figured heavily in this calamitous situation. Now was the time, Waite argued, to press for public ownership on a national basis.

On the railroad question, Governor Waite gained the distinction of being a prophet without honor in his own country. In the twentieth century nearly every country in the world except the United States has achieved public ownership of their railroad system in whole or in part. Up to the present, the United States has been content to engage in regulation of the railroads, except for the recent introduction of the skeletal Amtrak passenger service. However, a number of national railroad regulatory measures which resulted from the criticism of Waite and other reformers were passed in the early years of the twentieth century.

The Public Domain

From the founding days of the Republic to Waite's time, the question of the proper use of the vast land areas which the United States acquired was ever present. The main thread ran between those who believed land primarily belonged to the actual settler, usually a person of limited means, and those who favored a policy which heavily favored the exploitation of the land by a privileged wealthy few.[27]

A gradual democratization of land policy occurred early in the nineteenth century. The Land Act of 1796 provided for the sale of a minimum acreage of 640 acres at two dollars an acre; after several land acts, the minimum acreage in 1820 was reduced to eighty acres and the price to $1.25 an acre. The principle of aid to the small settler was further recognized in the Preemption Act of 1841, which established the right of settlement prior to purchase. However, large scale land speculation was common and land monopoly was aided by several land acts. In the 1840's George Henry Evans and his Labor Reform movement made plans to end excessive speculation in land and land monopoly through government gifts of land with inalienable titles. In 1862, with the accession of the new anti-slavery and free soil Republican Party to power, the long-hoped for Homestead Act, providing 160 acres of free land to those who would settle and improve it for five years, became a reality.

The Homestead Act together with its modifications to more arid, treeless conditions — the Timber Culture Act of 1873, the Desert Land Act of 1877, and the Timber and Stone Act of 1878 — became the basic land policy for the post-civil War decades. The 1841 Preemption Act remained in effect. Theoretically these land laws favored the settler, but the operations of them often favored the land grabber instead. Many would-be homesteaders were only hired agents of land monopolists. The actual homesteader often found himself on poorer land far removed from the railroad. After the passage of the Homestead Act until 1900, eighty-four out of every hundred new farms were acquired either through purchase or land subdivision.[28] The trend toward large-scale farming in the West was pronounced, and farm tenancy increased. The land acts of the 1870's mainly aided large cattle and timber companies in gaining control over large tracts of land.

Railroad companies received millions of acres of choice land from the government. The railroads often clashed with the settlers over land rights and sometimes unjustly deprived them of their land. Much good land was sold by the railroads to cattlemen, timber barons, and other powerful interest groups. An 1866 law left the door open to ruthless exploitation of mineral lands. By 1886, over twenty million acres of land were owned by foreign syndicates. Absentee ownership of land, foreign and domestic, was common. In the post-Civil War decades, monopoly in land grew as the corporation and the speculator became dominant.[29]

Reflecting the concern over the trends in land development, the first resolution in the December, 1889 platform of the Northern Alliance read:

> Resolved, that the public land, the heritage of the people, be reserved for actual settlers only, and that measures be taken to prevent aliens

from acquiring titles to lands in the United
States and Territories, and that the law be
rigidly enforced against all railroad corporations which have not complied with the terms of
their contract, by which they have received large
grants of land.[30]

The statement by the Southern Alliance and Knights
of Labor at the same time was similar:

We demand the passage of laws prohibiting
the alien ownership of land, and that Congress
take early steps to devise some plan to obtain
all lands now owned by aliens and foreign syndicates; and that all lands now held by railroad
and other corporations in excess of such as is
actually used and needed by them, be reclaimed
by the Government and held for actual settlers
only.[31]

Pressures such as these probably led to the passage of the 1891 land act which repealed the timber
culture acts and preemption laws, and amended the
Homestead Act and the Desert Land Act. This act was a
weak and inneffective law, however, and, as a leading
student of land history has noted, the corporate ex-
ploitative processes continued to threaten democracy
in America.[32]

The Populist Omaha Platform of 1892 echoed the
earlier sentiments of the Alliances and the Knights:

The land, including all the natural resources
of wealth, is the heritage of all the people and
should not be monopolized for speculative purposes,
and alien ownership of land should be prohibited.
All land now held by railroads and other corporations in excess of their actual needs, and all
lands now owned by aliens, should be reclaimed by
the government and held for actual settlers only.[33]

Adhering to the Jeffersonian-Jacksonian tradition,
Waite believed that the land should be primarily for
the actual settler. He ventured that "perhaps the most
general evil that afflicts mankind is land monopoly."[34]
There should be a wide division of land ownership in
the United States to insure a large class of independent debt-free farmers able to achieve their own livelihood, the Jeffersonian-minded governor asserted.
Large-scale speculation in land, or ownership and

control of large tracts of land by railroad or other
corporate interests were foreign to Waite's way of
thinking. This view was the source of the governor's
opposition to alien ownership, which he identified with
speculative enterprise by foreign syndicates and wealthy
Europeans.

Waite attacked the government gifts of land to the
railroads:

> So criminally wasteful has been the land
> policy of the United States that an area of pub-
> lic lands nearly equal to all the New England
> states and New York and Pennsylvania combined
> has been given away to railroad corporations.
> This insane policy of the government for the
> past thirty years has produced effects which en-
> danger the permanence of our free institutions.[35]

The governor voiced concern over farm tenancy and
mortgage indebtedness:

> The U. S. Census shows that 9,000,000 of the
> 12,000,000 homesteads in the Union are mortgaged,
> at an estimated average of $500 each. This makes
> the farm residence debt $4,500,000,000 and inter-
> est thereon at 7 per cent is $315,000,000 . . . .
> The Census Bureau gives the amount of farm mort-
> gages in Iowa at $198,634,957 and in Kansas at
> $235,000,000.[36]

A reckless national land policy, Waite charged,
had resulted in the loss of much valuable land in
Colorado. He said:

> Immense tracts of the best agricultural
> lands in Colorado have been gobbled up by alien
> land owners and in good part by fraudulent land
> entries. A large portion of the coal lands in
> the state, now belonging to individuals and cor-
> porations, were entered fraudulently as "agri-
> cultural land," and, until within the past two
> years no attempt whatever has been made by the
> state to secure any benefit from its title to
> its mineral lands, although such lands have been
> the chief source of the prosperity of the people
> of Colorado.[37]

68

Waite was not in favor of the Carey Land Bill of
1894 which authorized the President to grant a maximum
of one million acres to each public land state for purposes of irrigation, settlement and reclamation. He
asserted that the bill had been drawn up in the interest of private corporations who wanted arid lands for
cattle ranges and speculative purposes.[38]

History complicated the land question in some
parts of Colorado. A number of Mexican land grants
had been recognized by the United States after the
Mexican War. Six of these were wholly or partially
located in southern and western Colorado, causing difficulties between the owners of the grants and various
squatters and homesteaders. Governor Waite did not
view these grants with sympathy, but rather saw them
as obstacles to legitimate homesteading. He sent to
the Commissioner of the General Land Office in Washington a petition of settlers on Maxwell Land Grant
in southern Colorado to secure their claims.[39]

The complicated nature of the land claims dating
back to the Spanish and Mexican periods was apparently
something about which Waite had little or no knowledge.
The question of legitimacy of claims prior to the Anglo
invasion probably never occurred to him, just as the
rights of the Indians did not occur to him.

In his farewell message to the Colorado legislature, Governor Waite voiced a concern for the preservation of natural resources. A policy of land for the
settler had to be joined by a program of adequate public control over the nation's resources. Waite noted
that thousands of acres were idle due to water erosion.
Man had destroyed the timber resources indiscriminately
in the mountains, and now the snows melted too rapidly.

The Single-Tax

Davis Waite agreed with Henry George in deploring
land monopoly and excessive speculation in land. Beyond that they disagreed. Waite had slight regard for
either Henry George or the single-tax theory. He considered the single-taxers a divisive nuisance with, at
best, long-term answers when short-term answers were
needed. Henry George was a political opportunist,
Waite believed, who took the same stand as the status
quo conservatives on the issues that were really important.

The governor ridiculed the idea that landowners ruled the world; they were only vassals of the money power. He cited the example of England where the landed aristocracy "had gone down before the money power like grass before the mower." The 120,000 land owners in Great Britain in 1816 were now less than 20,000. In the United States, he continued, under a system of mortgages and trust deed encumbrances, the bulk of the land was quietly but rapidly being absorbed by the creditor class. Hence, the ultimate solution to social and economic problems had to deal with money, not land, he concluded.

Waite's _Union Era_ in the summer of 1892 noted that "Henry George, the great apostle of free trade, is at Chicago helping to nominate Cleveland. Mr. George is also a goldbug."[40] In writing to Ignatius Donnelly, Waite accused Henry George of polling 52,000 votes for mayor of New York as an independent candidate in 1886 and then selling out to the Democrats.[41]

Waite had some correspondence with single-taxers in the mid-nineties. During his second year as governor, when he had gained fame beyond the state, there apparently was some effort by single-tax adherents to woo him and other Colorado Populists to the fold. C. P. Cooper, General Secretary of the Free Land League of America, located in New York, called Governor Waite a "thinking man and a humanitarian," but disagreed with him on the matter of land ownership by large corporations. Productive use of the land by the corporations was the problem, Cooper said.[42]

A discussion of the single-tax in a Waite publication, _Our Nation's Crisis_, led to several rejoinders by single-tax advocates. Waite had accused George of being against free silver and public ownership of the railroads and of being a political opportunist. He reiterated that the single-tax was impractical. A single-tax advocate named James Robertson from Altoona, Pennsylvania, answered that Waite had no understanding of single-tax doctrine even though he claimed to have read _Progress and Poverty_. Robertson said George was not against government control of the railroads, but did not know how he thought about free silver. (Actually, Henry George had said in _Progress and Poverty_ that there was distress whether a country had paper money or gold and silver until the land problem was solved.)[43]

70

The single-tax was no more impractical than proposed Populist reforms, Robertson continued. He defended George's support of the Democrats on the grounds that the Democrats were for tariff reform and the single-taxers believed in free trade, and he accused Waite and other adherents to the Omaha Platform of insincerity in their land and transportation planks, charging that they believed only in financial reforms, and used the other planks to snare single-taxers and socialists. He concluded that Waite was bitter towards Henry George because George had campaigned against a Populist in Minnesota. [44]

Henry George and Davis Waite had one other thing in common besides their hatred of land monopoly and their passion for social justice. They both adhered to over-simplified solutions to cure the ills produced by industrial capitalism. George had his one-sided land emphasis, and Waite had his one-sided money emphasis.

However, with the growth of trusts and the increasing integration of finance and industrial capital in the nineties, one cannot help but feel that Waite was much closer to putting his finger on the real center of power in the United States than George, and was considered, like other militant Populists and socialists, more dangerous to the status quo as a result.

CHAPTER VII

LABOR

At the beginning of the nineties the Knights of
Labor and the craft unions of the town dominated the
labor scene in Colorado. The Knights were on the wane
from their high point in the mid-eighties, continuing
to have support mainly in the mining areas. The Western Federation of Miners appeared in Colorado in 1893
during Waite's administration, but did not figure in
his election. However, the Federation was of importance relative to the Cripple Creek strike of 1894.
The American Railway Union, led by Eugene V. Debs, also
appeared in Colorado in 1893.[1]

The Colorado State Federation of Labor, a branch
of the American Federation of Labor, was not organized
until 1896, but local craft unions and assemblies were
of importance. Chief among these was the Denver Trades
and Labor Assembly, founded in the eighties.[2]

Davis H. Waite was an active member of the Knights
of Labor. In his last year at Aspen before becoming
governor, he was secretary of Aspen Assembly No. 4001
of the Knights of Labor. George C. Rohde, who was co-
editor with Waite of the Aspen Union Era, was chairman.[3]
In 1891 Waite was also president of the Aspen Trades
Assembly.[4] After being elected governor he was invited
to transfer his membership in the Knights to a Denver
assembly, but this was not to be publicly broadcast
for fear of causing harrassment of the governor.[5]

The Knights probably had an important ideological
influence on Waite. His views of arbitration, strikes,
the eight-hour day, the general rights of labor, and
specific industrial disturbances were identical with
the positions of the Knights. On other questions such
as strict regulation of the railroads, a democratic
land policy, woman suffrage, and monetary inflation
there was also a similarity of views. This parallelism
may come as a surprise to those who identify Populism
simply with agrarianism or silver, but Terence V.
Powderly, head of the Knights of Labor, was a speaker
at the Populist Omaha convention, and several planks
of the Omaha Platform reflect the influence of labor.

The nineties was a decade of tumultuous industrial strife and numerous strikes and lockouts. These included the New Orleans general strike of 1892 — one of the first general strikes in U. S. history; the national coal strike of 1894; metal mining strikes and lockouts in such widely scattered parts of the Rockies as Coeur d'Alene, Idaho in 1892 and Cripple Creek, Colorado in 1894; the steel lockout and strike in Homestead, Pa., near Pittsburgh; and various railroad-connected strikes such as the Buffalo, N. Y. switchmen's strike of 1892 and the Pullman and Great Northern strikes of 1894.

The Homestead steel strike occurred during the summer in which Waite was nominated for governor. Henry Clay Frick had recently become manager of the Carnegie Steel Company in Homestead. Partial union-ization at the plant extended only to the skilled workers. Frick decreed an average slash in wages of 22 per cent. This and other proposals the workers rejected, but held out for a compromise settlement. A number of hours before the contract ended the company closed down the plant, thus causing a lockout of the workers. All the workers, union and non-union, stood fast against the company for several months.

The Carnegie Steel Company arranged with the Pinkerton Detective Agency to import several hundred men to take over the plant, paving the way for the use of a scab labor force and for breaking the strike. A gun battle lasting most of the day ensued between the workers and the Pinkertons, resulting in several dead on both sides. The Pinkertons were defeated and the workers were temporarily in control of the situation. The clash, however, caused the forces of labor to hate the Pinkertons for many years to come. By such man-uevers as obtaining the arrest of all the strike leaders and getting the governor of Pennsylvania to call in the National Guard, the company finally de-feated the workers and destroyed the union.

Waite's sympathies were strongly with the steel-workers. He saw the whole affair as an attempt to break the union. In a letter which came to light in 1903, Carnegie revealed to Frick that this indeed was his goal.[6] Noting that the Pinkertons had lost in the battle with the workers, Waite charged that the guns taken from the detective agency force belonged to the United States government, indicating to him that those in authority were aiding a private army. President Benjamin Harrison could not declare war on labor, he elaborated, but "Robert Pinkerton was allowed to maintain a private army and conduct war."

Waite had little use for Carnegie. He accused
him of trying to break the spirit of his workers, of
exploiting both his workers and the public at large,
and of being tied politically to President Harrison
and the Republican Party.[7]

Waite's sympathy to labor was manifest in other
ways during the 1892 gubernatorial campaign. Speaking
at the Denver Coliseum, the future governor referred
to the Biblical phrase that "the laborer is worthy of
his hire" and the Lincoln statement that "the laborer
is more worthy than the capitalist." He charged that
government generally legislated against labor. In five
states where labor problems had recently occurred, he
said it was simply assumed that the corporations were
right and the workers were wrong.[8]

In his inaugural address, Governor Waite took a
position similar to the Knights of Labor on the question of arbitration and strikes. He favored arbitration and was opposed to strikes and lockouts. In
establishments employing forty or more he urged compulsory arbitration. These arbitration procedures
would be conducted by members of the current judiciary.
The governor further suggested that general strikes
and lockouts be outlawed. Thus would the public welfare be ensured and industrial peace established. To
advance its cause, labor should basically rely on
legislation.[9] Lacking these procedures, Waite did not
hesitate to support striking workers in what he felt
was a just cause, a position also generally assumed by
the rank-and-file membership of the Knights. Many
Knights, as well as many in labor later, would have
questioned Waite's theoretical position in the light
of economic and class realities, emphasizing instead
the principle of collective bargaining and the right
to strike. Waite rather naively relied on what could
be obtained through legislation alone. But Waite did
not become a hero to labor on the basis of theory, as
we will see, although his stance was a relatively
advanced one for political officials of the period.

Governor Waite voiced another plea of the Knights
of Labor in opposing the use of convict labor in private business. This was a favorite device of some
employers for obtaining cheap labor as well as seeking
to drive down wage scales. Unemployment lists were
likely to rise as jobs became more dear. However,

state employment of convict labor on irrigation canals, public roads and bridges and similar projects was justified, he felt.

Other specific recommendations for the advance of labor in Colorado closely paralleled those of the Denver Trades Assembly: an eight-hour day law; an amended mechanics' lien law, sufficient to secure wages; an employers' liability law; an amended anti-child labor law, with penalties severe enough to prevent the growing evils of child labor; an anti-Pinkerton law, forbidding the employment in Colorado of a private armed force.[10]

Waite's views on the labor issue were tested early in his administration. In March, 1893, charges of neglect of duty were brought against John McNeil, the State Inspector of Coal Mines. The charges stemmed from a number of accidents and bad working conditions which prevailed in the coal mines of the state. Complaints of the miners included: lack of safety catches on the cages of the shafts, poor ventilation in the mines, inadequate communication facilities between the surface and the underground, and insufficient exits.

Public hearings on the charges were held in Waite's office in March and in June of 1893. The governor visited two mines at Lafayette. In his estimation the ventilation and safety provisions in these mines were not up to the requirements of state law. Waite claimed that McNeil "virtually admitted neglect in the performance of his duty" by pleading lack of funds for traveling expenses and other necessary items. This was not valid reasoning, Waite felt. McNeil, he said, should resign under such circumstances or face removal for neglect of duty. D. J. Reed eventually replaced McNeil.

Governor Waite believed that McNeil was a shield for the mine operators. Drawing attention to the Colorado mining law, Waite noted that "Sec. 17 mining laws requires that the Inspector shall see that these things be done and as he does not do them and persists in shielding the operations, he has not the confidence or respect of the miners, especially as the feeling in general that when communications have been sent to him in the past, complaining of anything in or about the mine, that he has sent the communications back to the employer, and the discharge of the men making these complaints has speedily taken place."

On the basis of the available evidence, it can be said that at the very least McNeil was not the type of inspector who would ever cause coal mine owners any trouble through criticism or aggressively working for reforms to better conditions in the mines. This was true despite the constant stream of fatal and non-fatal accidents. Sixty-three fatal accidents occurred in the mines during 1891 and 1892.[11]

Two reports are available on an inspection tour of the Rouse mine in Huerfano County following a fatal accident there on October 8, 1891. The reports are by State Inspector of Coal Mines John McNeil and J. C. Sharp of the Trades Assembly of Denver who went on the tour together with several others. In his report to Governor John L. Routt on October 29, 1891, Sharp called the accident needless. Noting that he understood timbering thoroughly as he was a carpenter, Sharp said that the timbering at the mine was poor.

McNeil's report differed considerably. Writing to Governor Routt on November 17, 1891, he called the accident inevitable. He did not notice anything about the general state of the timbering. Acknowledging that danger did exist at the point of the accident, McNeil remarked that the management was not aware of it, and that there was no reason why it should have been. The coal miners felt themselves responsible for their safety in their immediate working places, he said. Therefore, management should not be charged with "criminal carelesslessness."[12]

In his biennial reports as state inspector, John McNeil's recommendations consisted of a call for a bill to prohibit the mining of a vertical vein under a body of water.[13] McNeil's successor, D. J. Reed, a Waite appointee, made several recommendations: (1) employ only experienced men in areas with explosive gases, since employment of inexperienced men in such areas was a major cause of accidents. (2) Insure the just weighing of coal. Reed stated that the miners were entitled to a check weighman, especially since they were willing to pay for one. (3) Pay the miners regularly every two weeks in legal money. Irregular pay in company script good only at company stores had been a major grievance of the miners.[14]

The governor charged that coal monopolies dominated the state legislature, so that adequate money was not made available for the State Inspector of Coal

Mines to perform his duties properly.[15] He noted that
"the legislature of Colorado not only failed to provide for the necessary and legitimate expenses of the
mine inspector for 1893 and 1894, but also failed to
provide for the payment of similar expenses in 1891
and 1892." In general, the "mine owners fail to com-
ply with the laws made for the protection of the
miners."[16]

In 1893 and 1894 several strikes occurred in coal
mining regions in various parts of the state. Even
before the hard times of the depression years, bitu-
minous coal miners averaged $377 a year in 1891, which
was $61 below the average wage earned in the United
States for that year. The miners worked an average of
sixty hours a week in an extremely dangerous occupation.[17]

One of the more serious coal mining disturbances
developed in the late spring of 1894 in Huerfano County
near Walsenburg. Two thousand miners were on strike.
The miners demanded payment at regular intervals in
lawful money and freedom to trade where they pleased.
Also involved was the question of the correct weighing
of coal.[18] Waite sent a message to a rally of the
striking miners in which he said he did not favor
strikes, but that there was no excuse for the mine
companies not paying the men promptly. He urged the
miners to elect a Populist legislature to legislate
in their interests.[19]

In his farewell message to the Colorado state
legislature, the governor made several recommendations
on the subject of coal mining. These included: just
weighing of coal, to answer complaints that many tons
of coal were actually mined with no pay; payment of
coal miners every two weeks in lawful money, rather
than payment in script good only at the company store
(the company town system was especially evident in
southern Colorado coal mining areas); an examination
and report by the state coal mine inspector every six
months of every coal mine in the state with twenty or
more miners; an examination to judge whether mine
managers and superintendents were competent to hold
their positions.

The most serious national industrial strife in
1894 was the Pullman railroad strike. Originating at
the Pullman car company south of Chicago, it spread
over much of the nation's railroad system. The

employees of the Pullman Company lived in the company-owned town of Pullman, Illinois. Following the panic of 1893 wages were drastically reduced while rents and other living costs remained the same. The workers at Pullman organized branches of the American Railway Union, an organization led by Eugene V. Debs, which embraced all categories of railroad workers. The Pullman corporation owned and operated several miles of railroad, making the Pullman employees eligible to join. In May, 1894, the strike at Pullman began. Meeting in convention the next month in Chicago, the American Railway Union voted to boycott all Pullman cars in support of the strikers. The railroads refused to detach the Pullman cars, and the boycott became a strike, as the railroad workers declined to run trains with Pullman cars. The strike spread from California to New York, involving thousands of workers who had their own grievances stemming from the hard times. Under the direction of Attorney General Richard Olney, a railroad corporation lawyer, the federal government obtained an injunction against the strikers on the pretense of protecting the U. S. mail and interstate commerce in general. Eventually the railroads, with the aid of the Cleveland Administration, were able to break the strike and destroy the union.

Colorado was one of the states affected by the Pullman strike. Railroad disturbances rocked the state, especially at Pueblo and Trinidad. Trains were halted. There were reports of tracks blown up. Federal authorities in Denver enlisted several hundred United States deputy marshals and ordered them to take charge of railroads already under federal receiverships. The railroad workers disarmed fifty-two marshals at Trinidad where sympathy was strong for the strikers. By-passing Governor Waite, President Cleveland ordered five companies of troops from Fort Logan to Trinidad. Three hundred and fifty soldiers and one hundred deputy marshals were used to move three trains in Trinidad.[20] President Cleveland's injunction against the strike and the federal military actions were to Waite an invasion of states' rights. Waite wired Cleveland challenging the authority of the "federal court to recruit armed forces."[21] Cleveland ignored Waite.

Waite's position paralleled that of Governor Altgeld in Illinois, who had also protested the use of federal troops. Governors J. S. Hogg of Texas, Sylvester Pennoyer of Oregon, Lorenzo D. Lewelling of

Kansas, and William J. McConnell of Idaho also protested the federal interventions. Governor Waite suggested to Altgeld and Lewelling that the governors of all the states where federal troops had intervened should meet and issue a joint protest. Altgeld agreed, but felt that further action was futile until public sentiment, whipped into a frenzy by a press hostile to the strikers, had cooled.[22] Waite appeared in public wearing a white badge, the emblem of the railroad workers. He also avowed from the platform his sympathy with the strikers.[23]

During the dark days of 1894 there occurred Coxey's March on Washington in behalf of the unemployed. Jacob S. Coxey, an Ohio Populist reformer, originated the march to publicize his plan for public works projects for the unemployed. Issues of greenbacks would finance the projects. Several thousand men headed towards Washington from all parts of the country. Of the "Commonweal Army" of Coxey, Waite commented: "A most remarkable pilgrimage to Washington has commenced, destined perhaps to wield as powerful influence on the public welfare as the crusaders of the Middle Ages. - - - It is the right of petition that this movement represents." This right, Waite asserted, had been trampled by Congress for a quarter of a century. "If this motley crew of tramps and anarchists would erase from their banners that strange device: 'Peace on Earth and good will to man,' and instead ask Congress to sanction the scheme 'to refund the Pacific Rail bonds,' the whole outfit would be given free transportation to Washington and return in palace cars." Waite disagreed with those who said the march to Washington should be halted. Some "excesses" and a number of "campfollowers" and "spies" were to be found in "every such movement," but it was on the whole made up of "sober, intelligent, determined men."[32]

Waite concluded, "I can only speak for myself, but if the present Governor of Colorado ever calls out the militia in relation to the commonweal army, as it has been, and he understands it to be - - he will call out only the Commissary Department. It will be a mighty cold day indeed, when he chases up Coxey's army with anything but ambulances, food and clothing."[24] Waite protested that "Coxey who proposes that without one dollar's tax or cost to the United States four million men shall be employed in the construction of great works of public utility is called a fanatic and lunatic, whereas the real lunatics are the two old

parties which are piling up the indebtedness of the
nation. . ."[25]

While hardly guilty of the hysterical and reckless
charges hurled against it, Coxey's Army did not achieve
its purpose in Washington. Bills embodying his ideas
were introduced in Congress, but did not receive much
support. Instead, Coxey was arrested for leading his
men through the Capitol grounds, and sentenced to
twenty days imprisonment. He also was fined five
dollars for walking on the grass.

Waite suggested aid to the unemployed through a
public works program even if it did cost the government money. He argued that the country would gain in
several ways. Writing to Senator Stewart in a manner
which today seems forty years in advance of his times,
he said:

> The great problem of the age is how to
> supply work to the unemployed. The people must
> live; we have not as yet arrived to that Mal-
> thusian point of killing off the surplus popu-
> lation. Those who cannot earn a living do
> live, though perhaps poorly, at the expense of
> those who earn a living. All that loss would
> be saved if these unemployed had work. Not
> only that, but a thousand million dollars paid
> out by government for work on public improve-
> ments would make the best times we have ever
> experienced and at no cost to the people —
> besides the improvements would be worth their
> cost.[26]

The dramatic events which unfolded at Cripple
Creek in the early months of 1894 formed the chief
labor episode of Waite's career. Cripple Creek became an important gold mining center in 1891. In
1894 occurred the first crucial Cripple Creek strike.
This strike is also noteworthy as the first chapter
in the story of the Western Federation of Miners in
Colorado. The Western Federation was organized in
Butte, Montana in May, 1893. Several local Colorado
unions early became affiliated with the Federation.
Beginning in August, 1893, the miners at Cripple Creek
rapidly became organized in locals affiliated with the
W. F. M. The favorable outcome of the Cripple Creek
strike rapidly increased the popularity of the Western
Federation of Miners among the miners in Colorado.[27]

In 1894 Cripple Creek and Colorado Springs were both a part of El Paso County. Conservative Republicans and mining interests, centered in Colorado Springs, dominated El Paso County politics. On the other hand, local authorities in the various mining camps in the Cripple Creek area tended to be friendly to the miners. This was especially true at Altman where town officials were union men. When the gold rush to Cripple Creek began in 1891 unionism quickly developed. Many of the workers had been union members at other mining camps.[28]

The Cripple Creek strike must be considered against the backdrop of the eight-hour day movement and the Panic of 1893. Workers were now convinced of the rightness of the eight-hour day and increasingly resentful of longer hours. The depression of the mid-nineties produced a surplus of workers as many were unemployed. Many employers felt their bargaining power had increased. If a man did not like his terms of employment he could always be replaced. The shut-down in the silver mines had produced an abundance of unemployed miners.

Some mines had the eight-hour shift and others nine. The usual wage was three dollars a day. On August 17, 1893, H. E. Locke, the mine manager at the large Isabella mine, attempted to install a ten-hour day in place of an eight-hour day. Locke's efforts to intimidate the rebellious miners failed, and the order was cancelled. However, from that point tension continued to mount. Unionism spread. The miners agreed that they would quit work if further attempts were made to lengthen the work day. They expressed their desire for a uniform eight-hour day in the Cripple Creek area by February, 1894. In January, 1894, several of the largest producers announced a nine-hour day at $3.00 or an eight-hour day at the reduced wage of $2.50 a day to be effective February 1. The unions refused to submit to these alternatives. Several businessmen tried to get the mining companies to negotiate, but they refused.[29]

The men walked out on February 1 at all mines where the longer work day was in effect. The miners and their sympathizers termed the showdown a lockout, not a strike. Forty-one mines, mostly small, remained in operation on the eight-hour day. Also, two mines owned by W. S. Stratton continued to operate on a nine-hour day basis at $3.25 an hour. The struck mine owners attempted to obtain non-union men to run the mines. Clashes occurred between the strikers and the scabs. Several mines reclosed. The mines were placed under guard of a unit of armed deputies hired by the sheriff of El Paso County in conjunction with the mine owners. An injunction was obtained by the mine owners to prohibit strikers from interfering with the operation of the mines.

At this point Sheriff M. F. Bowers of El Paso County asked Governor Waite to send troops to preserve order. Waite sent three companies of militia under the command of Brigadier General E. J. Brooks. After conferring with El Paso County officials and Cripple Creek businessmen, State Adjutant General T. J. Tarsney and Brooks reported to Waite that the need for state militia had been greatly exaggerated. Waite, feeling that he had been hoodwinked into sending the troops as a further means of intimidating the miners, was livid with rage. He publicly announced that the militia had been sought on the basis of a "lying representation," and immediately ordered their withdrawal.[30] On two occasions Sheriff Bowers arrested a number of the miners, but they were released each time as none of the charges could be upheld.

Governor Waite blamed the large mine owners for the Cripple Creek difficulties and called the situation a lockout. "The inauguration of the Cripple Creek difficulties was by the few mine owners, and, as the facts prove, for their own selfish purposes," he declared. "it was originally a lockout and never a strike by the miners." Waite noted that the miners believed three dollars for eight hours was just since mining was laborious, especially at high altitudes. The profits were so much better at Cripple Creek than at the silver mining camps in the nineties, Waite charged, that "a large majority of the prospectors and mine owners in the Cripple Creek district" paid three dollars for eight hours even during the difficulties.

Waite felt that the large mine owner not only wanted a reduction in wages, but was quite content to stage a lockout until the arrival of the railroads when the cost of transportation would be greatly reduced. He also argued that a lockout would enable the large mine owner to more readily buy out the prospector and the small owner through a temporary depression in the value of mining property.

83

The railroad facts by themselves do not establish Waite's thesis, but they certainly support it. The Florence and Cripple Creek Railroad Company link to Cripple Creek was opened on July 2, three weeks after the mines reopened.[31] The Midland Terminal Railroad Company completed its last link to reach Cripple Creek from Divide in 1895.[32] Vernon Jensen has observed that a savings of three dollars a ton would occur for all ore shipped after the railroads reached the Cripple Creek district.[33]

Evidence that the affair was a lockout and that the question of the railroads was important is to be found in strongly anti-Waite sources. The anti-labor and Republican Greeley Sun said, "The owners of mines at Cripple Creek have determined to resume work on their properties now that the railroads have been built into the camp."[34]

Adjutant General Tarsney, close to the scene throughout the affair, commented, "In all fairness, it must be inferred that these were non-resident mine owners whose mines were closed. They had voluntarily closed them in order to save at least $3 per ton on freight of their ores from the camp to the railroad terminal, the press meanwhile persisting in prejudicing the public against the miners by reiterating that the lockout of the mine owners was a strike of the miners."[35]

Another important factor in the Cripple Creek situation, Waite believed, was the attempt of the mine owners to break up union activity in order to have a complaisant labor force in the future. The governor became convinced during the March disturbances that this was a goal upon which the operators and the police authorities in Colorado Springs were collaborating when the deputy sheriffs went to the Cripple Creek area to harass the miners and make mass arrests.[36] As to the position of the miners, Waite stated:

The Miners Union did use all legitimate means in its power to prevent miners from working at the reduced scale of wages. The Union was charged as is always the case with labor organizations in lockouts and strikes with intimidation and violence, but in all judicial investigations that have been connected with the Cripple Creek difficulties though many members of the Miners Union have been imprisoned as lawbreakers nearly all were discharged for want of evidence, and in the case of the Strong mine one person convicted under the charge of the judge as an accessory because a member of the Miners Union, and although sent to state prison for seven years, was pardoned by Governor McIntire as unjustly convicted — The experience of a century has taught them that the workmen can only rely upon peaceable and moral means. A resort to violence destroys public sympathy, ruins any reform, and these axioms are well understood.[37]

All was relatively quiet in the Cripple Creek area in April and the first half of May. Most of the smaller mines continued to operate under union conditions; the larger ones were closed. In May, the owners of the shutdown mines decided to reopen them on their own terms. A proposal of $2.75 for eight hours of work was rejected by the unions. The mine owners then determined upon a force of strikebreakers to operate the mines. They pledged money and arms to the county if it would recruit an army of deputies to guard the mines. The county commissioners agreed, and Sheriff Bowers proceeded to organize an army of deputies numbering twelve hundred.[38] Over a hundred deputies were recruited in Denver and transported to Cripple Creek by special train. The Greeley Sun commented, "Most of the men were formerly policemen or firemen under the old Denver fire board."[39]

In defense the miners began to prepare for a showdown rather than be intimidated. They established a military encampment at Bull Hill. Some of the striking miners attacked the Strong mine and captured a few workers and deputies. A few of the attackers engaged in destruction of property at the mine. John Calderwood, a miner at Cripple Creek and leader of the Western Federation of Miners, ordered all the miners to desist from further attacks and to refrain from destroying property. One brief skirmish occurred between small parties of miners and deputies, which resulted in at least one death on each side. Said the Pueblo Chieftain, "The mine owners have decided not to arbitrate differences with the Cripple Creek miners and trouble may begin at any moment." The paper spoke of a battle which could hardly be avoided.[40]

Upon learning of the rapid developments at Cripple Creek, Governor Waite immediately issued a proclamation asking the strikers to lay down their arms and declaring the army of deputies composed of men from several counties to be illegal. He ordered the deputies to disperse. The actions of Sheriff Bowers were outside the law, Waite declared, and were an usurpation of the powers of the governor.

Preliminary efforts at conciliation led by President William F. Slocum of Colorado College failed. John Calderwood stated that his union believed in arbitration and was willing to compromise. On May 28, two days after the proclamation was issued, Governor Waite arrived in Cripple Creek on a private train and met the miners on Bull Hill. He promised them that they would be protected from the deputies. The miners appointed the governor as their representative to make an agreement with the mine owners.

Delayed in Cripple Creek by four days of inclement weather during which time wild rumors of an attack on Colorado Springs circulated freely, Waite arrived on June 2, in Colorado Springs to negotiate with J. J. Hagerman who represented the mine owners. Agreement was reached on a tentative settlement, but several mine operators did not concur. Meantime, the building in which the meeting was held had been surrounded by armed men intent on lynching Governor Waite and mine union leader John Calderwood. Some quick-thinking and cool-tempered individual held the crowd at bay by pleading with them that acts of violence would bring disgrace to Colorado Springs. Waite and Calderwood hurriedly departed through a rear door and sped across campus to a carriage which transported them to the railroad depot where they boarded Waite's special train for Denver.

Newspapers, generally hostile to Governor Waite and the miners, fanned the flames of hysteria throughout the state. The Pueblo Chieftain spoke of the "gang of anarchists who at present control the government of Colorado."[41] The Denver Republican said, "The rebellion against civilized government at Cripple Creek must be suppressed. Lawlessness cannot be tolerated in any part of the state."[42] The same paper charged a few days later that Governor Waite was protecting violators of the law.[43] Papers sympathetic to the mine owners sometimes rather openly expressed their own desires for violence against the miners. "The delay of the Divide army in attacking the strikers had much increased the latter's confidence," one paper stated.[44]

In the Colorado Springs region newspapers openly
called for blood. One headline ran, "TO ARMS! El
Paso County Needs More Volunteers; Every Effort Will
Be Made to Put Down The Bull Hill Rebellion."[45]
Another paper screamed, "The rebellion at Cripple
Creek should be put down, there should be no compromise
with rebels."[46]

Reports circulated that mining attorneys in
Denver were advising the mine owners to ask President
Cleveland to call out federal troops on the basis that
the president had the power to protect the people in
their rights when the state authorities failed to do
so. If this call for federal action had been acted
upon, it would have established a close parallel with
federal intervention in the Pullman strike during the
same period. It would have been more difficult, however, for President Cleveland to call out the federal
troops in Colorado, where the problem was more local
in nature.[47]

Miners in other mining camps were preparing to
come to the aid of their fellow workmen at Cripple
Creek. In southwestern Colorado at the same town of
Rico, one hundred men had armed themselves and seized
a Rio Grande Southern train which they rode as far as
Montrose before receiving a telegram from Governor
Waite urging them to turn back. He indicated to the
miners that such a course of action could only damage
the cause of their fellow miners.[48]

On June 4, 1894, Governor Waite met in Denver
with J. J. Hagerman and another mine owner, David
Moffat. This time a settlement was successfully
negotiated to end the months of conflict. The settlement was a victory for the miners who had demanded an
eight-hour day with a daily wage of three dollars.

The agreement between the mine union and the mine
owners was as follows:

> For the purpose of settling the serious
> differences between employers and employees in
> Cripple Creek mining district El Paso County,
> Colorado — it is agreed by and between Governor
> Davis H. Waite, appointed by and representing
> the Free Coinage Miners Union No. 19, W. F. M. A.
> (Western Federation of Mines of America), its
> members and other miners of said district on the

one part, and J. J. Hagerman and David H. Moffat for themselves as mine owners and employers of mining labor in said district, on the other part, as follows:

1. That eight hours of actual work shall constitute "a day" divided as follows: four hours continuous work — then twenty minutes for lunch — then four hours of continuous work for which said eight hours of labor there shall be paid three dollars.

2. In the employment of men, there shall be no discrimination against union men or against non-union men.

3. The undersigned of J. J. Hagerman and David H. Moffat earnestly urge upon other mine owners and employers of mining labor in said Cripple Creek Mining District to accede to and act upon the foregoing agreement.[49]

The union, through their counsel, Governor Waite, made the demand originally for the employment of only union men. Later, Waite rescinded this demand in a compromise move leading to point two of the agreement. Hagerman also turned down any proposal promising no prosecutions against any of the miners.[50] The miners rejoiced over the settlement which had been reached.

The rejoicing proved to be premature. The deputies remained in the area, and the miners stayed in their camp. Governor Waite ordered the state militia to Cripple Creek to enforce acceptance of the settlement.[51] Sheriff Bowers and his army of so-called deputies, however, had no desire to let matters rest with the signed agreement. Cutting the telephone and telegraph wires, Bowers and his army proceeded on the night of June 6, to a locale a short distance from where the miners were camped. The next morning some minor skirmishes broke out between the miners and the deputies. Governor Waite immediately sent a truce order to Sheriff Bowers. On the same day the governor sent a telegram to Adjutant General T. J. Tarsney at Divide, a mining town close to Cripple Creek: "Go on with troops you have and take position between combatants. Preserve peace. Let Sheriff or U. S. Marshal pass through lines, but not any armed men from either

88

side. Miners and deputies have agreed on truce. Disarm neither side till further orders."[52]

Slowed by heavy rains, the state militia troops under the command of General Brooks did not arrive until the afternoon of June 7. The troops marched between the opposing sides. On June 8, Sheriff Bowers again attempted to march his deputy army against the miners on Bull Hill. The state troops had to chase the deputies. General Brooks threatened to fire on the deputies unless they turned back. Bowers' excuse for this adventure was that he had to serve warrants for the arrest of certain miners.[53]

The miners did not want the deputies to enter their camp, but were willing to surrender to the state militia. The militia marched to Bull Hill and took control. Waite again telegraphed to Tarsney: "Accept surrender of miners. Do not disarm them, but protect them with all your power. Make a cordon and keep armed deputies out. Advise sheriff to make no arrests. Use no force to compel any arrested man to go with the sheriff. Let that be voluntary. If the armed deputies resist your authority I will call out the reorganized militia to supress their insurrection."[54]

The deputies still refused to leave. Bowers objected to Waite that the militia should be aiding him in serving warrants and restoring the mines to the mine owners instead of blocking him from doing his duty. Waite warned Bowers: "It is ill advised to send out squads of deputies to arrest miners at this time. General Brooks is in the field to compel peace. He is ordered to prevent any arrests, or attacks, by armed deputies. The militia are under the orders of the Commander-in-Chief and not the sheriff. If the deputies resist the orders of General Brooks to suppress insurrection they resist the lawful powers of the state."[55]

Next Bowers claimed that he could no longer control his deputies. Waite warned Tarsney that if any deputies acted in defiance of the sheriff they were outside the law and should be handled as bandits. He ordered all deputies to disarm and disperse. The sheriff and his deputies finally realized that further resistance was futile. At a conference held at Altman further agreements were reached: the deputies were to disband, the mines were to be put in peaceable control of the owners, the state troops were to remain for at least thirty days, the miners were to give up all arms, and persons for whom Sheriff Bowers had warrants were to be arrested.[56]

Before disbanding, the mob of deputies let loose their frustrations on the citizens of Cripple Creek. They clubbed, kicked, and beat up many innocent people in a reign of terror lasting several hours.[57] The fact that none of the so-called sheriff's deputies, now openly a hoodlum mob, was ever arrested is an indication of the nature of the power structure in El Paso County in 1894.

Indictments were pressed against thirty-seven of the miners following arrests made by Sheriff Bowers. All but three indictments were dismissed. Two men were sentenced to seven years imprisonment for blowing up the Strong mine, the only incident in which there was evidence of violence by the miners. These two were pardoned before the expiration of the sentence. The other conviction was for a stage robbery incident.

The trials of several of the miners commenced in Colorado Springs in late June. Adjutant General Tarsney, a lawyer by profession, served as counsel for the miners. On the night of June 23, Tarsney was kidnapped from the Alamo Hotel, driven several miles outside Colorado Springs, then tarred and feathered. Several men were arrested, but no trial ever occurred. Governor Waite was outraged at the attack on Tarsney and offered a $1,000 award for aid in apprehending the criminals. He attacked the "leading citizens" of Colorado Springs for what he termed their "tacit approval" of the foul play against the adjutant general.[58]

Waite feared for the safety of the miners and their lawyers at the Springs, and expressed doubt whether a fair trial was possible. The governor vowed to send the National Guard for protection if the district judge of El Paso County deemed it desirable.[59] Various labor organizations praised Waite's defense of Tarsney and asked protection for the miners still in jail in Colorado Springs.[60] That Waite's fears were well founded was indicated by a letter that he received from eight jailed miners in October.

The miners wrote:

We see by the Rocky Mountain News that you will be in this city on October 8th and while here will you be kind enough to call at the county jail to see a few Bull Hill miners who are confined here, and can neither get a trial nor find out just what our bonds have been placed at. The authorities make no secret of the fact that they intend holding us as long as possible. Some of us have been here for over 4 months. We don't believe that you can either give us a trial or set our bonds, but we do believe that you are our friend, and we want to talk with you. It is not popular in this city to befriend us, but knowing you to be a friend of the working people we will anxiously look upon a visit from you during your stay in the city.[61]

In his report for 1893-94, Colorado Attorney General Eugene Engley summed up the Cripple Creek strike by saying: "I consider the governor's official course in what is known as the Cripple Creek war, as wise and patriotic. It is not too much to say that - - - the sheriff of El Paso County levied war against the state of Colorado. The sheriff of El Paso County had no authority in law to open recruiting stations and organize an army in Arapahoe County, to be transported and used in El Paso County, under the specious plea that such force, armed with Winchesters and cannon, were special deputy sheriffs of El Paso County."[62]

Among those high in praise of Waite's course of action at Cripple Creek was W. H. Harvey, of "Coin's Financial School" fame, who wrote to Waite: "For the first time in the history of strikes a Governor of a state has taken the side of humanity against capital and you have shown a comprehensive application of the true merits of the situation. I congratulate you with all my heart. The struggle, however, has only begun. Greed enthroned in power, and everywhere insolent and conscious of strength, is going to destroy the republic, unless it is saved by the middle and lower classes."[63]

As a result of the Cripple Creek episode many in the ranks of labor, especially in the West, held Governor Waite in high esteem. The Free Coinage Miners' Union of Altman, an affiliate of the Western Federation of Miners, asked the governor to deliver a Labor Day address. Invited were members of all unions in the West affiliated with the federation. An especially large contingent was expected from the Colorado mining camps.[64] Waite had become the hero of the miners in the West. His growing national fame was indicated by the fact that he spoke at large rallies for labor Populist candidates in Chicago in the fall of 1894.[65]

Contemporary non-labor and non-reform sources often harshly assailed Waite for his role in the 1894 Cripple Creek strike.[66] Later superficial and popularized accounts of the Cripple Creek incident, based largely on Denver newspaper accounts and so-called respectable contemporary sources, tend also to depict Waite negatively. However, a leading multi-volume general history of U. S. labor (Commons) and a specialized study of mining conditions in the West (Jensen) both portrayed Waite as a peacemaker successfully bringing about a just settlement of the Cripple Creek conflict. On the basis of the evidence there is no reason to dispute the portrayals by Commons and Jensen.

The reader may question Waite's dual role as state governor and labor counselor. However, the question must be asked whether bloodshed could have been avoided if Waite had not stepped in as a counselor. A related question is whether, under the circumstances in which labor was a decided underdog, a person with less authority than Waite's could have carried on negotiations with the mine owners on a basis of equality. The authority and power of El Paso County was completely in the hands of the mine owners. As Commons has noted, the Cripple Creek strike of 1894 was a good example of the rugged class war which gripped the mountain states during this period.[67] Neutrality in any event was almost impossible. The only conclusion possible from the previous examination of the facts is that the original drive to violence, the continuous will to violence, and almost all the actual violence were on the mine owners' side. Waite shrewdly realized that there was no essential contradiction involved in being a friend of labor, gaining a just settlement, and keeping the peace.

Two differing philosophies were in conflict in the Cripple Creek clash. Both assumed the right of private ownership of productive property. The mine owners and their sympathizers assumed that the business of society was business. They believed in the supremacy of profit making and the rights of the property owner. The businessman had the right to dictate terms to labor and otherwise to run his business as he saw fit. "Social responsibility" was not a phrase in the

92

mine owners' vocabulary. If labor troubles developed, it was expected that local, state, and federal authorities would atuomatically respond as needed to preserve property and to keep labor "in its place." Conflict with Governor Waite did not occur over technicalities such as his dual role, but over the fact that he refused to play the usual role of a governor as a front man for propertied interests.

Waite and many of his followers believed in cooperating among what they termed the various producing classes: businessmen, farmers, labor. They believed in public regulation and control, with emphasis on curbing special privilege and aiding the underdog. In labor disputes, this meant favoring genuine arbitration and negotiation, not intimidation and violence. At the mines this philosophy meant distrust of the power of the large mine owners and sympathy for the miner in unionizing and obtaining better working conditions.

Following the defeat of his bid for re-election in 1894, Waite became temporarily bitter with labor, as he did also with the women (see chapter on woman suffrage). Both, he believed, had betrayed him. He acknowledged the support of the Western Federation of Miners and of the remnants of the Knights of Labor outside of Denver. He was especially bitter towards the Trade Assemblies of the cities and made the dubious claim that "the 'organized' workmen of Denver almost to a man voted Republican."[68] Officially, the Denver Trades Assembly adhered to a non-partisan political position.

Governor Waite was piqued that he was not invited to the national convention of the American Federation of Labor which met in Denver in late 1894. "I shall not attend — not that I care for this personal insult from Gompers & Co."[69] Despite the snub by the Gompers bureaucracy, Governor Waite very likely had many admirers among the rank and file of the A. F. L.

After Governor Waite left office, he was eagerly sought as a spokesman for labor. In 1895, for example, he gave the Labor Day address in Tiffin, Ohio.[70]

Davis H. Waite is undoubtedly as great a friend as the working man has ever had in the Colorado governor's office. He was staunchly pro-labor, putting the welfare of people ahead of considerations of profits and corporate property rights. After the election in 1894, James Hogan, a regional director of the American

93

Railway Union, spoke for many when he said, "One thing, Governor, you have been true to poor toiling humanity. I don't believe there is a miner who descends in his shaft but who loves and reveres the only Governor known in history who called out the militia to check the carnage of Hessian deputies."[71]   Edward Boyce, president of the Western Federation of Miners, made a similar statement in noting that Waite was the only governor ever to call out the soldiers to protect the workers.[72] His grave in Aspen, Colorado is marked by an impressive monument erected by the Western Federation of Miners.

CHAPTER VIII

WOMAN SUFFRAGE AND OTHER REFORMS

Among the far-reaching social changes accompanying the advent of the industrial revolution in the United States and in several countries of Western Europe during the nineteenth century was the alteration of the position and role of women. In the United States in the first half of the nineteenth century women worked in more than a hundred industrial occupations. In 1880, women workers gainfully employed numbered 2,647,000; by 1890, the number had risen to 4,005,500, or 17.2 per cent of the total work force. The pay was characteristically much less for women than for men.[1] Women were employed in factories, especially in the textile industry, as well as in service occupations such as laundering, and in various household occupations. Women were also beginning to invade professions hitherto denied them such as medicine, theology, and law.[2] Due to the large growth of public education in the United States in the nineteenth century, many entered a more traditional field for women, the teaching profession.

The nineteenth century thus altered radically the notion that woman's place was in the home. Yet well into this same century, a woman was legally considered a perpetual minor. If unmarried, she was the ward of male relatives; if married, she was part of her husband's property. An unmarried woman or a widow had some independence in the ownership of property and in earning her own living, but she could enter few occupations.[3] Politically and legally, woman was quite restricted, and in the economic area, she faced gross discrimination in occupation and pay. One large group, the Black woman, faced special difficulties, first as a slave and later as an emancipated person in the white man's world.[4]

An organized woman's right movement had its inception in 1848 with the Seneca Falls Convention in New York. The convention grew out of discrimination which faced women who were active in the anti-slavery movement. National woman's rights conventions were held annually nearly every year thereafter. State and local organizations grew in many areas. The chief efforts of these groups were focused upon removing the formal barriers to women, legal and occupational, and gaining the suffrage for women.

In answering the challenges presented by this conflict between the old and the new, women resorted to several strategies. After the Civil War, some working women became associated with the trade union movement, and a few even managed to become leaders.[5] The National Labor Union and its leader, William Sylvis, were quite sympathetic to the problems of women in industry and to the organization of women.[6] Later the Knights of Labor played the most important role of any nineteenth century labor group with its broad organizational appeal, including a demand for organization of workers regardless of sex. At the high point in 1886, the Knights had one hundred and thirteen women's assemblies chartered.[7] There is record of at least one of these assemblies in Denver, No. 3324.[8] The Knights were strong advocates of woman suffrage.

A few successes and many failures were recorded nationally before the Colorado Populist success with woman suffrage in 1893. Widows with children of school age gained a vote on school issues in Kentucky as far back as 1838. In 1861, Kansas granted school suffrage for all women. Fifteen other states followed in the 1870's and 1880's. In 1887, Kansas granted municipal suffrage. Several states such as New Hampshire, Massachusetts, and Montana gave the vote to tax-paying women on tax questions.[9]

Women gained the vote in the territory of Wyoming in 1869. The leader, Mrs. Esther Morris, and the governor of the territory both were influenced by woman's rights forces before coming to Wyoming. Some accounts even state the territorial legislature passed the woman suffrage bill as a joke on the bachelor governor. This is possible due to the very small legislature, nine in the Senate and eleven in the House, with six votes being needed for passage in each body.[10] The territorial legislatures in Utah and Washington also voted for woman suffrage, but these were canceled by Congress and court decisions respectively.[11] The first state to attain statewide woman suffrage was Wyoming in 1890. The provision was written into the state constitution.

There were a few abortive attempts to introduce woman suffrage in Colorado before the Populist era. In 1868, the question was raised through a bill in the territorial legislature, but received practically no consideration.[12] Two years later, Territorial Governor Edward McCook recommended the franchise for women in his annual message to the legislature. This time there was some public discussion of the issue as well.

The Constitutional Convention of 1876 provided the next setting for the issue. A petition by a thousand citizens was presented to the convention. The minority report of the Committee on Suffrage favored woman suffrage. On the floor of the convention a proposed amendment for extension of the vote to women was turned down by a 24 to 8 vote.[13]

Through instructions of the Convention, the First General Assembly of Colorado, meeting in 1877, passed a law putting the proposition to a vote by the general male public. Following strenuous campaigning led by the Woman Suffrage Association, the measure was defeated at the polls by a better than 2 to 1 margin.[14] Women did obtain the right to vote in school elections through the state constitution in 1876.[15] An effort to extend the franchise to women in municipal elections lost out in the legislature in 1881.[16]

Accounts of woman suffrage in Colorado note that the movement was dormant in the eighties. However, as regards Davis Waite and woman suffrage, the eighties were probably quite important. During this period, Waite was a member of the Knights of Labor which were quite active in Colorado and in his home county of Pitkin. Woman's rights, including woman suffrage, was, as already mentioned, a part of their program. In 1887, the Sixth General Assembly included eight members of the Knights. The Knights were especially active in lobbying during this same session. One of the laws passed stated that corporations must provide suitable seats for women workers.[17] The Workingman's Party was organized in Pitkin County in 1887, a reflection of the emphasis on politics by the Knights to gain their goals. Among the planks of their platform was one calling for woman suffrage.[18]

In Waite's weekly, the Aspen Union Era, there were references to the Knights and woman suffrage such as the following quotation taken from The Michigan Patriot:

> The Knights of Labor at the recent General Assembly declared in favor of woman suffrage

and reaffirmed the plank in the declaration of principles which asks for women equal pay for equal work. The Knights of Labor are and have been since the first organization of the order, far in advance of the other industrial organizations on the question of the rights of women. No true labor organization can deny to women the right to their individuality and the same freedom of action granted to men.[19]

The organized suffrage movement in Denver began to rouse itself from slumber in 1890 with the visit of Matilda Hindman to the state to solicit aid for the suffrage campaign current in South Dakota.[20] However, there is little evidence on the surface during the early nineties either inside or outside the Populist ranks to suggest that women suffrage would win in Colorado in 1893.[21]

At the Pueblo Populist state convention in May, 1892, there was one lady delegate, Mrs. Emma Curtis of Canon City. She was to become a leading member of the Waite Administration.[22]

A plank for woman suffrage was not to be found in the Populist Party Omaha Platform of July, 1892. Woman suffrage was originally included in the St. Louis Platform in February of the same year, but later erased. The reasons given were that suffrage was a state question and that a political platform must not be "loaded down with unnecessary issues, no matter how excellent."[23]

The post-Omaha Populist state convention in Denver in July adopted the Omaha Platform. Mrs. Mary Elizabeth Lease, a leading Kansas Populist, and Mrs. Curtis were among the speakers at a rally during this convention.[24] A Mrs. Washburn thought the ladies did not receive their proper share of attention at the convention. She had a resolution on political equality for all, but did not present it.[25]

Governor-Elect Davis H. Waite began to feel the pressure for woman suffrage late in 1892 from some reform elements. Quitman Brown, a Populist rancher from Yuma, Colorado, wrote to Waite urging woman suffrage to combat the "saloon menace." He suggested women over twenty-one be given the vote in municipal, school, and judicial elections.[26] A week later, Brown elaborated on his views in a second letter to the governor-elect by saying he was against full suffrage for women at present. If woman had a vote on the state level, she would choose the Prohibition Party and endanger the Populists. Brown reasoned that a local women's vote would eliminate the saloon and thus the Prohibitionists. Women could then safely be given the vote on the state and presumably national levels.[27] One Denver correspondent wrote to Waite recommending woman suffrage for all elections. Said she: "Women have tried to bring about reforms but have failed to an extent because they could not vote."[28]

In his Inaugural Address to the Ninth General Assembly, Governor Waite recommended the extension of woman suffrage to all municipal elections. He noted that women had gained the right to vote in school district elections several years before, but that the "heavens have not fallen, and the efficiency of the public schools has been greatly improved."[29]

The Rocky Mountain News described the inaugural references to woman suffrage in glowing tones: "The greatest demonstration, however, was during his references to woman suffrage. They were so well put that the audience fairly rose and cheered, the demonstration being renewed under the leadership of a lady in the gallery, who leaned over and waved her handkerchief enthusiastically as a signal to others."[30]

In April, 1893, during the regular legislative session, Waite vetoed a bill which would have provided for greater equality between the sexes in property rights. The veto message follows:

This bill repeals Section 223 of the General Statutes which reads as follows:

Section 26, Chapter 18, General Statutes (223)

No covenant express or implied in the deed of any married woman shall have any effect to bind such married woman, or her heirs, save so far as to pass to the purchaser named therein all her present estate described thereby expressed to be conveyed.

The present law seems designed for the protection of married women. It will be time enough to put her on equal legal terms with men, when she has equal rights with men as to suffrage.[31]

99

A bill to submit the woman suffrage question to the voters was introduced in the House by a Populist, Rep. J. T. Heath of Montrose.[32] It passed both houses mainly due to the Populist vote, but not without badly needed help from the Republicans. The House tally was 34-27, with 22 Populists, 11 Republicans, and one Democrat in favor, and 3 Populists, 21 Republicans, and 3 Democrats against. In the Senate, the margin was 20-10, with 12 Populists and 8 Republicans supplying the majority and one Populist, 4 Republicans, and 5 Democrats being in opposition.[33] The measure was signed by Governor Waite on April 7, 1893. At the general election on November 7, 1893, a victory was won for woman suffrage by a vote of 35,798 to 29,451, a majority of 6,347.[34] Counties which returned a Populist majority in the 1892 elections favored woman suffrage by 6,818 votes; Republican and Democratic counties were against the proposal by a margin of 471.[35] Colorado thus became the first state to attain woman suffrage by a vote of the males of the state.

After the election, Helen M. Reynolds, a leader of "The Equal Suffrage Association of Colorado," thanked the governor for his support of the woman suffrage bill, and said that the victory in Colorado represented the greatest achievement yet for equal rights.[36]

The Women's Christian Temperance Union of Colorado, another leader in the contest for woman suffrage, was also quite warm in its praise of Governor Waite's role, "Believing that your influence in both your official and private capacity was a potent factor in securing the passage of the Equal Suffrage bill in the legislature and its subsequent approval of the people, the Women's Christian Temperance Union of Colorado desires to express appreciation of this service in the cause of moral reform."[37]

The most detailed elucidation of Waite's views on woman suffrage appeared in his North American Review article several months after the election on woman suffrage.[38] Waite felt that two basic principles could be cited in favor of equal suffrage. First, there should be no taxation without representation. Waite argued that women were taxed and had no representation, since it was incorrect to say that husbands and sons represented them. Furthermore, the fairer sex was certainly unrepresented if unmarried. Secondly, "suffrage should be based on intelligence. . . .

100

If a woman has the mental ability to protest against unjust laws, and to demand enactments calculated to promote the general welfare, why should not her wishes, and most especially when taxed as a citizen, be consulted in the exercise of the powers of government?"

Since liberty was in danger, Waite thought that the entrance of women into politics might help the forces of reform. "Certainly there is little hope of the future, unless women, admitted to suffrage, acquaint themselves more thoroughly than men with political affairs, and 'come up with greater zeal to the help of the Lord against the mighty' in providing a remedy for the fearful condition of this nation, the result of the positive acts of conspiring monopolists, and the hitherto criminal negligence of the mass of the voters."

The governor labeled the eventual effects of woman suffrage "a matter of conjecture." He remarked that "in Wyoming and Washington, to my knowledge, no extraordinary progress has been made in the line of political reform that can be traced to female suffrage, and in Colorado sufficient time has not yet elapsed to speak understandingly of the result." Waite felt that there was no validity to the usual arguments against women being in politics. To the argument that the right to vote would pull woman out of her element and "defy nature," Waite stated that women had never had a fair chance. He thought that women were weaker physically and even, in line with much current and traditional thought, that they were "perhaps, as a mass, mentally weaker than men." However, there were doubts on the latter point, he conceded, since higher education had been closed to women until a few years ago. True, women were limited by the child bearing function, but this was no reason against voting or holding office.

Another objection commonly raised to equal suffrage was that women did not fight in wars. The governor contended that battles were not won wholly on the field. In the Civil War, Waite noted, women in "their own legitimate way," accomplished as much or more than the warriors.

As to woman suffrage and partisan politics, Waite remarked that there was nothing partisan in itself about the issue. In all states, men of all parties favored or opposed woman suffrage, "but there is no doubt that in Colorado the women owe suffrage to the

Populists. The Populists in the General Assembly
nearly all supported the bill, but a majority of the
members of both the old parties voted in opposition.
The law was recommended by a Populist governor, the
bill was introduced by a Populist representative, at
the general election the Populist Party in the state
supported the measure; but nearly all the Republican
counties and all the Democratic counties voted against
it." Waite forecast "no Republican or Democratic State
will ever confer equal suffrage upon women, because
Republicans and Democrats, as political parties, do
not believe in the doctrine of equal rights." Governor
Waite saw the Populists as both the political and
economic hope of women. "The Populist Party will, at
no distant day, not only redeem women from political
servitude, but also emancipate man and woman from
industrial slavery."

During the campaign of 1894, the governor reiterated his belief in equal suffrage and stated that
"suffrage should be based on intelligence, not the
accident of birth, sex, or wealth."[39] Co-education
had paved the way for equal suffrage, and the Populists
had then taken the lead in putting it into effect.
However, despite the fact that women now had a role to
play in politics, this did not change or add to the
issues in any way. There were no issues that particularly interested or affected women as such. Her lot
and problems were simply those of mankind as a whole:

> There are no arguments in this campaign
> that should be peculiarly addressed to woman.
> . . . It is true that the Women of Colorado
> owe suffrage to the Populist Party. The elec-
> tion returns prove this, but if this were all
> it would not be worth mentioning. The same
> arguments which convince a man should convince
> a woman. If the women have not learned, or will
> not learn, that the condition requires a change
> in its financial policy to save the owners their
> mortgaged homes, to increase the prices of
> products of the farmer, the mechanic, and the
> manufacturer, so as to pass the cost of produc-
> tion, and increase the wages of labor. . . . If
> in short the women are not convinced that the
> question of morals both belongs to politics and
> must dominate our politics to preserve our
> liberties, then the present condition of affairs
> must continue till they produce their inevitable
> result, and reduce the common people of the

United States to industrial slavery, just as is now the case with the common people in the old world. But I have faith in Man, why should I not have faith in Woman?[40]

Women were quite active along partisan lines in the campaign of 1894. Each party had a woman candidate for Superintendent of Public Instruction.[41] According to one writer, the "Republicans especially made an appeal for the woman vote, posing as the guardians of morality and of law and order."[42]

The 160,000 votes cast for governor in 1894 were almost double those of 1892, apparently due mainly to woman suffrage. While Governor Waite lost in his bid for re-election, he received a vote of over 66,000 in 1894. His winning vote in 1892 had been 44,242. Governor Waite was quite disappointed and bitter about the downfall of his administration. In casting about for reasons for his defeat, he came to firmly believe that the majority of the women had voted against him. As a result he turned strongly against woman suffrage. He charged that the Republicans had corruptly used an ignorant woman vote to overthrow Populism in Colorado.

Waite expressed his feelings to Ignatius Donnelly quite freely:

Twenty-five thousand kind girls in the state voted Republican because their employers wanted them to, so badly as to see that they were registered, went with them to the polls, and attended strictly to them. These girls neither knew or cared how they voted. 15,000 gamblers and lewd women in Denver voted Republican as the Populist state administration had stopped public gambling and Sunday dram-drinking.

Equal suffrage in Colorado has brought to the polls at least 30,000 ignorant hired girls, whose votes are purchasable and at the disposal of the wealthy classes who have hired their services. The right of suffrage should be based on intelligence. Female suffrage I hope will hereafter be opposed by all Populists, although it may be best to say nothing about it in the party platform.[43]

Waite was not alone in connecting the 1894 election results with woman suffrage. One newspaper commented: "Denver and the larger cities went over-whelmingly one way owing, it is believed to the energetic work of the women."[44] Mrs. Phila Bliven of Durango, a strong supporter of Waite, unloaded her bitterness towards her own sex in a letter to the governor: "Last November I fought the woman suffrage movement, and six weeks ago I said, 'Alan McIntire will sail into office in the arms of the Colorado women and they called me a woman hater.' God help me, I was never so near hating my own sex as I am tonight when the news of your defeat comes to me. . . . I consider your stand as regards the woman suffrage movement the one mistake of your public career."[45]

What element of truth there is in Waite's charges is hard to determine. That fraud or corruption existed in elections during Waite's period of time was common knowledge. A Republican machine which ruthlessly dominated Denver politics had been openly challenged by Governor Waite on the gambling and clean government issues in the Denver Fire and Police Board controversy. Under the circumstances women in houses of prostitution presumably could be persuaded rather easily to vote Republican. The national election of 1896 illustrated how employers could coerce employees into voting the "right" way. Waite apparently assumed women could be coerced more easily than men, but he offered no evidence to support his charges.

In any event, Waite's figures are grossly exaggerated. Out of the emotion of the moment, Waite had announced that 25,000 to 30,000 votes out of about 85,000 for the Republicans were from "controlled" women. The Republicans had a plurality of 18,608 votes in Colorado in 1894. Arapahoe County which included Denver was responsible, it is true, for a heavy percentage of this margin, 17,546 votes. Denver and Colorado Springs were the two strong centers of anti-Waiteism. Except for these two cities, Waite carrried the state by approximately 2,000 votes. There was no need to blame woman suffrage, however, for the adverse vote in Denver and Colorado Springs. The conservative press and the Republican organizations had sufficiently fanned the flames of hysteria against Waite over the Cripple Creek strike, the Denver Fire and Police Board controversy, and the general cry of "radicalism."

Despite the fact Colorado was the only state to extend woman suffrage between the 1892 and 1894 elections, analysis of the results does not indicate any startling differences between Colorado and other states in the western half of the United States in the 1894 election. The Colorado Populist vote in 1894 was 41.37 per cent; Nebraska was the only state to register a higher percentage vote for Populism.[46] Thus it is difficult to charge that Populism in Colorado lost relatively due to thd entrance of woman suffrage. One observer concluded that "for the most part" women "voted in harmony with their husbands and male relatives."[47] There seems to be no evidence to indicate that there was any large scale divergent woman's vote as such. Theoretically, Waite's campaign for clean government in Denver should have appealed to women and helped to offset pressures from the opposite direction.

One national Populist spokesman, Eugene V. Debs, rebuked Waite in a comradely manner for his renegade views on woman suffrage:

I do not agree with you in regard to woman suffrage, although I have great respect for your views and opinions. You are doubtless embittered on account of immediate results and, I confess, not without good cause. I admit the force of your argument, but it seems that with anything like equal chances we would soon have a host of able and courageous women on the rostrum and on the hustings who would more than compensate for the disadvantage you point out.[48]

After the election the defeated governor went on a speaking tour. Among the roles he now played was that of serving, in effect, as an agent of the anti-woman suffrage forces. Since he could speak as one of the few having experience, apparently his words carried some weight. After Waite's lecture in St. Paul, Ignatius Donnelly wrote to him: "The statements you have made here ended woman's suffrage in the People's Party."[49]

In the few years Waite continued before the public eye anti-suffrage forces in other states occasionally sought counsel from him. In 1897, Mrs. Elizabeth S. Crannell of Albany, New York, wrote to Waite asking for methods of getting woman suffrage repealed. She claimed many Colorado women wrote of their desire to limit the vote to males and that they believed it to be necessary for the welfare of the state. Mrs. Crannell was disillusioned with the women leaders in the national equal suffrage associations, and argued that they were all Republicans and Democrats opportunistically playing both sides of the fence to serve their ends.[50]

At least one woman Populist leader in Colorado became bitter about woman suffrage. Mrs. Alice Faulkner of Denver had been president of the Woman's Populist League in 1895-1896. She had become generally disillusioned about all political parties, and doubted the intelligence of the people in politics. Woman suffrage achieved nothing, she said.[51] Other woman Populists in Colorado did not agree with Mrs. Faulkner. Mrs. Evangeline Heartz, a Denver Populist who was elected to the state legislature in 1896, received credit for several reform laws enacted in the late nineties. These included a law requiring school boards to hold open meetings, a law setting up a board of arbitration, and a law providing greater protection for railroad employees. In gratitude, the railroad employees gave Mrs. Heartz a large box of candy with the inscription, "The Thanks of 5,000 railroad men."[52]

In the period from 1894 to 1900, ten women were elected to the Colorado state house of representatives. Women filled other posts including the office of state superintendent of public instruction. Thus, women not only voted, but a number of them became politically active at an early stage.[53] In January, 1899, the Colorado legislature, on the basis of the results in Colorado, recommended that woman suffrage be extended to all other states and territories.

In commenting on the outgoing Waite Administration in early 1895, the Rocky Mountain News had praised Governor Waite and the Populist Party as mainly responsible for the advent of woman suffrage in Colorado. Ironically, despite the later renegade role of Waite, it can still be stated that the chief legislative accomplishment of the Waite Administration was woman suffrage.

Other Political Reforms

During his tenure as governor, Waite proposed the direct election of United States Senators, and the initiative and referendum. In his inaugural address he asked the Ninth General Assembly to memorialize

106

Congress: "That a constitutional amendment be submitted to the States, providing that United States Senators be elected by a direct vote of the people."[54] In his extra session proclamation, he proposed an amendment to the state constitution that would make the instruments of the initiative and referendum applicable to state legislation, thus giving the citizen a chance to initiate laws through petition and to vote on certain referred legislative proposals. The latter proposition lost in the House by two votes. The call for the direct election of United States Senators and the initiative and referendum was common among Populists. Both demands were included in the Omaha Platform.

An Australian ballot law had been passed in Colorado in 1891. Colorado was only one among many states which passed such a law in the early nineties. The Australian ballot is an official ballot printed at public expense, which contains the names of all the candidates for the different offices. The voter marks the ballot in the secrecy of a voting booth. In his inaugural Governor Waite commented, "The Australian ballot, though cumbersome, is correct in principle. The people of the state have become somewhat familiar with it, and I recommend no change except such as is necessary to relieve the law of complicated and useless requirements."[55] The Australian ballot proposal was also included in the Omaha Platform. Each of the above devices was seen by the Populists as a means to bring government closer to the people and to offset the trend toward government by a privileged elite.

Waite was opposed to capital punishment and asked the state legislature to outlaw it. Capital punishment had been abolished in Michigan, Wisconsin, and Kansas, he said, with the result that the percentage of crimes had diminished in those states and the percentage of convictions for murder in the first degree had increased. Waite urged that punishment for murder in the first degree should be changed to life imprisonment. Colorado Attorney General Engley agreed with Waite: "I believe that Colorado has become sufficiently civilized to abolish that relic of barbarism known as the death penalty. Statistics demonstrate that wherever the death penalty has been abolished, homicide has decreased. The theory that the death penalty is a deterrent to crime is no longer tenable."[56] However, the state legislature did not act on Waite's request on capital punishment. Two years after Waite left office, in 1897, Colorado did abolish the death penalty only to restore it in 1901.[57]

Governor Waite was also known for the pardons that he gave. One newspaper editor remarked, "Governor Waite had a soft heart — opposed to capital punishment, he granted reprieves to all criminals sentenced to death until his term expired. As ex-officio member of the board of pardons, he was ever ready to grant clemency. One of his last official acts was to grant a pardon to a man who had never served his sentence."[58]

Waite gave 113 pardons during his two years as governor. Sixty-six of these were penitentiary pardons. He also issued twenty-two commutations and seventeen respites from execution. As nearly as can be determined, Governor John L. Routt, who preceded Waite, gave forty-nine penitentiary pardons, and Governor Albert W. McIntire, who served after Waite, gave thirty-eight penitentiary pardons.[59]

Before coming to Denver as governor, Waite had a record of concern over the questions of liquor and gambling. As justice of the peace in Pitkin County, he had a reputation for meting out severe sentences to gamblers and Sunday closing law violators. He asked for the election of aldermen in Aspen who would close "the gambling hells and saloons."[60] By one count, there were twenty-nine saloons in Aspen in 1892.[61] As a member of the Kansas legislature in 1879 he voted for prohibition in Kansas. However, he apparently considered himself a temperance man by 1895, but not a "political prohibitionist."[62]

The Denver City Hall War

In the early nineties, Denver was a Republican stronghold in which gambling and the saloon flourished. State and municipal laws on gambling existed, but they were not enforced. The Denver Charter of 1893 gave the city council the responsibility "to prohibit and suppress dance houses, tippling houses, dram shops, opium houses, gaming, and gambling houses."[63] Many gambling places were open all night. Criminal elements gathered there. The police engaged in sporadic raids to make occasional arrests, but not to enforce the law. Many Denver property owners, businessmen, and lawyers benefited too much from the status quo to bother about the law. "The gamblers, often in alliance with the

108

police, constituted a powerful political element and were largely responsible for the chronic disorder and corruption attendant upon county and city elections. Gamblers were sometimes threatened with prosecution by politicians and thus blackmailed into support."[64]

The Denver Fire and Police Board, with its vast powers of appointment and removal, had been a center of political corruption. Sufficient protest was mobilized in 1891 to pass an act by which the members of the Fire and Police Board were to be appointed by the governor of the state. No more than two of the three commissioners were to belong to the same political party. In this manner Governor Waite became directly involved in Denver politics. In his efforts to achieve honest government, Waite clashed with two sets of his own appointees to the Board on the issue of gambling. In each instance, the governor charged the board members with protecting the gamblers rather than enforcing the laws on gambling. In the first dispute Waite removed two Populist appointees. In the second more serious dispute a Populist and a Democrat were involved. This was the famous episode of the so-called Denver Civil War.

The ousted board members, refusing to vacate, barricaded themselves in their offices and adjoining apartments and turned City Hall into a fortress manned by their firemen and policemen and a body of "deputy sheriffs" recruited by the gambling elements. The Republicans supported the ousted board members. The governor ordered out the state militia to enforce the board changes, and an armed conflict almost resulted. An appeal to the state supreme court averted a clash. The court confirmed Waite's power of appointment and removal, and the third of Waite's boards was installed. This board closed the gambling establishments for the remainder of Waite's term. Sunday and midnight closing laws were enforced, and prostitution was confined to certain areas of the city.

Waite asserted "that the Republicans of Denver were in league with the gamblers and lewd women is indisputable." Gamblers "have always demanded and received a consideration for their votes." The governor also commented, "The wealth and aristocracy of the city was a unit against the governor." He was particularly incensed by what he considered desertion by the very moral forces he should have been able to rely on — the churches, YMCA and WCTU. "The entire religious

sentiment of the city, acting in harmony with the
gamblers and lewd women had denounced the state executive as an anarchist, usurper, and tyrant," he
declared.[65] What moral protests were made by such
groups came only after "arrangements made with their
political co-laborers and bosom friends — the gamblers
and lewd women" had ceased.

Waite was irked by the failure of the clergy to
refer to the Populists as the one responsible for
gambling reform. That there was at least some appreciation of Waite's efforts, however, was reflected in
the message he received from the Denver branch of the
WCTU upon the closing of the gambling places: "Such
fearlessness for the right and suppression of vice,
adds one more step to the onward march of progress for
the uplift of humanity."[66]

Tariffs and Taxes

As late as 1888, Waite championed the protective
tariff in a typically Republican manner. In the <u>Aspen
Times</u> of June 28, 1888, there appeared this announce-
ment:

A CHALLENGE

> Being myself a friend of the cause of
> labor, and anxious that it should make itself
> felt in the politics of the country, and be-
> lieving that a tariff for the protection of
> American industry is essential to the pros-
> perity of the laboring men, I invite the labor
> organizations of Aspen, who, as I am informed,
> are mostly free traders, to a public discussion
> of the question: Free Trade or Tariff for
> Revenue vs. A Tariff for Protection of American
> Industry.
>
> Davis H. Waite[67]

Aspen, June 20, 1888

Judging from his later comments on the tariff,
Waite must have lost the challenge. In 1892, Waite's
newspaper, the <u>Aspen Union Era</u>, announced that the
"tariff is a chestnut."[68] The tariff was of benefit
mainly to the trusts which obtained a monopoly of the

110

American market and pegged prices artificially high. Carnegie and others in the steel industry had in this manner become millionaires.[69]

Waite saw the tariff as a side issue which politicians debated in order to cover up the real issues. References to the tariff in his speeches were rare. The tariff benefited only the rich, he asserted: "The working men of America must cease to look to the tariff for relief from their many woes. Of what avail are cheap goods, if one has not the money with which to buy at any price? Of what avail are protected industries, if that protection benefits only the capitalist and the employer? . . . The tariff is the rich man's issue, but the working man derives no benefit from either the protection or the free trade side of the question. As a source of revenue, a high tariff rigidly enforced could be made most serviceable but with over 10,000 miles of frontier, it is probable that more goods are smuggled into the country than pay duty."[70] Hence, Waite saw little use for the tariff for either of its traditional uses, revenue or protection.

Waite felt that the current tax systems were unjust and inefficient. He deplored the heavy reliance on the property tax and advocated the income tax and the inheritance tax. Real and personal property taxes were difficult to assess fairly. More stringent laws would not help, as loopholes were always possible. Waite recommended the exemption of a homestead or "improved and inhabited premises" up to a valuation of one thousand dollars. In addition, all household furniture should be exempt. This would place the bulk of the taxation on "a class much better able to pay than the great mass of the small holders."[71] A single tax or any other tax system which is definite would be preferable to the property tax, Waite said. He favored a graduated income tax which would begin at either the $1,500 or $2,000 income level.

S. H. Allen, an associate justice of the Supreme Court of Kansas, suggested to Waite that "a graduated income tax could be made all sufficient. I have no hesitancy in saying in public and private, that I am in favor of doing away with multi-millionaires, and of accomplishing this purpose through the national taxing machinery."[72] The turbulence of the early nineties with its more sharply drawn class lines had produced similar sympathies in Waite. Writing in his

111

post-gubernatorial days to E. D. Benson, he saw the
legal power of taxation as a potent weapon to control
trusts and corporate power and to ensure the liberties
of the individual. Through the income tax, redistribu-
tion and greater equalization of income were possible.

Waite forecast prophetically that the 1895 Supreme
Court decision invalidating the income tax would soon
be overruled:

> It is true the decision of the United
> States Supreme Court on the income tax stands
> measureably in the way of the goal to be sought,
> but that decision is like the Dred Scott decision,
> a complete overturn of both the form, practice,
> and theory of government. The Dred Scott
> decision logically carried out made slavery
> the normal condition of all the entire juris-
> diction of the United States and that was the
> object of it. It failed, and the income tax
> decision will also fail. Even if the United
> States cannot remedy completely the evils of
> the present law system, the states can to some
> extent and so far as possible, I favor legisla-
> tion of that kind — liberal homestead exemption,
> graduated income tax, and inheritance tax.[73]

The Subtreasury Plan

Before Waite became governor he was a strong
proponent of the subtreasury plan; there is little
mention of it in his later writings and speeches.

An elaborate development and defense of the subtreasury idea was presented by Waite in the National
Economist (Washington, D. C.), in January, 1892. C.
W. Macune, the editor of the National Economist, had
originated the subtreasury plan at the convention of
the Southern Alliance in December, 1889.[74] Waite's
proposal was a merger of his greenback and banking
ideas with the basic subtreasury concept.

> 1. An entire change in our financial policy,
> the abolition of all banks of issue, and the
> right to issue full legal tender to a spec-
> ified amount based on the actual wealth of
> the United States to be confined to the gen-
> eral government and that money to be issued

directly to the people, upon good security.

2. That the general government when required by the producer shall warehouse the agricultural crops of the nation upon reasonable terms, and advancing money to the owners if requested, to the extent of 80 per cent of the market value of the crops warehoused.

Waite's arguments on point one were similar to those already noted in the sections on greenbackism and banking. The government should issue full legal tender treasury notes on good security at a rate of interest not to exceed two per cent, he said. He advocated the inclusion of real estate security as the best and most tangible form of security. This was an idea advocated by many northern reformers to broaden support for the basic idea of the subtreasury plan contained in point two.

As to the second point, Waite averred that the present system "under exclusive control of private enterprise" had led to capitalistic combinations and commissions for freight and storage, which had limited farming profits. Under the proposed government warehouse plan, the government would enter the agricultural warehouse business to the extent of advancing eighty per cent of the market value of the crops stored at reasonable rates in order to tide the farmer over hard times. The farmer could not plant, harvest, and market his crops without pecuniary assistance under the current setup. Money was difficult to obtain except on "extortionate terms amounting to partial confiscation." The farmer had been compelled to make "forced sales" each year at below cost of production. Waite maintained that his proposal was not class legislation, as all owners of real estate and their products would be treated alike. He ridiculed the more radical idea that the government should buy and dispose of all agricultural products. The main point was that the government should deal directly with the people so as to eliminate the "money monopoly middleman."[75]

In his advocacy of government aid to agriculture Waite was again ahead of his time. Waite suggested that the first proposition of the subtreasury plan would probably accomplish all that was necessary to restore prosperity. He thus admitted that the subtreasury plan as usually construed was secondary to him. This view probably accounts for his slight

113

mention of the plan after 1892 when it had generally lost favor. The Southern Alliance had fathered the subtreasury idea in 1889, but by the summer of 1892 the Omaha Platform spoke only of the alternative of the "sub-treasury plan . . . or a better system."

Education

Education assumed a significant importance to Waite in assuring the success of a democratic politics. Yet the "tendency of the age" toward "a concentration of wealth and power" had adversely affected the institutions of education too, he said. Education and the arts "have been made the instruments of despotism and of the upbuilding of oppressive combinations, whose effects are more and more the degradation of the people." He believed that "education should humanize; it should elevate the people in a moral and physical sense."[76]

The governor was no believer in the ivory tower scholar. The scholar must be committed to the welfare of the people and against monopoly and special privilege. "In the present contest between the common people and the tyranny of the law of corporate and private greed, it should be and is the highest aim of the scholar to work for humanity, to labor that the golden rule shall become the law of nations, and the right of the citizen to 'life, liberty, and the pursuit of happiness' shall no longer be a dream."[77]

Waite was much concerned about the democratization of the educational process. He said, "It is much more necessary that children generally should be well grounded in the common branches of knowledge and thus supplied with the tools of improvement, than that a few should be taught at the public expense the refinements of culture, philosophy and the arts. Let the education at the expense of the people be severely practical and let us have no aristocracy in the public schools." In Colorado, Waite thought that there was too much inequality of educational opportunity. Some children in Denver, Boulder, Greeley, Colorado City, and Pueblo attended fine schools and had well-trained teachers. But many counties in the state, due to poverty, kept their schools open only three months a year.[78] The continuation of this process in Colorado and other states, Waite declared, could only strengthen the trend towards rule by a special elite in the United States.

CHAPTER IX

RELIGION, RACE, NATIONALISM, AND PREJUDICE

Religion and Reform

Waite was interested in religion as it related to morality and politics. If religion did not further the cause of human liberty and social justice it was of no value. The governor was not concerned with mysticism, dogma, ceremonial, or church organization. He was not a member of any church.[1] He attacked orthodox Christian doctrine which held that man by nature is depraved and that Christ must intervene to save man. This was contrary to reason, experience, and law, Waite said. Ignorance was the source of all sin and was the only devil; ignorance, not sin, was responsible "for the fix we are in."[2] In these statements Waite showed his kinship to the philosophy of deism.

Waite believed in a God of Righteousness who guided the destiny of mankind and whose way triumphed eventually despite the oppressor and despite the churches themselves. At his inaugural, the governor prophesized, "When the old thirteen colonies rebelled against the British government, there was to the human eye or understanding, not the least hope of success. So now the hosts of monopoly are pressing the people into a Red Sea, but the same God, who, through many ages and in many times, opened a way of escape for the oppressed of so many races, still rules the destinies of nations, and He will so order it that this last, greatest, and best of free governments shall never perish from the earth."[3]

Arguing against the view that religious instruction was necessary, Waite asserted that no necessary connection between religion and morality existed. "We do not believe religious instruction is at all necessary. Universal history disproves it. The history of the church itself disproves it, for the church's standard of morality has risen and fallen with the times through which it has lived." The churches might proclaim adherence to an absolute and eternal moral standard, but, to Waite, the moral standard of religious institutions was relative to their environment. In the Middle Ages the church "seemed to have no more powers of endurance against evil than common mortals. There is absolutely no question but that it resorted to the vilest practices to maintain its existence."[4]

Waite subscribed vaguely to an idea of Natural Law which was not to be identified with Christianity or any other religion, but which governed all religious institutions. Morality was innate. Human beings were essentially good. Given the proper environment, the morality of the human heart would find expression. "Christianity and religions of every short are subject to the great laws of Nature, and that morality comes, not from religious teaching, but from an inborn spirit of love and justice in the human heart which under favorable conditions always asserts itself." These comments of Waite's suggest elements of Emersonianism.

The governor declared that great men who had never known Christianity had been active in the cause of liberty and progress. Many "professing infidels and atheists" had a high level of morality and integrity. "The great mass of the leaders who are today struggling to save the nation from industrial slavery are indifferent to religious instruction or religious principles. Man's conception of justice is entirely separate and apart from religious convictions."[5]

Getting closer to politics, Waite cited the need for the churches to be on the side of liberty and moral right. Although Christ was crucified 1900 years ago, almost every government was "Godless" though "nominally Christian." Jesus could have reigned as King of the Jews, and driven out Caesar, Waite maintained, but he had a higher mission to "establish principles more powerful than armies, more enduring than the dynasties which built the pyramids." In his own day, nothing was a "more humanizing, philanthropic, or Christian duty than to so control governmental affairs, as to do equal and exact justice to all men."[6] The idea that morals could be separated from politics was "a great heresy." It implied that politics and religion operated on different planes. The piety of the churches had been throttled from their infancy by this erroneous notion. The churches had too often been on the side of evil. "The American churches, for example, had been the greatest bulwark of chattel slavery," Waite continued. "An industrial slavery has succeeded more cruel and relentless than was ever African slavery.[7] How should the contemporary Christian act? If a

116

Christian prayed for good rulers and voted for corrupt ones, he was a hypocrite. If a churchman did not protest against the open purchase and sale of votes, he stood damned as much as for any sin. The number and magnificence of churches might increase, but this in itself meant nothing.

"The church cannot oppose reform," Waite proclaimed. God had created of one blood all the nations of the earth. The confessing Christian must squarely meet the implications of this statement. He must face the challenge of political corruption. Christ had paid his tax; there must have been some justice in it. But the modern system of taxation was inequitable and "rotten." Waite cited Cook County, Illinois as an example. Christ would not pay his tax in Chicago, Waite asserted. God would topple "the golden image with its feet of clay." The Republic would not perish. The same God who led four million Negroes from slavery would emancipate seventy million from industrial slavery. "He will not allow seventy million of His people, black and white, to lose their liberties and their religion in the horrors of an industrial slavery more merciless than Moloch."[8]

Waite was a strong advocate of separation of church and state. He wrote: "No law should be enacted respecting any establishment of religion, or prohibiting the free exercise thereof, and no person should be denied any civil or political right or privilege, or capacity, on account of his opinions concerning religion. No appropriation should be made from any public fund, or moneys whatever, of anything in aid of any church or sectarian society, or to help support any school, academy, seminary, college, university, or other literary or scientific institution, controlled by any grant or donation of land, money or other personal property to any church or for any sectarian purpose."[9]

On the separation of church and state with more specific reference to education, Waite commented, "Let the Catholic hierarchy teach its religion if it will, but let it never have a single dollar of the public school fund for that purpose. Let it send its pupils to the public schools if it wants to do so, but let no fact of history remain untaught on that account. Let it exercise a censorship over the thoughts of its followers and maintain a monarchical religious institution if it please, but let it not

117

attempt to bulldoze American citizens into silence because they chance to criticize its conduct in either or all of these matters. Our public schools, and the rights of free speech and thought, are too dear to American hearts, and too necessary to the maintenance of liberty and establishment of justice, to be sacrificed upon the altar of the ruling powers of any religious denomination."[10]

The American Protective Association and Roman Catholicism

In his temporary bitterness and disillusionment over the election results of 1894, Waite believed that the Roman Catholic Church had played a prominent role in the defeat of Populism in Colorado. In a letter to C. T. Beatty, national secretary of the American Protective Association, a nativist and anti-Catholic organization of the 1890's, Waite made the preposterous statement that the entire Catholic vote in Colorado had been turned over to the Republicans between the Saturday before election and election day. He said that the Bishop in Colorado and nearly all the clergy had been "actively at work" for the People's Party during the campaign because the anti-Catholic A. P. A. "was supposed to have dictated" the Republican nomination. Some blamed the supposed change, Waite said, on a Republican contribution of $50,000 to certain bishops for what the Republicans called "religious purposes."

Waite's post-election opposition to woman suffrage and his post-election anti-Catholicism were closely related. According to him, nearly all the hired girls in Denver were Catholics and were subject to the control of Catholic priests. Opposing woman suffrage, he told Beatty, "It puts a tremendous power for evil into the hands of the Catholic priests and gives them in almost every city and state, the balance of political power, which they will use to destroy the free school system of the United States and to put active Catholic politicians in power. I never realized this fact until too late in my own state."[11] Waite offered no facts to support his contentions. There is evidence that at least one Roman Catholic priest, a Father Malone of Denver, did publicly call for the defeat of the Populists. He claimed that the A. P. A. was operating inside the Populist Party, a charge he did not substantiate either.[12]

118

Beatty hoped that Waite might become a member of the A. P. A., and wrote to him the, following:

I was much pleased indeed to receive your favor of the 1st inst. for I have often thought and hoped that matters would so shape themselves in the near future so that should an independent party be formed, that the party you are interested in and it might coalesce. Personally, we agree on the money question, and, it seems to me, that when the matter is discussed at a meeting soon to be held, composed of delegates from every State in the Union for the purpose of considering the advisability of forming a new American Party, one of the planks of the platform should embody your ideas. Do not think that the convention above referred to will be the supreme A. P. A. Convention to be held in May. It will be a convention composed of delegates from the different Patriotic Orders of the United States, and will be composed, I believe, of some of the brightest men in this country. The oath of the A. P. A. Order published in this year's World Almanac page 115 is not correct. We take no obligation prohibiting the employment of Roman Catholics. From what you say I believe you could conscientiously take all of our obligations and that you would be in hearty sympathy with our Order.[13]

No evidence exists that Waite joined or considered joining the A. P. A. Adequate reasons are to be found in Waite's own comments to Beatty on the A. P. A. in Colorado. Waite was, temporarily at least, attracted by the anti-Catholicism of the American Protective Association; he was repelled by its ties to the Republican Party in Colorado, and by its political hypocrisy.[14] He wrote to Beatty: "In this state your organization is numerous and active. It early took possession of the inside Republican ring of Denver, and in nominations 'put none but Americans on guard', etc. Most of the A. P. A. have always been active Republicans and they are so anxious to defeat the Populists and redeem the state that they united with those not in sympathy with their order in the nomination of a man for governor who was brought up a Catholic and whose wife also claimed she is a Catholic, and then a corrupt bargain was made to bring to the support of the Republican ticket the influence of the Catholic Church, innocently supposing that they would cheat the

119

Catholics after election out of the consideration."
But the A. P. A. was mistaken, said Waite, and got
only a "fragment" of the "loaves and fishes," and "are
howling in impotent rage." Concluded the governor,
"I am glad of it."[15]

One Populist leader who corresponded with Waite
exhibited a strong anti-Catholic bias. Paul Van
Dervoort, Nebraska Populist, wrote to Waite, "I am
glad you approved of my dab at the Catholics. They
deserve more than that. They talked some of our people
into working against A. P. A. and they hired others
and drove all the A. P. A. people to the Republicans
and then they went there, too. We could combine the
great mass of the A. P. A. vote in 1896."[16] Later,
Van Dervoort wrote in a similar vein to Waite, "We can
get the A. P. A. vote if our people had sense. I like
your courage. It is the kind that sees ahead and says
it."[17]

One Denver Populist was quite upset over Waite's
anti-Catholic utterances and cited facts which contradicted his assertions about the Catholic vote:

I cannot understand how any man who pro-
fesses to stand on the Omaha Platform could make
himself a tool in the hands of the A. P. A. to
circulate their anti-Catholic doctrine. The
majority of Populists in this precinct last fall
were Catholics. Every English-speaking Catholic
in this precinct voted the straight Populist
ticket. I know as I canvassed the precinct three
times and I could tell how most of the people
voted. I know of many other Catholics in other
precincts and districts all over the city who
worked earnestly as well as voting for the Populist Party. If the Catholic hired girls of Denver
were as ignorant as your informants they would
indeed be a sorry lot.[18]

It is probable that the above Populist correspondent knew whereof she spoke. The A. P. A. dominated
the local and state Republican conventions in Colorado
in 1894, and was able to get its candidates nominated
for office. In their eagerness to defeat Populism in
the 1894 election, the Colorado Republicans freely
accepted A. P. A. support and condoned the anti-
Catholicism of the A. P. A. The Republican administration of Albert W. McIntire, which had been elected in
1894, did not allow a single Roman Catholic to hold
office.

120

The Denver Fire and Police Board controversy was the occasion for Waite's contact with an organization similar to the A. P. A. The Patriotic Order Sons of America charged Governor Waite with discrimination against its members in police appointments. The governor received the following resolution from the order:

Whereas the Governor of this state has by and through his lately appointed partisan police board declared an open and aggressive war upon all members of the Patriotic Order Sons of America;

And whereas a large number of the members of this order, lately occupying positions on the police force, have been preemptorily discharged or forced to resign, by the said police board, without cause, save and except, that they were members of this order;

And whereas such treatment is contrary to the spirit of American citizenship, and a direct insult to true American manhood, as viewed from the teachings of this order.

Therefore be it resolved, that Camp No. 15, P. O. S. of A. hereby enters a most solemn protest against such treatment, and declares the same to be an unwarranted and unjustifiable assault upon a particular class of citizens who are and ever have been a true liberty loving body of men.

Resolved, that this camp place the band of open censure so far as in its power lies, upon the present administration and hold it accountable for its unjust attack upon members of this order as above stated.[20]

Governor Waite answered that he did appoint a partisan board including two Populists, but that "no member of the P. O. S. of A. or the A. P. A. or any similar organization has been removed to my knowledge from the police force or fire department or been compelled to resign therefrom because he was a member of the P. O. S. of A. or any other similar organization, political or religious. The removals and resignations from both the police and fire departments were for participation in the insurrection against the attempt of the Governor (since declared legal by the Supreme Court) to take possession of the City Hall." Waite concluded, "I am not a member of the P. O. S. of A. or the A. P. A. or the 'Loyalty and Liberty League,' or any kindred organization nor am I a member of any church, but I do believe in that doctrine of the Omaha Platform of 'equal rights for all and special privileges to none.'"[21]

Anti-Semitism

Basic to the attack on Populism by the "new critics" has been its identification with anti-Semitism. In an article in 1951, Oscar Handlin maintained that the origins of American anti-Semitism were to be found in the Populist movement.[22] This was in sharp contrast to the thesis of Carey McWilliams that American anti-Semitism originated with the rise of industrial capitalism.[23] Others during the fifties echoed Handlin's line. Peter Viereck accused the Populists of "Jew-baiting." Even Henry Ford's anti-Semitism was linked to a youthful Populist background by Viereck. However, Viereck stretched the meaning of the term "populism" to include anything agrarian in the late nineteenth century.[24] Richard Hofstadter in his Age of Reform asserted that basically American anti-Semitism could be traced to the Greenback-Populist tradition.[25]

In the 1960's, the Handlin-Hofstadter theme was challenged. Walter T. K. Nugent, in his study of Kansas Populism, found that the Populist forces there were not anti-Semitic.[26] Norman Pollack has severely questioned the validity of Handlin's sources in the latter's attempt to link anti-Semitism and Populism. He maintained that Handlin's case rested mainly on one source, Caesar's Column, by Ignatius Donnelly. Hofstadter also relied heavily on Caesar's Column in presenting his thesis. Pollack acknowledged that there were examples of anti-Semitism in Donnelly's book, but argued that this aspect had been grossly exaggerated in the total picture. Furthermore, Donnelly's anti-Semitism was ambivalent in nature and the humanistic content of the book had been ignored.[27]

Proper perspective is also necessary in approaching the subject of Waite and anti-Semitism. In the Waite Papers, a collection of his speeches and correspondence, there are two obvious anti-Semitic statements by him. Writing to Senator Stewart of Nevada, he

122

remarked, "With government pecuniary aid, instead of opposition, instead of turning us over to the tender mercies of Jew extortioners, the recuperative powers of the American people are almost beyond conception."[28]

While describing the rise of the "money power" in one of his speeches, Waite referred to Alfred de Rothschild as a "Jew banker in Belgium" who went to England where he established the House of Rothschild. Waite then proceeded to describe how the House of Rothschild as a prominent part of the English "money power" had built its empire of finance and had become a force which "controls czars, emperors, kings, lords, and commons" and was above all laws and constitutions.[29] In another speech which dealt with the English "money power" the governor asserted that English money brokers, the Barings, had taken control of Argentina.[30] These references would seem to substantiate the claim of Walter T. K. Nugent that the name Rothschild has more of an English than a Jewish significance, as it was the English "money power" that Waite was attacking.[31]

Another term with debatable anti-Semitic content is "shylock." The determining factor for both the name Rothschild and the term Shylock would seem to be the context in which these words are used. In a letter to Ignatius Donnelly, Waite said, "The arguments in behalf of the creditor class, and against money as dishonest, are the stock arguments of Shylock against the seventy cent dollar and the fiat greenback."[32] Criticizing Senator John Sherman's alleged servitude to the "money power," Waite commented in a speech, "Both as Secretary of the Treasury and as a United States Senator no measure to increase the profit of the bondholder and of the Shylocks of Wall Street lacked Sherman's support.[33]

However, even the terms "Rothschild" and "Shylock" rarely occur in Waite's letters, speeches, and articles, or in the letters to Waite from a representative list of Populists and reformers. Letters from Colorado Populists to Waite are remarkably free of anti-Semitic expressions.

It would appear to the present writer that the thesis that the Populists had less association with anti-Semitism than the population as a whole would be much closer to the truth than the contrary view of Hofstadter and Handlin.

The Blacks

Jack Abramowitz in his provocative article on the Black and Populism stated: "The collapse of Populism in 1896 put an end to a movement that had every chance of producing a truly emancipated South in which the Negro would have been accorded a respectable position which might in time have broken down hostility and suspicion between Negro and white."[34] He thus called attention to the crucial importance of the question of Black-white cooperation in southern Populism. The earlier Tom Watson and other more foresighted Populists had understood that Black-white unity was the key to Populist success in the South.

The question of the Black was not confined to the South. The first involvement of a Black in the third party occurred in Kansas in 1890 when the Independents named a Black, the Reverend Benjamin F. Foster of Topeka, as candidate for state auditor. He received 112,000 votes, and ran 6,000 votes ahead of his ticket. At least one Black delegate from Kansas attended the Omaha Convention in 1892.[35]

In 1890, the Black population in Colorado was 6,215, or a little over one per cent of the state total. There were 3,045 Blacks in Denver, and nearly a thousand in Pueblo.[36] In August, 1892, a Constitutional Convention of an organization of Colorado Blacks convened in Denver. The organization had been formed the previous December to help achieve equal opportunity for all citizens regardless of color. One of the convention resolutions read: "Resolved, that we condemn all labor organizations which condemn a laborer because he is black." The state central committee of the organization was composed of Blacks from Arapahoe, Boulder, Clear Creek, El Paso, Lake, Las Animas, Pueblo, and Pitkin Counties. No mention of the Populist Party was made in the report of the convention.[37] A week later, the Langston Club, a group of Denver Black Republicans, met and adopted a resolution supporting the Republican ticket "from A to Z."[38]

John W. Dickinson of Georgetown appealed to Waite for the establishment of a Black Populist weekly in Denver to enlist Negro support for Populism and to offset the influence of two Denver Black Republican weeklies.[39] It is not known whether Waite acted on this appeal.

In one speech Waite expressed his sympathy for Civil War emancipation, but revealed his paternalistic picture of the Black: "I believe there is a just God who provides over the destinies of nations and who compelled North and South to emancipate four million poor and ignorant black slaves."[40] He was also against the Fifteenth Amendment. "The elective franchise was given to the Negro in the South with all his unfitness," he declared.[41] This would seem to indicate that Waite was not conscious of the vital importance of Negro-white cooperation to Populist success in the South.

One bit of evidence suggests that some Blacks looked upon Waite as a friend of their race. The Reverend John J. Smallwood, President of the Temperance, Industrial, and Collegiate Institute of Claremont, Virginia, wrote to Governor Waite in late 1894 that his school needed fifty thousand dollars to erect a new building. He asked Waite for $1,500, and promised to give Waite's name to the new structure. The Reverend Smallwood continued, "We are all working people. We believe you to be a true friend of the workingmen and to our race."[42] It is not known how Waite reacted. However, the correspondence and speeches of Waite indicate a general lack of consciousness of the special problems faced by Blacks.

The weakness of Waite on the Black question was a common one among Populist leaders and the general Populist movement, and, indeed, a common weakness of the whole society in which he lived. But far from being racists as Viereck has charged, the most advanced thinkers of the period on the Black question were Populists.[43] C. Vann Woodward has noted that never have the two races cooperated more closely in the South than during the hey-day of Populism.[44] Thomas Watson was the brave leader of these Southern Populist forces. In the North, Eugene Debs urged the unity of all workers regardless of color.[45] Perhaps Henry D. Lloyd had the clearest insight of any northern Populist leader on the Black issue. He stated that the Black question of the South was the key to the future. The ability of the workingmen to organize and win their rights and the success of the drive against the forces of monopoly depended on the success in achieving Black-white unity, he said.[46]

The Indians

Early territorial and state administrations in Colorado were particularly harsh and vicious in dealing with the Indians. They were acting, of course, in behalf of white land and mineral grabbers. Following the slaughter of the Indians at Sand Creek in southeastern Colorado in 1864, Indian retaliation became the pretext for removing the Cheyenne and Arapahoe Indians from eastern Colorado. The Ute Indians of western Colorado became the next victims as people poured across the Divide in search of gold and silver and land. The Utes were forced to retreat step by step until they were removed from Colorado to Utah in 1881.[47]

Today, as a result, surrounding states such as Arizona, New Mexico, and Oklahoma have considerable Indian populations, but Colorado contains no Indian land except for an insignificant overlapping of reservation boundaries and state borders in the southwestern corner of the state.

Waite arrived in Colorado at a time of anti-Ute hysteria. Apparently he adopted the prevailing white attitudes without question. When he became governor, white settlers in western Colorado were still complaining that the Ute Indians were crossing over the boundary into their old hunting grounds.

Governor Waite wrote to President Cleveland in May, 1893, that the troubles resulted "from the fact that the Indians are allowed by the U. S. Indian agents to wander away from their reservation." The difference in cost of upkeep was then pocketed by the Indian agents, the governor asserted. The Indians destroyed the wild game in their hunting excursions and frequently destroyed also the cattle of the settlers. They did not consume the meat, but sold the hides to the agents.

Waite argued that the Ute Indian Reservation in southwestern Colorado was large enough and had sufficient game to support the Indians. However, the Indians wandered into eastern Utah, and back into northwestern Colorado. The extinction of the deer was inevitable in the latter area, he said. Large herds of elk, which were abundant two years ago, were almost gone. Colorado had efficient game wardens and good game laws, and could protect itself from the "outrages

126

of individual hunters or ordinary hunting bands." But
it was difficult to protect the state's borders "from
a band of marauding Indians" composed of one hundred
to one hundred and fifty who were here today and many
miles away tomorrow.

Governor Waite asked that an order be given to
the effect that the Indians "be positively prohibited
from leaving their reservations for hunting or pilgrimage purposes in N. W. Colorado."[48]

In November of the same year, Governor Waite wrote
to the Secretary of the Interior that the Ute Indians
were in Rio Blanco or Routt County west of Meeker
"slaying deer by the thousands for their hides." Waite
noted the claim of certain Indian agents that the
Indians had a right to go anywhere in Colorado on lands
originally belonging to them, but expressed no sympathy
with this view. There were no treaties, he remarked.
The Indians should be forced to obey the general laws
of Colorado the same as the white man. Waite thought
this demand was legitimate, despite the peculiar circumstances of livelihood which the white man had forced
upon the Indians. Again, the governor concluded with
the request that the Indians be kept on their reservations.[49]

Waite did not conceive that there might be an
Indian side to the problem or that land containment
had caused the Indian difficulties. His concern for
reform did not extend to the Indians. Also, he seems
to have been scarcely aware of the different history
and culture of the Spanish-speaking peoples to be
found in southern Colorado.

Chinese and European Immigration

Anti-Chinese sentiment was strong in the West in
the late nineteenth century. Colorado was no exception. Waite addressed an anti-Chinese gathering at
the Aspen courthouse in March, 1892. He signed the
article in his own newspaper advertising the meeting.
In his article he complained that some scheduled
speakers had later declined, and that the meeting was
not to be addressed only by the "radical element in
Aspen."[50] Occasionally, anti-Chinese material appeared
in the Aspen Union Era, including a three-verse anti-
Chinese poem which spoke of the Chinese swarms to be

found "in every crack and crevice and under every kettle or pan."[51] In one speech Waite lamented, "Chinese immigration, confessedly transient, wholly foreign, abjuring citizenship, recognizing in both civil and criminal matters, as superior to our own tribunals the tyrannical edicts of a secret organization, flourishes and is rapidly introducing coolie competition to American labor in nearly all parts of the country."[52]

Certain remarks by Waite on the newer southern and eastern European immigration were not more enlightened. "A limited amount of pauper, criminal, and contract immigration might be assimilated to our institutions, but not the deluge of such undeniable immigration as the past few years has poured into the country from the most ignorant and degraded people of Europe."[53] Writing to Ignatius Donnelly, the governor said, "It (woman suffrage) has the same fatal error as the policy . . . that allows the Italian, the Hungarian, the Pole and the pauper immigrants from Europe 'to declare their intentions,' and vote before they know one word of our language."[54]

In 1893 at Cripple Creek a group of native American workers attacked an Italian immigrant labor group. In his official report to the Secretary of State of the United States on the incident, Governor Waite noted that the sheriff and the police did not act properly to protect the Italian immigrants. As an "abstract question" and under treaties with Italy, the subjects of Italy were entitled to the protection of life and property, he said, "but in equity and according to the principles of the Constitution, America was made an asylum for the oppressed of Europe and all nations, with the expectation and understanding that the subjects of Italy or any of the countries of Europe who might seek our shores should come with a view of renouncing their allegiance to foreign potentates and becoming citizens of the United States. I confess I have but little sympathy with contract labor which is imported for the purpose of reaping the advantage of our higher rates of labor only, and with no honest desire to acquire American citizenship, whether that class of people come from Europe, Asia, or Africa."[55]

Waite thus revealed his prejudices against Italian immigrants, illustrated by the unfounded assumptions that they could not possibly desire citizenship and that they had dangerous ties abroad. These were all too common views of the times.[56]

Despite his pro-labor views, the governor did not understand that unionization of the workers, not restrictions on immigration, was the answer to employer attempts to pit native labor against immigrant labor. Education and greater opportunities would be the answer to political manipulation and other problems generally associated with the immigrant, not restrictions on immigration of supposedly inferior people.

Nationalism and Foreign Affairs

Similar to many Populists, Waite voiced anti-British sentiments at a time when the British Empire was the dominant force in the world. These sentiments were directed mainly towards the Briitsh rulers and British imperialism, often referred to, perhaps simplistically, as the "British money power," due to obsession with the money issue. Few today would take at face value, though, his assessment of the control of the British over American politics in the late nineteenth century via monetary policies.

The governor asserted that "the British money power . . . controls the world and under Republican and Democratic rule in this country for the past thirty years has made the United States one of England's provinces . . . Not Pharoah nor Attila, not Nero nor Caligula; not the great Caesar or Napoleon, not all combined have occasioned the woes that within the past century, the British money-power has brought upon the sons of men."[57] In their correspondence Waite and Donnelly agreed that a special effort should be made to attract the Irish to the Populist cause, because, as Donnelly put it, they were "fighting England just as we are."[58]

Waite was against any proposal for an international monetary conference, which, he felt, would be dominated by European powers. Said Waite, "I denounce the entire international conference business as un-American, and as without warrant in our Constitution or organic laws. In all our history is no instance in which the rights of this nation have been submitted to European arbitration that they have not been ruthlessly sacrificed with the most defiant injustice. The northeastern and northwestern boundaries and the Alabama claims are conspicuous instances, in which, by the decision of foreign arbitrators, the United States were deprived of their rights."[59]

The governor attacked the _Alabama_ claims settlement with Britain. The Alabama and other Confederate cruisers were built and manned by the British and had swept United States commerce from the seas and "destroyed our shipping interests," he said. Yet the tribunal awarded only fifteen million dollars to cover the value of the ships and cargoes actually destroyed. "Not one cent" was awarded, Waite charged, for merchants whose commercial interests were "blocked or destroyed."[60]

The governor continued, "There is only one international conference that is at all in consonance with republican principles and republican theories, and that is a conference composed of delegates from all the republics on this continent of America." The First Pan American Conference had met in 1891, he said, but it revealed that the United States delegates, Republicans and Democrats, were not in favor of the free coinage of silver, though many Latin American countries were.[61] The United States dominated the conference, and its wishes unfortunately prevailed.

What was needed, Waite implied, was a declaration of independence by the Americans from the European money power, and an adoption of free and unlimited coinage of silver and government currency by all the Americas. Waite saw a United States-Mexico financial agreement as the first major step in this direction.

Writing to Porfirio Diaz of Mexico, Waite said:

> The prosperity of my own country, Senor, is no less threatened than is that of yours. We have the advantage that our nation is more populous, more extensive in area, and more wealthy than Mexico, but you have one great advantage over us, that you have the free and unlimited coinage of silver. Supplement that with the issue of government currency. Within four years the Administration of the United States now upon the side of the European money-power, will be so changed that the influence of the United States government will favor such a joint financial policy for the United States and Mexico . . . and there will be such a rallying to the support and enforcement of the 'Monroe Doctrine,' as shall be invincible against any force the enemies of mankind can bring against us.[62]

As part of the development of inter-American relations, Governor Waite favored the construction of a Nicaragua canal to connect the Atlantic and the Pacific. The United States and the Central American republics should jointly build and manage the canal, he said, but the United States should have control of it. The government would finance and build the canal, which would be open to the commerce of the world.[63]

With the coming of war with Spain in 1898, Waite adopted the imperialist argument. He declared, "The original territory of the United States, within the present century, has been tripled in extent, and not only without injury to the government or people, but with the most extraordinary benefit to both. We need Hawaii, we need the Philippine Islands and we need the Nicaragua canal — not that we should enter upon a career of conquest, or by the strong hand take from any weak nation her territory, but we need a protectorate, a foothold — justly obtained in all these places and many more." The United States must become a great naval power, Waite asserted, or be without either influence among nations or even means of self-defense; it must be prepared in terms of an irrepressible conflict between right and wrong, "or the republican idea of self-government vs. the idea of despotism." Waite continued that "it would be disgraceful for this nation to make a war for conquest; but in a just war like that against Spain, from whose government Cuba should have been wrested twenty-five years ago, our duty is clear." In conclusion, Waite quoted approvingly the following statement of Senator Henry Teller in the United States Senate, "Wherever our flag flies by right of conquest or by consent of the people, there it will remain, and the party or the man who proposes to take it down will reckon with the great body of the American people who believe it the best flag and the best government, and better calculated to bring peace and prosperity to mankind than any other flag and government under the sun."[64]

During this same period, Waite's closest parallel, the reform Governor of Illinois, John P. Altgeld, became associated with the anti-imperialists. Unlike Waite, Altgeld drew a careful distinction between internal expansion and imperialism. Internal expansion had involved setting up new states equal with the old and with the citizens of each state having equal rights; imperialism meant conquest of people inhabiting other lands and ruling them against their will.[65] Altgeld's

131

analysis, however, ignored the plight of the American Indian who was victimized by the internal expansion across the North American continent.

The issues of the Spanish-American War and American imperialism are, of course, beyond the period of the real Populist movement. But it is interesting to note that a number of former Populist colleagues of Waite's had views on the Spanish-American War and imperialism which contrasted sharply with his. Ignatius Donnelly, Henry D. Lloyd, Eugene Debs, Thomas Watson, and James Weaver, among others, were sharply critical of the Spanish-American War and American expansion.[66]

CHAPTER X

WAITE AND THE NATIONAL POPULIST MOVEMENT

The national Populist Party was a loose coalition composed of several elements; agriculture, silver, labor, and middle-class reformers and idealists, though it had a strong agrarian base. The common desires and the differences of these forces were the key to the initiation, the path of development, and the final fusion and dissolution of Populism. Differences were both strategic and tactical. As Populism reached its zenith in 1894, and the depression brought fear to the conservative and radical-mindedness to the downtrodden, a division between moderate and radical elements became sharper within the Populist ranks also. The former favored silver and fusion; the latter favored the Omaha Platform and party independence. This strategic argument unfolded mainly during the period when Davis Waite had achieved national stature as a Populist reformer.

Tactical questions were also important. How to achieve unity between the South and the West to bring Populist victory at the polls was a sectional matter of no small concern to Waite and many others. The fine dividing line between principle and compromise was a problem with which many politicians have wrestled. Whether to leave out certain planks in the program in order to attract a larger following was a problem which divided even the more reform-minded Populists. The highly individualistic and sometimes colorful personalities of the leading Populists were an important aspect of the Populist story, especially since the coalition was an unstable one, and there was never a dominant leader of Populism. The purpose of this chapter is to trace the unfolding of this drama with special reference to Davis Waite.

At the founding convention of the Populist Party in Cincinnati in May, 1891, many shades of opinion were expressed. A radical minority threatened to issue a minority report and did succeed in assuring a platform-making convention in St. Louis on February 22, 1892. Waite was a delegate to this St. Louis conference as a representative of the Farmers' Alliance and the Knights of Labor. As he later wrote, he "participated in the preliminary debates and skirmishes which revealed the fact that hardly two persons in all the

133

crowd were agreed upon any one thing. The crank, the
fad, the single-idea man, the fierce bigot and the
uncompromising fanatic were there in full force, and
in their fighting clothes. There was no greater con-
fusion at the building of the Tower of Babel and it
seemed impossible to reconcile these hostile forces."[1]
A platform was adopted at St. Louis.

This platform was essentially reaffirmed at the
national nominating convention of the Populist Party
in Omaha in July, 1892, although a number of resolutions were added. Of the Omaha Platform Waite declared:
"It is conceded to be the grandest political document
issued since the Declaration of Independence and like
it will be immortal."[2] The Omaha Platform became
Waite's political bible. It was his guiding star by
which he measured everything through the shifting sands
of Populist maneuvering in the years that followed.

Waite favored L. L. Polk of North Carolina for
the Populist presidential nomination at the Omaha Convention in 1892. Polk was President of the Southern
Farmers' Alliance. Waite commented, "We think it
politic to nominate Polk for the reason that in order
for the People's Party to succeed, WE MUST BREAK THE
SOLID SOUTH." The South was a debtor section and "a
field for plunder" under "our financial system," he
said. The South was in a state of bankruptcy as the
crops did not "bring the cost of production." But the
South had faced ostracism since the Civil War as old
prejudices still existed. It was time to forget sec-
tionalism and nominate a Southerner. "We believe the
nomination at Omaha of L. L. Polk for President means
victory this very year."[3] The political need to nominate a Southerner became a constant theme of Waite's,
causing him to wish that James G. Field of Virginia
had been nominated for President and Weaver for Vice-
President in 1892, and to support Senator Benjamin
Tillman of South Carolina for a time in 1896.

Waite did not favor going outside the Populist
ranks simply to nominate a well-known politician.
Judge Walter Q. Gresham and Senator William M. Stewart,
two possible presidential nominees, were silverites,
but were Republicans in all other respects, Waite believed. The People's Party, he felt, should not engage
in temporary expedients of this kind. He saw the
People's Party as a permanent organization with a
crusading mission similar to 1776 and 1861. He was
suspicious of any move which seemed to suggest fusion

with the Democrats and Republicans. "The People's party has come to stay. It proposes to take possession of this government, and will play second fiddle to no political organization under heaven."[4]

Expanding on the theme of the destiny of Populism, Waite asserted, "The People's party is no toy; it is no plaything; it is no passing fancy; it is not a fleeting chimera of the brain. It is a tremendous power that has been acquiring strength and momentum for many years and when at last its history shall be read, it will exhibit the landmark of the emancipation of the laboring masses from industrial slavery."[5]

Though Waite wanted candidates and leadership to consist only of proven reformers, he was willing to accept into the Populist ranks those who supported the People's Party only on the silver issue. The People's Party "hopes to receive the assistance of the men who are today proposing to support it on the silver issue. We hope that they will ultimately see the justice of our full demands and the soundness of our methods of securing them."[6]

The basic division within the Populist Party began to manifest itself in 1892. The more conservative element leaned toward emphasis on the silver issue; the more liberal element stressed a broad program of reform based on the Omaha Platform. Waite was aligned with the latter grouping, which became more militant in its demands as the economic crisis of 1893 burst upon the nation. The conservative grouping, ever fearful of sweeping reforms and socialistic tendencies, centered in the wealthy silver mining interests and the more well-to-do farmers. Among the millionaire Populist mine owners were Senators William M. Stewart of Nevada, Senator John P. Jones of Nevada, Charles E. Lane of California, and George F. Hearst of California. The conservative elements were rebuffed at the 1892 Omaha Convention with free silver being simply one among many planks in the platform.[7]

In 1893 several midwestern Populist leaders became intimate with the American Bimetallic League and its President, A. J. Warner. Western mine owners dominated the League. Herman E. Taubeneck of Illinois, the national executive secretary of the Populist Party, received heavy contributions from the silver interests. James B. Weaver, Populist presidential candidate from Iowa, and Senator William A. Peffer of Kansas, became

135

associated with Warner. The national committee of the Populist Party stressed the silver issue in a statement calling for party gatherings on the Fourth of July. Some Populist leaders talked of removing from the Omaha Platform any of the planks which might prove objectionable to the silverites.[8] Silver propaganda was swinging a number of local Populist leaders to a strictly silver position.[9]

The silver issue itself reached a fever pitch in the summer of 1893 with the threatened repeal of the Sherman Silver Purchase Act. Weaver presided at a giant national silver rally on August 1 in Chicago, sponsored by the American Bimetallic League. Waite gave his famous "Bloody Bridles" speech at this gathering; however, silver remained only an issue to Waite, not a panacea or a substitute for the Omaha Platform. Indeed, Waite used silver in this speech to rally the anti-monopoly forces.[10] The American Bimetallic League met in December, 1893. Writing to Ignatius Donnelly, Waite termed this meeting a failure. He said that it had treated all political parties alike although the Populists were the only party in favor of free and unlimited coinage of silver.[11]

Waite urged national Populist leaders to stand firm on the Omaha Platform. He opposed any attempt to turn the Populist Party into a silver party. This theme was combined with a plea for greater South-West unity in the letters he wrote in late 1893.[12]

In reply to Waite, Tom Watson of Georgia declared he was also strongly against the single silver plank as a Populist platform. On South-West unity Watson said to Waite: "I heartily concur with you in the desire to see the West and the South form a political alliance. If such men as Tillman (Ben Tillman of South Carolina) and yourself take hold of the movement I shall not doubt the results."[13]

From the Populist viewpoint, South-West unity was highly desirable, but Waite seems to have underestimated the potential support in the industrial northeastern United States, especially from the ranks of labor. Watson also underestimated this same potential.

Senator James Kyle of South Dakota, a front runner for the 1892 Populist presidential nomination, wrote to Waite that he was against compromise, but then proceeded ambiguously to note, "We must keep an eye on our next platform and so construct it as to bring the financial issues alone to the front. In this way we shall provide a refuge for a large body of Democrats and Republicans."14

Waite charged that Weaver wanted to drop the Omaha Platform for the silver issue and fuse with the old parties. Weaver protested, maintaining that the "old parties" were unreliable "upon every issue" in the Omaha Platform. The People's Party was the only one making an honest effort to obtain bimetallism, Weaver said. On fusion with the Democrats and Republicans, Weaver asserted, "I am not, nor have I ever been in favor of fusing with them directly or indirectly. But I am in favor of a straight middle of the road fight from start to finish. After we have made our nominations I have no objections to other organizations meeting and endorsing our candidates, provided it is done in an open, frank, and straightforward manner."15

H. E. Taubeneck, Populist Party national secretary, was upset by Waite's position on the December Bimetallic League meeting and declared to him that the Populist Party had "compromised nothing, or surrendered nothing." He said, "The People's Party will never agree to support a silver republican or a silver democrat so long as I can prevent it."16 While disavowing fusion, neither Weaver nor Taubeneck directly answered Waite on the issue of silver versus the Omaha Platform.

Included among those sending messages of support for Waite's defense of the Omaha Platform and political independence were John W. Breidenthal, Chairman of the Populist Party of Kansas; H. L. Loucks of the Farmers' Alliance and Industrial Union of South Dakota; and I. E. Dean of the Farmers' Alliance and Industrial Union of New York. Breidenthal wrote, "I am disappointed in the action of General Weaver in attempting to sidetrack the people's party. I have been his personal friend and warm supporter for many years, having voted for him twice for president, but I certainly think he is making a mistake in this matter."17

A major Populist Party crisis occurred in the late 1894-early 1895 period following the 1894 elections. The party had gained one and a half million votes, considerably better than the one million count of 1892, despite the fact that it was an off-presidential election year. Labor Populism had especially made gains. Populism in Illinois led in achieving a coalition of farmers and city workers.[18] More radical stirrings in Populist ranks, related to the hard times of 1893 and 1894, caused uneasiness among a number of the more conservative Populist leaders. At a silver conference held at St. Louis in November, 1894, H. E. Taubeneck and A. J. Warner asserted that the Populist Party must rid itself of the "cranks and socialists" and organize a silver party instead.[19] The controversy came to its sharpest focus in the Populist Party conference on December 28 and 29, 1894, in St. Louis. The first attempt to oust the more reform-minded element from the movement occurred at this time.

Waite was concerned that the St. Louis conference should not change the Omaha Platform. He launched a letter campaign against the conference, and found that others were also unfavorable to it. George F. Washburn, Populist national committee member from Boston, wrote, "If the silverites bolt our movement, simply because we refuse to abandon everything else for silver, then I say, let them go. We can get along better without them, than they can without us."[20] The Colorado delegation at St. Louis would be dominated by straight silverites, but the "times are hard," Waite commented, and the majority of the Populist Party "would stand by the Omaha platform," and would recognize no change except by a national convention "duly authorized."[21] Said Waite: "I shall stand squarely on the Omaha platform, until that platform is changed by a Populist national convention, duly called and composed of the regular delegates of the people's party, without the admission of any outside delegates."[22]

The divisions within the party at this time were illustrated in a letter from Paul Van Dervoort to Waite. Van Dervoort of Omaha wrote to the governor, "I am delighted to know how you stand (on the St. Louis conference) but we will all have to be there to beat the game. Taubeneck, Turner, Peffer, McKeighan, Allen, Stewart, Jones, the whole Washington crowd will be there to bring about the change. Unless we rally our forces we will be beat. I shall take the position that nothing but a national convention can change the platform. No self constituted crowd can change the voice of 1700 delegates. Don't fail to come and bring your friends. Geo. F. Washburn is all right and Morgan."[23]

At the St. Louis meeting efforts to defeat the

more reform-minded elements failed. Instead, the radicals launched a successful counter-offensive under the leadership of Henry D. Lloyd who presented a Declaration of Principles demanding adherence to the Omaha Platform.[24] A resolution was passed advocating public ownership of all monopolies which were specially public in nature; an end to government by injunction, and no more use of federal troops in industrial disputes, an obvious reference to the Pullman strike; a limit on fortunes which could be acquired through inheritance; and free and unlimited coinage of silver.[25] The theme of the meeting was anti-monopoly, and this was expressed in the slogan of the gathering, "Down with monopolies and millionaire control. Up with the rights of man and the masses."[26]

In the same month in which the reformers scored a victory in St. Louis, labor Populism received a setback in Denver. Under the leadership of Samuel Gompers, the American Federation of Labor refused to endorse independent political action and an alliance with Populism. This happened despite the fact that a majority of the rank-and-file probably desired such an alliance. Many members of the Federation ran for office as Populists in 1894, and many delegates came to the convention with instructions to promote the cause of Populism. Despite the fact that Governor Waite was a champion of labor, he was not invited to the convention, as previously noted.[27] The convention's action cast a shadow over the budding labor-farmer coalition essential to the continued growth of Populism. It is likely, as one student of Populism has noted, that the failure to achieve a strong labor-farmer alliance ultimately doomed the Populist movement.[28] In the elections of 1895, the labor vote for Populism in the large cities, which had increased dramatically in 1894, was perceptibly lower.[29]

Early in 1895, the National Watchman, an official Populist journal, called for conservative support for the party from businessmen and professional people and for the ouster of "socialistic" elements in order to achieve electoral success.[30]

Meanwhile, Taubeneck and other more conservative-minded Populist leaders continued their offensive despite the setback at St. Louis. Early in January, 1895, Taubeneck wrote to W. S. Morgan, a radical Populist leader from Arkansas, that the Populist Party desperately needed friends and that there was danger its Washington national headquarters would have to be closed.

Taubeneck noted, "My record since the P. P. has been organized is a consistent one. I would not change it if I could. The party will either adopt my policy or we will never succeed as a party."[31] Three weeks later Taubeneck characterized himself as a practical politician compared with Morgan whom he accused of being in a "dreamland living on theories and abstract ideas." He asserted that "more delicate complications confront our party than ever before. I feel confident from the best information I can receive that a new party will be organized, and if so, no new recruits will come to the Populist ranks, except from the socialists and communists, and we will lose a great number of the best element in our party."

Taubeneck was referring to the National Silver Party which was formed a few months later. He continued, expanding on his theme that the more radical reformers were ruining the People's Party:

The Farmer's Tribune of Des Moines has made it impossible for Senator Stewart, Jones and the silver men in our party to remain with us. Mr. Loucks of South Dakota has placed us in such a position that there is no way out of it, except to repudiate him, when he openly and above board advocates socialism. The "Wealthmakers" of Nebraska, and the "People's Call" in referring to the silver question as simply a "bait to catch the silver men" has done us infinite harm. The Topeka "Advocate" is on the same line — you cannot tell whether it is a single-tax organ, a socialist paper, or a People's Party paper. The "Nonconformist" is gone. It has joined the socialism which the American people will not endorse. I am not a socialist or communist in the remotest sense, and I will fight it to the bitter end. If the dreams of Harry Lloyd, Tom Morgan, Brother Loucks, and others, is to be the policy of the party then there is no hope for victory.[32]

In the spring of 1895 Taubeneck revealed again his concern chiefly for the silverites when he wrote to Waite: "I was in hopes that the gold bugs would control the Illinois convention and force the free silver element out of the party, but I fear that will

140

not take place." He foresaw a "great danger" that the Democrats and Republicans would both hold their silverites, and there would be thus no accessions to the Populists.[33] Waite, at the same period, expressed satisfaction to Donnelly that the Populist "regulars" were standing firm on the Omaha Platform. He reported a long talk with Weaver, in which Weaver had insisted that the new silver party was sincere on the silver issue and the call for the abolition of banks of issue. Waite disagreed, proclaiming it stood only for silver. He said that "the General swore by all the bald headed gods that if that proved to be the case he would drop the new party like a hot potato."[34]

During 1895, ex-governor Waite combined speaking tours with his journalistic endeavors, including his publication of Our Nation's Crisis. By the fall of 1895, the Populists and other political parties were maneuvering in earnest for the 1896 campaign. The main topics of discussion among the Populists were the possible candidates and whether the convention should be held before or after the Democratic and Republican conventions. Waite favored an early convention in Dallas.[35] He desired the nomination of a Southerner.

The silver-oriented Populists wanted a late convention; the more reform-minded Populists were divided, with many like Waite favoring an early convention in order to seize the initiative. H. L. Loucks declared, "Now is the time of holding the convention, the sooner the better." He agreed with Waite that "a Southern man would be our strongest card for 1896." Loucks revealed the continuing internal strife in the Populist leadership: "Taubeneck has proven himself wholly incapable and his recent manifest shows plainly that he repudiates the Omaha platform and should be forced to resign."[36] George Washburn hesitated to bring a Southerner "to the front as a candidate" yet. He thought a later Populist convention might benefit from dissatisfaction at the other party conventions.[37] W. S. Morgan saw "much weight in Waite's argument," but had one objection: if the Democrats split, the Populists could welcome the dissidents.[38]

In November, 1895, Waite wrote a dramatic appeal to Governor Altgeld of Illinois for unity between the Populists and the northern and western Democrats. He assumed the southern Democrats were disintegrating and the Populists would fall heir in the South. Both old major parties were captives of the money power, he

141

said, but he appealed to the principles of the Democratic Party of Jefferson and Jackson which were "immortal" and were "now at issue before the American people." Waite asserted that Field should have been nominated in 1892, and that the Populists would nominate a Southerner in 1896. How his proposed Populist-northern Democrat unity was to be achieved he did not say.[39]

William Jennings Bryan declared in a letter to Waite in late 1895:

> The campaign of 1896 is in my judgment all important, and I have announced that I shall not support a gold standard man for president even if such a one is nominated by the democrats. I know that the Populists have no faith in the ability of the silver democrats to control the next national convention but I believe that there is a reasonable chance . . . I believe that there should be an agreement upon a ticket which can be supported by all silver men and I think that ticket ought to be taken from the West and the South. It is not well to select candidates too early, this congress may develop some strong men. If the Populists and silver party meet after the Dem. and Rep. conventions it will be possible to take advantage of the circumstances as they exist then. I am inclined to think that Donnelly's plan of a union on candidates but each party having its own platform is the most feasible plan. We can all agree on silver at 16 to 1, but when you take up the subject of paper money you find three classes among the silver men. . . .[40]

The People's Party national executive committee met on January 17, and 18, 1896, at St. Louis. The silver-conservative faction was in control. It did not attempt to alter the Omaha Platform as it had a year ago, but it did try to insure control of the national convention. The convention was to be held after the Democratic and Republican conventions.[41]

Plans were later made to have the Silver Party meet at the same time as the Populists. Reporting to Waite immediately after the meeting, Ralph Beaumont lamented that "the silver element ran things and we are to have our convention after the others have had theirs. We are to modify our principles so as not to

142

hurt the sensitive feelings of the dissatisfied of the two old parties."[42] Edwin Burdick agreed with Waite's estimate of the national committee meeting that "just a few were running things at the top for their own ends" and were "out for their own power."[43]

In the spring of 1896 Waite's attention focused on "Pitchfork Ben" Tillman, the Democratic Senator from South Carolina who sympathized with the Populists and espoused many of their ideas. Earlier Tillman had predicted to Waite the disintegration of the two old parties, and an alliance of southern Democrats, western Republicans, and Populists. Defeat would probably occur in 1896, but victory awaited this alliance "inevitably" in 1900. Tillman assured Waite "the principles of Jefferson and Jackson can never die," and stated he would urge "the alliance of those seeking financial relief, from the coinage of silver and issue by the government of all paper money."[44]

In March, 1896, Waite endorsed Tillman as the Populist candidate, though Tillman was a Democrat. Waite assumed that both the Democrats and the Republicans would nominate "goldbug" candidates and write "goldbug" platforms. He expected Tillman and the South Carolina delegation would bolt the Democratic convention.

Waite wrote to Tillman expressing his fears about the direction of the Populist Party:

> The Bi-Metallic League of Jones-Sibley-Warner-Bryan-Weaver and Taubeneck who are to meet at St. Louis, Mo. on the same day with the Populist National Convention, expect to control the nomination for the Presidency. . . . I have got down to the very inside of the bi-metallic organization, and a more rotten and vile conspiracy never existed. They want and are determined to have no other reform but the free coinage of silver. That they want or will permit any war on the banks or monopolies of any kind whatever, either trust or transportation, is sheer deception. They are raising funds in Denver — raising them from the bankers of this city — Republican and Democratic alike and none of them Populists.[45]

A Republican bolt was unlikely, Waite told Tillman. Senator Henry Teller of Colorado might be nominated as a silver candidate, but he was "a coward" and would

not bolt the regular nomination of his own party.
(This was poor prophecy as Teller did bolt.) Democratic silverite bolters might try to encourage Tillman
to run, Waite continued. But they were not reformers,
and Tillman was. The Democratic bolters would nominate
Bland,[46] but he would not bolt, so "they are at work
on Bryan because he will bolt and they can rely upon
him as exclusively silver and because he has been one
of the main figures in the Bi-Metallic League."

Waite proceeded to tell Senator Tillman how to
bolt the Democratic Convention and bring Waite's plan
to fruition:

> In the first place when you bolt the nomi-
> nations and platform of the National Democratic
> Convention at Chicago you must state as the causes
> something more than the failure of that convention
> to put a free coinage of silver plank in its plat-
> form. You must assign as a reason the failure of
> the convention to reaffirm the old Democratic
> principles of Jefferson and Jackson in their war
> upon banks of issue and trusts and corporation
> monopolies. Without mentioning the Populist or
> the Silver Party, or alluding in any way to the
> Omaha platform, plant yourself squarely upon the
> free coinage of silver at 16 to 1 and eternal
> war upon banks of issue and monopolies. Put
> yourself in general terms in sympathy with the
> great reform movement and the Populist National
> Convention will nominate you for President in
> spite of all the bi-metallists this side of hell
> and in spite of Messrs. Weaver and Taubeneck.
> Then we have the silver men in a hole, and compel
> them to endorse your nomination and you will
> never get their support in any other way. . . .
> Because you are a thorough reformer I favor your
> nomination for the Presidency.[47]

Shortly thereafter, Tillman wrote to Waite that
the silver men would control the Democratic Convention.
The danger existed, he said, that the Democrats would
name a compromise candidate who will sell out the true
reformers.[48]

Tillman apparently said or did nothing to further
Waite's scheme to nominate him for President on the
Populist ticket, hoping instead for a reform-minded
Democratic nominee.

During April, Taubeneck and Weaver met in Denver with a number of local Populists and silverites. Waite was ignored.[49]

In May, L. D. Raynolds of the Chicago Express declared that the Democrats were headed for a silver candidate and a silver platform. It had been a mistake for the "true Populists" to think that a late convention was best, he asserted. The Populists were trapped: either fusion and death, or no fusion and be charged with being enemies of silver.[50]

Paul Van Dervoort of Omaha agreed with the observations of Tillman and Raynolds. He indicated to Waite that "Taubeneck and Co." were busy trying to line up delegates at the Populist National Convention, who would endorse the Democratic nominee. Bryan already claimed the needed votes for the nomination, Van Dervoort maintained.[51]

However, writing to Ignatius Donnelly in May, Herman Taubeneck would continue to claim that the Democrats did not know what they would do. The Republicans would nominate McKinley and write either a gold standard platform or straddle the money issue. Splits in the West would result, which "will give us the electoral vote of nearly all the Western States." The Democratic administration and the "goldbugs" would probably control the Democratic Convention, Taubeneck continued. The South and the West would rebel over silver, leading to large scale bolts which would benefit the Populists. "It seems to me that at no time since our party was organized have the prospects for a great victory been so flattering as today," he observed.[52]

By May, 1896, Waite, while continuing to adhere to the Omaha Platform, was more earnestly seeking principled compromises. Rather than see the reform Populists face isolation, he was willing to agree to a platform based on the financial issue alone, provided the entire money question, not just silver, was included. He said, "I am willing to take the stump abstaining wholly from all personal attacks and advocating a reunion with the bimetallists on the financial issue, but the whole of it, not a part . . . I concluded to accept that compromise, believing that if we could only get a fight on between Wall St. on the one hand and the United South and West on the other, that all necessary reform issues would naturally and rapidly drift into the controversy. My Populism means something more than silver and I can never agree to the Omaha platform being whittled down to that single issue."[53]

When Bryan was nominated by the Democrats, Waite was astounded and jubilant. Writing to Ignatius Donnelly, he exclaimed: "To my utter surprise the Democratic Convention at Chicago went back to the old democratic doctrines of Jefferson and Jackson and have nominated a good and true man on the platform. Of course I support him. . . . The silver game was to nominate Teller but it failed. Bryan has not been in the silver 'cabal,' but the silver crowd must support him."[54]

Waite contradicted earlier statements he had made about Bryan and the silverites. In a previously noted letter Bryan sent to Waite late in 1895, Bryan clearly revealed himself to Waite as a silver man above all else. The clue to Waite's change is to be found in his letter to Donnelly, and in a later statement that he supported Bryan because the Democratic platform included the main reforms of the Omaha Platform.[55] Waite was probably influenced, too, by the role he must have known that Altgeld had in the Democratic Party Convention.

At the National Populist Convention, Waite supported Bryan and was against a "middle of the road" or different nominee. Marion Butler of North Carolina, Ignatius Donnelly and Jacob Coxey, the Texas delegation, and some others, Waite noted, were in the middle-of-the-road camp at this point. Waite said, "If the decision is against Bryan, it will be by delegates from the Northeast and other states that cannot give any electoral votes . . . A middle-of-the-road nominee cannot carry a single state north or south, and I don't know as a division will prevent Bryan carrying a single state north or south."[56]

However, Waite opposed the Democratic Party vice-presidential nominee, Arthur Sewall, whom he characterized as "a national banker, a railroad monopolist, and a foe of organized labor."[57] The Populists nominated their own vice-presidential candidate, Tom Watson of Georgia, with Waite's warm support.

Curiously, while Waite supported a combined Populist-Democratic presidential candidate, he would not countenance the same thing on the state level. Instead, he ran on a straight Populist ticket for governor in opposition to a Populist-Democratic fusion ticket.

He received scant support, but stubbornly remained in the race until the end despite efforts of some local reform Populists to get him to resign from the ticket.

Waite had, in fact, been caught in a great dilemma, causing him to be on both the "middle of the road" and the "fusionist" sides at the same time. He wanted to support a candidate like Bryan who had a chance to win and who, he believed, truly espoused a Populist-type program; he also desperately wanted to preserve the separate identity of the Populist Party. No doubt he labored under illusions about how much the latter goal was possible through a separate Populist vice-presidential candidate.

Tom Watson, the Populist vice-presidential nominee, found himself in the same dilemma. He saw no contradiction between being on a Bryan-Watson ticket and supporting Waite's 1896 gubernatorial bid. Watson had hoped to help Waite in his campaign and told him, "My heart is with you. It is to such men as you that Populism must look to save it from utter wreck."[58]

After Bryan's defeat, Watson told Waite, "Like yourself, I feel no regret over the failure of the Patterson (Colorado) fusion ticket. Our party will have to be reorganized and the fusion heresy stamped out. It seems to me that our national committee is discredited. The figures show that a change of less than 25,000 votes would have elected Bryan. Who doubts that an honorable recognition of the Populists and their nominee would have given him more than that?"[59]

In an election post-mortem, Governor Altgeld of Illinois discussed with Waite the problems both the Democratic and Populist reformers had faced. Referring to Waite's criticism of Sewall, Altgeld noted, "At the time of the Convention, Illinois put Sibley in nomination for Vice President and stuck to him as long as there was any show. I felt that he was the right man. . . . The campaign has demonstrated that Sewall did not help us any but I am inclined to think now that the fight is over that we would have been beaten no matter whom we had on the ticket."

Altgeld blamed Bryan's defeat on three main causes. First, there were "the hard times for which we were

held responsible and augmented by the fact that the
restoration of McKinleyism was believed by many of the
people to be a sure promise of prosperity."

Second, "all the corporations, the newspapers,
the big merchants, the manufacturers and the banks
united against us. The banks sent for every man who
owed them any money and required him to pay up unless
he would agree to vote for McKinley and in our State
nearly all of the manufacturers discharged and paid
off their men on Saturday evening or Monday evening
prior to the election and said to them that if McKinley
were elected they would come back Wednesday morning,
but if McKinley was not elected they need not come back
at all as the establishment would not be able to go on.
These men went home and talked with their wives and
the wives remembering the awful experience they had
had when they were without bread became alarmed and
induced their husbands to vote as the employer wanted."

Third, "there was collected this year and distributed with a lavish hand an amount of boodle such
as was never collected before in this country and comprehensive schemes of fraud were carried out."

Of the future, Altgeld commented: "There may be
some difference of opinion but after all activity is
the main thing. . . . Personally, I do not see how
any party can accomplish anything in Colorado unless
it has the support of the Populists there."[60]

Writing to Bryan, Waite listed two basic errors
he believed were committed in the 1896 campaign. "The
first great error was in the nomination of Mr. Sewall.
. . . Whatever may have been the motive or intentions
in the nomination of Sewall, that nomination was a
surrender to Wall St., an attempt to placate the money
power, to convince it that the nomination of Bryan was
only a strategical move, and that really the party
would remain as it had been, the creation of monopoly."
The second error was that "the silver element was
allowed to overslaugh the true reformers of the People's
party, who had no part or lot in the matter of the
campaign." Waite cited Minnesota as an example where
he said Donnelly and other true reformers had been
kept in the background. Waite asserted that "yourself
and Gov. Altgeld were the only speakers in all the
presidential campaign that dared say anything but silver and these declarations were no detriment to the
Democratic party and were all that held our party in

line, but the 'silver' element is opposed to all other reforms." While stating that Bryan was the logical reform candidate for 1900, he warned that "the active assistance of the radical reformers of the People's Party must not be rejected and despised."[61]

Waite also placed some blame on Populist Party organization for the 1896 debacle. There was no means to hold it to principle. It had the same caucus system, the same committees, the "rotten delegates," and the bossism of the old parties. The "rights" and the action of the rank and file were handed over to an "inside ring," Waite asserted. "A few leading officials of the People's Party by as bald trickery in the way of bossism, bogus proxies, and paper delegates as ever distinguished 'Tammany Hall,' assumed supreme control of the party and exercised that control without consulting the popular will and without appeal." He especially singled out Taubeneck for criticism, and blamed him for calling a late convention "for the sole purpose that the Populist Party should become an annex of the Democratic Party and ratify its national ticket."[62] Waite reiterated that the highest authority of any political party was its national convention.

After 1896, Waite continued his lecture tours and his publishing endeavors as long as his health permitted. Late in 1897, in the midst of a speaking tour, he wrote to his wife, Celia, of his hopes for the future:

Am still stumping in Iowa and had a specially enthusiastic meeting at New Market. House was just jammed. Our campaign is making some headway. We do not expect to carry the state. Weaver's cursed fusion has been too well arranged for that, but the Democrats, I think, cannot carry the election. If fusion fails in Ohio and Iowa, and I think it will, the scheme will be seen to be impracticable, and our People's Party organization can be saved. There seems to be no Populist or Democratic fusion in Colorado or Greater New York. If we can only save the Populist organization and get rid of the traitors like Weaver, Butler, Allen, Taubeneck, Sockless Simpson, Cyclone Davis, and various other scoundrels too numerous to mention, who have more or less control of the party machinery — there is hope in the future, not in my time, but certainly in Frank's (Waite's small son), and possibly people

149

a good deal older. I am beginning to get over that feeling of discouragement that has weighed me down all the past year, and I feel that there is hope in the future. I attended a Democratic meeting yesterday at Osceola. The speaker advocated fusion, but many of his arguments were populist, and sound on economic questions. Politics and political issues are becoming better understood each year, and if the people are capable of self-government, which is the great problem to be solved — they will eventually save the country.[63]

APPENDIX A

WAITE AS PORTRAYED IN THE POPULIST REVOLT

By JOHN D. HICKS — FACT AND FICTION

Since The Populist Revolt by John D. Hicks
continues to be the basic history of the Populist
movement, his portrayal of Waite is of some interest.[1]

Hicks' view of Waite is strongly negative.
Judging from the footnotes, his sources were almost
entirely secondary. The only exceptions were the
Colorado House Journal and the People's Party Paper.
The latter was apparently the only Populist source
used. No Colorado Populist sources were used. In
fact, no Colorado sources were noted except the House
Journal. Inadequate source materials combined with
basic unwarranted assumptions and lack of proper background material in detailing the chief episodes of
Waite's career resulted in a very one-sided and inac-
curate portrayal of Waite.

The whole tone was set for the discussion of
Waite and his administration with the statement that
his "whole personal appearance" and the "occasional
frenzy of his rhetoric" were the mark of a "narrow-
minded fanatic."[2] How does personal appearance suggest
a fanatic? Does the fact that Waite had a beard make
him a fanatic? If so, there were numerous fanatics
in existence, including people of every conceivable
viewpoint, among whom would be listed the "goldbug."
Judged by the clothes they wore, there is no criteria
for determining whether Grover Cleveland or Benjamin
Harrison or Davis Waite was or was not a fanatic. If
the "occasional frenzy" or rhetoric suggests a fanatic,
then, again, there must have been a large number of
fanatics in the United States, including the editors
of the reputedly staid New York Times, almost every
Colorado newspaper editor, and other groups and indi-
viduals too numerous to mention. Flowery speech and
Biblical allegory were common in late nineteenth
century America. Finally, the adjective "narrow-
minded" coupled with the noun "fanatic" suggested
something ipso facto wrong with a person of crusading
zeal.

With this unfounded but basic attitude about Waite thus established in the reader's mind, Hicks proceeded to describe Waite's legislative program, the Denver City Hall War, and the Cripple Creek strike of 1894. In discussing legislation, no mention was made of woman suffrage, the only significant Populist legislative accomplishment. Hicks noted at the beginning of the section on Waite that Populism won in Colorado because of silver, but the Populists elected to state administrative posts, including Waite, were more reform-minded. Yet, when legislation was discussed, the division between silverites and more reform-minded Populists was ignored. Thus, it was made to appear that, in the overriding of a veto by the governor, it was simply a matter of a reasonable legislature, which included many Populists, dealing with an unreasonable governor. An example is railroad legislation. Waite wanted a commission with real powers, but vetoed the bill repealing the existing railroad law, calling it better than nothing. No hint was made that Governor Waite wanted railroad legislation similar to that in other states. The entire matter, instead, centered about Waite's assumed neuroticism. Thus, the fact that Colorado was left without any law regulating railroads was mainly significant in displaying the "immense chagrin" of the governor and in causing him to grind his teeth over the "great satisfaction of the railroads."[3]

Hicks stated that Waite's Mexican dollar plan "failed to impress" Colorado Populists, the Colorado legislature, and Tom Watson. What he did not say was that a number of Populists and silverites sympathized with Waite's idea, and that similar ideas were being discussed in other states.[4]

Failure to include adequate background information also placed Waite in a very unfair light in both the Denver Fire and Police Board and Cripple Creek situations. Hicks called Waite's second set of replacements on the board "both Populists."[5] Actually, one was a Populist, and the other was a Democrat. After describing the efforts at barricading and arming City Hall to prevent Waite's last set of new appointees from taking office, Hicks stated that, to the governor, this was open insurrection against the state. Could anyone in Waite's position have considered the situation otherwise? According to Hicks, the "army" at City Hall consisted of "policemen and firemen" and "several hundred deputies" of the Arapahoe County sheriff. The nature of the deputy sheriffs was not disclosed, and there was no mention of the large percentage of the gambling and associated elements who had barricaded themselves in City Hall.[6]

Hicks never mentioned what the issues were in the Cripple Creek strike. Yet he accused Waite of gaining notoriety for himself and unpleasant advertising for Colorado by his conduct. He admitted Waite avoided bloodshed in the conflict, but contended that if Waite had been more tactful there would probably have been less danger of violence. But, from the description of the events by Hicks, it is clear that the main threat of violence came from the forces opposed to Waite. Hicks further accused Waite of twice failing to bring about a settlement while serving as counsel for the miners. Not only is this another misstatement of fact by Hicks, but it leads to misrepresentation of that which followed. Waite, of course, did participate as counsel for the miners in the basic agreement which was reached with the mine owners on June 4, 1894. The state militia was called out after June 4 not because Waite failed to conclude an agreement with the mine owners, as Hicks implied, but because the illegal army of deputy sheriffs, employed to attack the miners, failed to respect the agreement.

That there could have been a connection between the mine owners and the army of deputy sheriffs under Sheriff M. F. Bowers of El Paso County is not even hinted in Hicks' account. The sheriff emerged as a kind of hero and the national guard was accused of shirking its duty for failure to act before the agreement.[7] Apparently, what Hicks meant was that the national guard should have aided the mine owners in crushing the resistance of the striking miners, a customary practice in the late nineteenth century. By his reasoning on the Denver Fire and Police Board controversy and the Cripple Creek situation, Hicks put himself in the strange position of appearing to condemn Waite for threatening to meet force with force to uphold civil authority threatened by violence mainly organized by outlaw elements, while, on the other hand, appearing to damn him for not using force against striking miners seeking a peaceable redress of their grievances.

Note: Another general history of Populism,
Lawrence Goodwyn's Democratic Promise: The Populist
Movement in America, appeared in 1976. Due to the
restricted definition of Populism by the author, there
is very little material on Davis H. Waite and Colorado
Populism.

APPENDIX B

A NOTE ON THE HISTORICAL BACKGROUND OF ANTI-SEMITISM

There is need to put the matter of anti-Semitism in correct perspective before trying to relate it to Populism. During the Middle Ages, the Jews were outcasts in the closed system of a feudalistic Christian Europe. They existed at the margin as peddlers and money-lenders, the latter a role Christians could not perform because of Church doctrine against usury. These activities began to be respectable in the late medieval period as Christians became merchandizers and bankers, replacing the Jews who in several instances were driven from the country as in England in 1290.

In early modern times the Jewish people found a more free and tolerant attitude in at least certain places such as Holland and the North American colonies. These were places characteristically where the old order was most thoroughly demolished or never existed in a full blown state. But in all Christian societies latent anti-Semitism was never far below the surface and prejudices did hang on.

Thus, in the United States the first Jews appeared in the Dutch colony of New Amsterdam (New York) in 1654 and were allowed to stay as a prejudiced Pete Stuyvesant was overruled by Dutch authorities and settlers.[1] They were welcomed especially in liberal Rhode Island and at least tolerated in several other colonies. However, Jewish citizens in several colonies experienced political restrictions on voting and office holding, as did Roman Catholics and some unorthodox Protestant groups. In some instances, these restrictions continued for a number of years after the Revolution of 1776.

Many Jews welcomed the liberating tendencies of the American Revolution, the French Revolution, and the European revolutions of the early nineteenth century. They actively supported these revolutions. Gains were made in ending medieval ghetto restrictions and winning the rights of citizens. Even a few monarchs and aristocrats such as Joseph II of Austria caught the new spirit of freedom of the early bourgeois and abolished some of the worst features of anti-Semitism in Austria.

155

Gains were often tenuous and partial. Early in U. S. history some Federalists, the ultra-conservatives of their day, tried to use anti-Semitism as one means of discrediting the Jeffersonians, since many Jews were naturally attracted by the liberal ideas of Jefferson.[2]

By the late nineteenth century more ominous signs were appearing. The bourgeois had stabilized their power and were fearful of further democratic advance. They preferred alliances with the aristocracy rather than the workers and peasants. Anti-Semitism became a weapon of political reaction. In Germany, Bismarck, representing the large industrialists and landowners, used anti-Semitism as a weapon to crush any democratic-minded opposition to his autocratic power and his militarization program. Political rivals were castigated as Jewish conspirators, while Bismarck was pictured as representing what was truly German.

In France, the Dreyfus affair occurred in 1894 while Waite was governor. An aristocratic French officer was found to have given military secrets to Germany. To protect him, a scapegoat was made of Captain Alfred Dreyfus, first Jew to be a member of the French Army general staff. Anti-Semitism was rampant in France. Political reactionaries fanned the flames of anti-Semitism in order to try to destroy the Third Republic itself. Republicanism, they charged, had led to treason by Jews. Again, latent mass anti-Semitic feeling had been deliberately aroused in a Christian country, but it is important to note that the instigators were the ruling classes.

In eastern Europe, where the old aristocratic order still remained more intact, anti-Semitism was also on the rise as a weapon to suppress democratic reforms. Pogroms occurred in Czarist Russia and attacks on Jews intensified in Rumania and Austria.[3]

In the United States, Carey McWilliams has indicated that anti-Semitism has served as a "mask for privilege"[4] to protect the interests of the rich and powerful. It is commonly agreed that the first notorious and well-known case of anti-Semitism in the post-Civil War United States occurred against the New York banker Joseph Seligman in 1877, when he and his family were rebuffed at the Grand Union Hotel in Saratoga Springs, New York. Within a few years exclusion of Jews became common in Eastern resorts.[5]

The leading industrial and financial circles in the United States have practiced not only social exclusiveness but business discrimination against the Jew regularly for a hundred years, as more recent studies than McWilliams have continued to indicate.[6]

Furthermore, with the mass immigration of Jews into the United States in the late nineteenth century, it is apparent that anti-Semitism was added to the arsenal of racism and national prejudices to keep workers divided and unorganized, leading to more effective exploitation. Many Jewish immigrants became part of the eastern urban industrial work force, entering into competition with non-Jewish workers for the available jobs, housing, etc. Under the circumstances, it is not surprising that latent long-time anti-Jewish animosities would surface again as carryovers from the "Old World."

What all this has to do with the preposterous claim that anti-Semitism in the United States originated in the Populist-Greenback ranks in the western plains and mountain areas where the Jewish population was very small and could hardly have been noticed much less seen as a threat is hard to say. It seems that eastern urban-oriented historians like Oscar Handlin and Richard Hofstadter tended too readily to project back into the past common political concepts about Midwest conservatism in the twentieth century. Also, the Handlin-Hofstadter theories, flying in the face of all previous evidence to the contrary and buttressed by few facts, fitted all too well into the neo-conservative Cold War patterns of the fifties. While Allan Nevins and others were glorifying big business with laudatory estimates of the Fords and the Rockefellers, other historians were attempting to pin the crimes of the ruling classes on the people's movements themselves.

NOTES

Chapter I

[1]John D. Hicks, The Populist Revolt, A History of the Farmers' Alliance and the Peoples' Party (Minneapolis: University of Minnesota Press, 1931). The link between the Alliances and the Populists is made especially clear in this work, which is still considered a basic source on both the Farmers' Alliances and the Populist Party. However, the work is marred by racism, prejudice against the more militant reformers such as Davis H. Waite, and the minimizing of labor involvement in the Populist movement. See also Solon J. Buck, The Agrarian Crusade (New Haven: Yale University Press, 1920).

Chapter II

[1]Labor Day Programme, September 2, 1895, Tiffin, Ohio, Waite Papers, Colorado State Archives and Public Records, Denver.

[2]Biographical data on Davis H. Waite was assembled from the Waite Papers in the Colorado State Archives in Denver, the Leon W. Fuller and Virgle Bessor theses on Colorado Populism, and from interviews with Mrs. Frank Waite of Palisade, Colorado, and Miss Quantrille D. McClung, a former librarian at the Denver Public Library, who was engaged in compilation of data on the governors of Colorado while the author was engaged in research on this work.

[3]Correspondence, Waite Papers.

[4]Information about Waite's illness and death was obtained through the courtesy of Mrs. Frank Waite, daughter-in-law of the governor.

Chapter III

[1]Leah M. Bird, "Minor Political Parties in Colorado," Colorado Magazine, XIX (November, 1942), 208-13; Richard C. Welty, "The Greenback Party in Colorado," Colorado Magazine, XXVIII (October, 1951), 301-11.

[2]Joseph R. Buchanan, The Story of a Labor Agitator (New York: The Outlook Co., 1903), pp. 110, 247.

[3]Anna Rochester, The Populist Movement in the United States (New York: International Publishers, 1943), pp. 47-49.

[4]Leon W. Fuller, "History of the People's Party in Colorado" (unpublished Ph.D. dissertation, University of Wisconsin, 1933), pp. 43-44; Hicks, The Populist Revolt, p. 158.

[5]Aspen Union Era, November 26, 1891.

[6]Ibid., April 14, 1892.

[7]Aspen Times, March 28, 1888, and April 4, 1888.

[8]Aspen Union Era, September 17, 1891.

[9]Ibid., August 20, 1891.

[10]Ibid., August 4, 1892.

[11]Ibid., November 5, 1891.

[12]Fuller, "History of the People's Party in Colorado," pp. 48, 66.

[13]Waite's Magazine, I (October 1, 1898), 3.

[14]Aspen Union Era, August 4, 1892.

[15]Rocky Mountain News, September 13, 1892.

[16]Ibid., September 14, 1892.

[17]Fuller, "History of the People's Party in Colorado," p. 52.

[18]Denver Republican, July 29, 1892.

[19]Ibid.

[20]Rocky Mountain News, July 29, 1892.

[21]Ibid., October 23, 1892.

[22]Virgle M. Besser, "The Administration of Governor Waite and the Populist Party in Colorado, 1893 to

1895" (unpublished M. A. thesis, University of Colorado, 1924), pp. 40-42.

[23]Trinidad Chronicle and Fort Collins Courier, quoted in Denver Republican, September 10, 1892.

[24]Waite's Magazine, I (October 1, 1898), 4.

[25]Ibid.

[26]Ibid.

[27]Fuller, "History of the People's Party in Colorado," p. 96.

[28]Ibid., pp. 96-97. Members of the Republican Party in the state assembly came mainly from law, business, and farming backgrounds. Mining and farming were the chief occupations of the Populist members.

[29]Rocky Mountain News, January 11, 1893.

[30]Inaugural Address of Governor Davis H. Waite to the Ninth General Assembly of the State of Colorado (Denver: The Smith-Brooks Printing Co., State Printers, 1893).

[31]Session Laws of Colorado, 1893, pp. 394, 351-56, 397-403, 365-71, 356-57, 376-97, 436-37, 305, 131-236, 242-43, 256-58.

[32]Fuller, "History of the People's Party in Colorado," p. 113.

[33]Waite's Magazine, I (October 1, 1898), 4. In Waite's Magazine, Waite used the third person in referring to himself.

[34]Letter Press Books of the Governors, IX (March, 1893 - March, 1894), Colorado State Archives, Denver. Hereafter cited as Letter Press Books.

[35]Waite's Magazine, I (October 1, 1898), 30.

[36]Ibid., p. 4.

[37]Fuller, "History of the People's Party in Colorado," pp. 203-04.

[38]House Journal of the Extra Session of the Ninth General Assembly of the State of Colorado (Denver: The Smith Brooks Printing Co.), pp. 38-39.

[39]Fuller, "History of the People's Party in Colorado," pp. 216-18.

[40]Ibid.

[41]Annual Message of Governor Davis H. Waite, January 4, 1895 (Denver: State Printers, 1895); Session Laws of Colorado, 1894, pp. 33-38, 45-59.

[42]Session Laws of Colorado, 1894, pp. 59-84.

[43]Aspen Union Era, September 17, 1891.

[44]C. L. Swords and W. C. Edwards, Sketches and Portraitures of the State Officers and Members of the Ninth General Assembly of Colorado (Denver: Carson, Hurst and Harper, 1893).

[45]Rocky Mountain News, February 4, 1893.

[46]Information on the above-mentioned persons was gathered from correspondence in the Waite Papers.

[47]Report of the Attorney General of Colorado, 1893-94; Fuller, "History of the People's Party in Colorado," pp. 196-98.

[48]Rocky Mountain News, February 16, 1893, p. 5.

[49]Rocky Mountain News, February 17, 1893, p. 5; Letter Press Books, VIII (October 19, 1892 - March 24, 1893), 404-06.

[50]Executive Records, State of Colorado, VIII (July 6, 1893), 308-10. Hereafter cited as Executive Records.

[51]Executive Records, IX (May 16, 1894), 60-66.

Chapter IV

[1]Francis A. Walker, "The Relation of Changes in the Volume of the Currency to Prosperity," Economic Studies, I (April, 1896), 33, 41; Merle Curti, The

162

Growth of American Thought (New York: Harper, 1951),
p. 555.

[2]Aspen Union Era, April 14, 1892.

[3]"The most dangerous foes to reform are those
professed reformers who, acknowledging the evils that
exist, support the financial system which produced
them. Their mission appears to be to obstruct and
divide reformers. They compose a sort of guerrilla
corps, who dress in the uniform of progress and repeat
as occasion requires some shibboleth of reform." From
Waite Speech Collection, Waite Papers.

[4]Throughout history, "a contraction of the currency, the steady decrease in the prices of all products and in the wages of labor, and a constant increase
in the purchasing power of money, which the scarcity
of money inevitably occasions, always has and always
will result in the loss of national prosperity and
liberty and end in a night of barbarism." From Waite
Speech Collection, Waite Papers.

[5]"This arbitrary act of oppression (the Currency
Act) destroyed the good times in the colonies, compelled a great loss of property in consequence of the
inability to pay debts, and Dr. Franklin says, was a
far greater cause of the Revolutionary War than the
Stamp Act or the tax on tea, although these latter
were made more prominent because directly connected
with the first outbreak in Boston." From Waite Speech
Collection, Waite Papers.

[6]Congress authorized the issuance of greenbacks
totaling over $400,000,000 to aid in financing the
Civil War. Buck, Agrarian Crusade, p. 109.

[7]Buck, Agrarian Crusade, pp. 78, 83, 94; Dr. R.
Dewey, Financial History of the United States (Boston:
Massachusetts Institute of Technology, 1903), p. 382.

[8]Philip S. Foner, History of the Labor Movement
in the United States (New York: International Publishers, 1947), I, 420-23.

[9]Ibid., p. 428.

[10]Ibid., p. 484.

[11]Aspen Union Era, September 24, 1891.

[12]"There is no doubt whatever that this government could pay all its expenses of every kind and even much more by the issue of additional greenbacks without the collection or levy of one dollar tax or revenue, because the increase thus made to the currency of the country would be much less than the natural growth of population and business, but the two per cent interest on loans to the people by the government of a sufficient amount to properly perform the business of the country would afford sufficient revenue to pay all the legitimate expenses of an economical administration and thus eliminate the question of taxation from the national issues." Aspen Union Era, August 13, 1891.

[13]"It (money) does not grow on trees. It is not dug out of the ground, it is not produced by labor. It is a creation of the law." From Waite Speech Collection, no title, no date, Waite Papers.

[14]Aspen Union Era, May 12, 1892.

[15]William H. Harvey, Coin's Financial School (Chicago: Coin Publishing Co., 1894), p. 49.

[16]From Waite Speech Collection, no title, no date, Waite Papers. Governor Waite also wrote a letter to William H. Harvey on November 31, 1894, in which the same views were presented. Also see letter of William H. Harvey to Governor Waite, November 29, 1894, Waite Papers.

[17]Waite to E. D. Benson, Seattle, May 27, 1895, Waite Papers.

[18]See the chapter on Waite and national politics for a fuller exposition of this theme.

[19]Norman Pollack, The Populist Response to Industrial America: Midwestern Populist Thought (Cambridge, Mass.: Harvard University Press, 1962), pp. 133-37.

[20]Hicks, The Populist Revolt, p. 317; Martin Ridge, Ignatius Donnelly, The Portrait of a Politician (Chicago: The University of Chicago Press, 1962), p. 328.

[21]C. Vann Woodward, Tom Watson, Agrarian Rebel (New York: Rinehart and Co., 1938), p. 431.

[22]Chicago Times, December 28, 1894.

[23]Chicago Times, January 30, 1895.

[24]Pollack, The Populist Response to Industrial America, p. 136.

[25]Ibid., p. 122. Also, Waite to Donnelly, April 22, 1895, Donnelly Papers.

[26]Henry Demarest Lloyd, "The Populists at St. Louis," Review of Reviews, XIV (September, 1896), p. 302.

[27]Governor Lorenzo D. Lewelling of Kansas to Waite, December 19, 1894, Waite Papers.

[28]Aspen Union Era, June 30, 1892.

[29]Ibid.

[30]Waite to Ignatius Donnelly, July 10, 1895, Donnelly Papers.

[31]"The Hill Banking System," by Davis H. Waite, Aspen Union Era, June 30, 1892.

[32]Waite Speech Collection, no title, no date, Waite Papers.

[33]U. S. Department of the Treasury, Annual Report of the Secretary of the Treasury, 1896, p. 218.

[34]Report on Mineral Industries in the United States at the Eleventh Census: 1890 (Washington, D. C.: Government Printing Office, 1892), p. 42. Also see diagram opposite p. 42. These figures are at best only approximations and differ according to the source as the census itself notes on page 50 in listing estimates of various sources. One point is clear: Colorado was the leading silver-producing state in 1889 followed by Montana, Utah, Nevada, and Idaho in that order - p. 56. It is a point of curiosity why Montana and Utah did not become Populist strongholds like Colorado, Nevada, and Idaho. Apparently, there were other ingredients involved besides the mere presence of silver.

[35]Ibid., p. 76.

[36]Harold U. Faulkner, Politics, Reform, and Expansion (New York: Harper and Row, 1959), p. 103.

[37] Ibid., p. 205.

[38] Aspen Union Era, February 25, 1892.

[39] Percy Stanley Fritz, Colorado The Centennial State (New York: Prentice Hall, Inc., 1941), p. 332.

[40] Denver Republican, April 26, 1892.

[41] Inaugural Address of Governor Davis H. Waite, pp. 21-24.

[42] Ibid., p. 23.

[43] Speech by David W. Waite to the Colorado State Silver League Convention, Denver, July 21, 1893, Waite Papers.

[44] New York Times, July 12, 1893.

[45] Waite to Ignatius Donnelly, April 22, 1895, Donnelly Papers. See Edward Flower, "Anti-Semitism in the Free Silver and Populist Movements and the Election of 1896" (unpublished Master's thesis, Columbia University, 1952), pp. 19-22. He refers to an anti-Semitic work published in Chicago in 1895 by Ebenezer Wakely, The Gentle Ass and the Judean Monetary Establishment, in which Luckenback's affidavit appears in the appendix.

[46] Davis H. Waite, "Are the Silver States Ruined?" North American Review, LXXXI (January, 1894), 26.

[47] Message of Governor Davis H. Waite to the General Assembly of Colorado, January 10, 1894. Waite noted: "The free coinage of gold and silver was designed and expected to be continuous, and Congress had no right to demonetize either gold or silver or to close its mines to the free coinage of either metal. Upon a proper case made in the United States court we are bound to presume that the courts would so decide because the facts and merits of the case demand such a decision. Were this all that the Constitution of the United States contains upon this matter the state might even resume coinage as a right lapsed to it, but another clause absolutely prohibits a state from coining money. This clause has prevented me from recommending anything like token money, or bars stamped with weight and fineness."

[48]Waite to President Porfirio Diaz of Mexico, September 19, 1893, Waite Papers.

[49]Denver Republican, October 11, 1893.

[50]Message of Governor Davis H. Waite to the General Assembly of Colorado, January 10, 1894.

[51]Colorado House Journal, 1894, pp. 81-82; Fuller, "History of the People's Party in Colorado," p. 215.

[52]Denver Republican, January 12, 1894.

[53]Waite to Ignatius Donnelly, December 19, 1893, Donnelly Papers.

[54]Senator William M. Stewart of Nevada to Waite, January 2, 1894, Waite Papers.

[55]Governor Sylvester Pennoyer of Oregon to Waite, December 26, 1893, Waite Papers.

[56]B. I. Bailey to Waite, June 18, 1894, June 22, 1894, and August 18, 1894, Waite Papers.

[57]Governor L. D. Lewelling of Kansas to Waite, December 16, 1893, Waite Papers.

[58]Herman Taubeneck to Waite, January 10, 1894, Waite Papers.

[59]Ignatius Donnelly to Waite, December 13, 1893, Waite Papers.

[60]Charles S. Thomas to Waite, October 9, 1893, Waite Papers.

[61]Thomas B. Buchanan to Waite, November 20 and November 25, 1893, Waite Papers.

[62]Waite to J. N. Ashby, Watson, Colorado, April 9, 1894, Waite Papers.

[63]Senator Marion Butler of North Carolina to Waite, May 18, 1896, Waite Papers.

[1]Critics of Populism give the impression that the Populists were neurotic and unreal in their attacks on Wall Street and monopoly. However, these critics offer no facts to support their allegations. The studies of Gustavus Myers, Ferdinand Lundberg, G. William Domhoff, C. Wright Mills, Victor Perlo, Paul A. Baran, Paul Sweezy, Harry Laidler, Anna Rochester, Henry Demarest Lloyd, Matthew Josephson, Thorstein Veblen, S. Menshikov, Estes Kefauver and others; the revelations of the Pujo Committee in 1913, the Temporary National Economic Committee (TNEC) in the 1930's, the Kefauver and Celler congressional committees in the 1950's, and the Patman congressional committee study in 1962; the Sherman and Clayton Anti-Trust Acts and later anti-trust acts and governmental actions all make it crystal clear that the Populists were living in a very real world indeed.

That some Populists may have been guilty of oversimplified, conspirational-type criticisms of growing economic monopoly, or may have offered oversimplified programs or panaceas to meet the challenge of monopoly, does not negate the essential validity of the Populist criticism of economic concentration.

It is true that far more trusts were formed in the immediate post-Populist period, especially from 1897 to 1904, despite the Sherman Anti-Trust Act. This would seem to indicate that the Populists were correct in their criticisms of the Sherman Anti-Trust Act and prophetic in their understanding of the economic trend of the times and its social and political implications.

[2]Hicks, The Populist Revolt, p. 440.

[3]Ibid.

[4]Ibid., p. 441.

[5]Waite Speech, "Mission of the Populist Party," Waite Papers. In this speech, Waite used statistics gathered by George K. Holmes, an economist who was a specialist on wealth for the 1890 census.

[6]Ibid.

[7]Faulkner, Politics, Reform, and Expansion, p. 91. See also George K. Holmes, "The Concentration of Wealth," Political Science Quarterly, VIII (December, 1893), 593; Wilford I. King, The Wealth and Income of

the People of the United States (New York, 1915);
Thomas G. Sherman, "The Owners of the United States,"
Forum, VIII (November, 1889); Charles B. Spahr, The
Present Distribution of Wealth in the United States
(New York, 1896). All are noted in Faulkner together
with some of their revealing statistics.

[8]Aspen Union Era, November 19, 1891.

[9]Fifth Biennial Report of the State Inspector of
Coal Mines of the State of Colorado for the Years 1891
and 1892, pp. 5-6. Statistics were compiled from the
table, "Product and Character of Colorado Coal Mines
for 1892," enclosed on p. 5.

[10]C. F. & I. News, October 7, 1963.

[11]Georgetown Courier, January 5, 1895.

[12]Leroy R. Hafen and Ann Hafen, The Colorado Story
(Denver: Old West Publishing Co., 1953), pp. 281, 387.

[13]Waite Speeches, Waite Papers, no title, no date,
Box 11.

[14]Aspen Union Era, February 18, 1892. It is true
that formation of the steel trust did not occur until
1901 with the organization of the U. S. Steel Company.

[15]Aspen Union Era, January 7, 1892.

[16]Waite Speeches, Waite Papers, no title, no date,
Box 11.

[17]Ibid.

[18]Sometimes critics of Populism belittle the
Populists with their constant reference to the term
"money power." These critics caricature Populism by
assuming that the Populists had in mind a vile conspiracy by a handful of bankers. However, Henry D.
Lloyd and Eugene V. Debs clearly used the term "money
power" to mean "monopoly" in their speeches and writings. The two are used inter-changeably. Other
Populists such as Davis Waite used the term more
ambiguously, but it is clear that Waite often used
the term "money power" in the broader sense to refer
to monopoly, ruling class, the "power elite" of C.
Wright Mills, the "economic royalists" of Franklin
D. Roosevelt, the "military-industrial complex" of

Dwight D. Eisenhower, or whatever other term, loosely applied, might be used to describe the dominant political-economic forces of an industrial capitalist society.

[19]Waite Speeches, Waite Papers, no title, no date, Box 11. While Waite's portrayal of early America has an element of truth, it is an idyllic exaggeration. Colonial America and the early decades of the new independent republic were also times of sharp class distinctions, social struggles, and considerable differences between rich and poor, not to mention the plight of millions of slaves.

[20]Waite Speeches, Waite Papers. Material presented above was gathered mainly from the speeches "Mission of the Populist Party," and "The People's Party."

[21]Letter Press Books, IX, 150.

[22]Ibid., IX, 148.

[23]Ibid., IX, 291.

[24]Waite to Donnelly, May 26, 1893, Donnelly Papers.

[25]Senator William Stewart, Nevada, to Waite, September 19, 1895; Waite to Stewart, November 7, 1895, Waite Papers.

[26]Waite Speeches, Waite Papers, no title, no date.

[27]"Governor Waite's Baccalaureate Address Delivered at the State Agricultural College at Fort Collins to the Graduating Class of Ninety-Three," Waite's Magazine, I (October 1, 1898), 31.

[28]Hicks, The Populist Revolt, p. 441.

[29]Waite Speeches, Waite Papers, no title, no date, Box 11.

[30]Foner, History of the Labor Movement, II, 328.

[31]Waite to E. L. Benson, Seattle, May 27, 1895, Waite Papers.

[32]B. Franklin Hunter, President, National Club of Philadelphia, to Waite, October 25, 1894, Waite Papers.

[33]Foner, _History of the Labor Movement_, II, 304-05.

[34]F. G. R. Gordon, Manchester, New Hampshire, to Waite, February 27, 1897, Waite Papers.

[35]William Harrison Riley, Townsend Centre, Mass., to Waite, October 11, 1894, Waite Papers.

[36]Norman W. Lermond, Thomaston, Maine, to Waite, February 29, 1896, Waite Papers.

[37]With the usual emphasis on Debs as a labor leader and a Socialist, it is sometimes forgotten that Debs was a Populist who was seriously considered by many Populists as their nominee for President in 1896, a move which Debs himself discouraged.

[38]Ray Ginger, _The Bending Cross_ (New Brunswick: Rutgers University Press, 1949), p. 177.

[39]Eugene V. Debs to Waite, July 17, 1895, Waite Papers.

[40]_Ibid._

[41]Debs to Waite, December 7, 1895, Waite Papers.

[42]Debs to Waite, December 21, 1895, Waite Papers.

[43]Debs to Waite, January 7, 1899, Waite Papers.

[44]Caro Lloyd, _Henry Demarest Lloyd_ (New York: G. P. Putnam's Sons, 1912), II, 279.

Chapter VI

[1]Solon Buck, _The Granger Movement_ (Cambridge: Harvard University Press, 1913), pp. 12-13.

[2]William Larrabee, _The Railroad Question_ (Chicago: Schulte Publishing Co., 1898), p. 88.

[3]Buck, _The Granger Movement_, pp. 12-15; Buck, _The Agrarian Crusade_, pp. 23, 45; Robert E. Riegel, _The Story of the Western Railroads_ (New York: Macmillan Co., 1926), pp. 130-34, 221, 223, 283, 285-87, 289, 293; Hicks, _The Populist Revolt_, pp. 60-74; Fred A. Shannon, _The Farmer's Last Frontier_ (New York:

171

Farrar and Rinehart, Inc., 1945), pp. 295-303.

[4]Buck, The Granger Movement, pp. 123 ff.; Buck, The Agrarian Crusade, pp. 25-76.

[5]Buck, The Granger Movement, p. 213.

[6]Fred Shannon, American Farmers' Movements (Princeton, N.J.: D. Van Nostrand Co., 1957) pp. 149-51.

[7]James H. Baker and Leroy R. Hafen, eds., History of Colorado (Denver: Linderman Co., Inc., 1927), II, 817.

[8]Robert G. Athearn, Rebel of the Rockies: A History of the Denver and Rio Grande Railroad (New Haven: Yale University Press, 1962), see early chapters.

[9]Aspen Times, January 1, 1888.

[10]On the subject of eastern and foreign controls over railroads in Colorado, see Robert E. Riegel, The Story of the Western Railroads, pp. 219-291. The question of early foreign and eastern controls over one of Colorado's own railroads, the Denver and Rio Grande, is well illustrated in Robert G. Athearn's, Rebel of the Rockies, pp. 5, 6, 37, 76, 107, 149, 151, 170, 175, 176, 195.

[11]Buck, The Granger Movement, pp. 198-99.

[12]Riegel, The Story of the Western Railroads, p. 141.

[13]Report of the Railroad Commissioner, Colorado, 1891-92, p. 4.

[14]Ibid.

[15]Ibid., p. 5.

[16]Ibid., p. 15.

[17]Aspen Union Era, August 4, 1892.

[18]Inaugural Address of Governor Davis H. Waite, pp. 35-43.

[19] Ibid.

[20] Buck, The Agrarian Crusade, pp. 32, 50, 52, 55-56; Buck, The Granger Movement, pp. 164, 178.

[21] Letter Press Books, IX, 23-33.

[22] See letters concerning railroad passes in the Waite Papers: Edward T. Jeffrey, Denver and Rio Grande, to Waite, December 14, 1892; Jeffrey to Waite, December 17, 1892; Charles E. Gast, Santa Fe Railroad, to Waite, January 4, 1893; Charles Wheeler, Union Pacific, to Waite, March 14, 1894, and accompanying Waite notes refusing the passes.

[23] William Garner, Trinidad, Colorado, to Waite, January 6, 1893, Waite Papers.

[24] E. T. Jeffrey to Waite, June 28, 1894; Waite to Jeffrey, July 1, 1894, Waite Papers.

[25] Waite Speeches, Waite Papers, no title, no date, Box 11.

[26] Waite Speeches, Waite Papers; Waite to Senator William Stewart of Nevada, November 7, 1895, Waite Papers.

[27] Roy M. Robbins, Our Landed Heritage: The Public Domain, 1776-1936 (Lincoln: University of Nebraska Press, 1962), p. 9. The theme of land settler vs. land monopolist is central throughout Robbins' book. For evidence of the same conflict specifically in the post-Civil War decades, see Fred A. Shannon's, The Farmer's Last Frontier, pp. 51-75.

[28] Shannon, The Farmer's Last Frontier, p. 51.

[29] Robbins, Our Landed Heritage, pp. 207-90; Shannon, The Farmer's Last Frontier, pp. 51-75; Ernest S. Osgood, The Day of the Cattleman, Phoenix, ed.; (Chicago: University of Chicago Press, 1957), pp. 48-49, 99-100, 103-104, 203, 211.

[30] Shannon, American Farmers' Movements, p. 148.

[31] Ibid., p. 150.

[32] Robbins, Our Landed Heritage, pp. 296-97, 301, 303.

[33]Hicks, The Populist Revolt, p. 443.

[34]Inaugural Address of Governor Davis H. Waite, p. 12.

[35]Ibid.

[36]Waite Speeches, Waite Papers, no title, no date, Box 11.

[37]Inaugural Address of Governor Davis H. Waite, p. 13.

[38]Inaugural Address of Governor Davis H. Waite, p. 12; Annual Message of Governor Davis H. Waite, 1895.

[39]Executive Records, VIII, 365-66.

[40]Aspen Union Era, June 23, 1892.

[41]Waite to Donnelly, December 11, 1894, Donnelly Papers.

[42]C. P. Cooper, General Secretary, Free Land League of America, Brooklyn, N. Y., to Waite, August 19, 1894, Waite Papers.

[43]Henry George, Progress and Poverty, 50th ed. (New York: Robert Schalkenbach Foundation, 1953), p. 6.

[44]James Robertson, Altoona, Pa., to Waite, June 5, 1895, Waite Papers.

Chapter VII

[1]Foner, History of the Labor Movement, II, 256.

[2]Bureau of Labor Statistics of Colorado, Seventh Biennial Report, 1900, pp. 219-24.

[3]Aspen Union Era, April 14, 1892.

[4]Aspen Union Era, November 5, 1891.

[5]M. J. Welch, Secretary of State Assembly, Knights of Labor of Colorado, Denver to Waite, November 20, 1892, Waite Papers.

[6] George Harvey, *Henry Clay Frick the Man* (New York: Scribner, 1928), pp. 164-65.

[7] *Rocky Mountain News*, October 16, 1892.

[8] *Ibid.*

[9] *Inaugural Address of Governor Davis H. Waite*, pp. 14-16.

[10] *Ibid.*, p. 20; *Denver Republican*, July 3, 1892.

[11] *Fifth Biennial Report of the State Inspector of Coal Mines of the State of Colorado*, 1891-92, pp. 7-8.

[12] J. C. Sharp to Governor John L. Routt, October 29, 1891, and John McNeil, State Inspector of Coal Mines, to Governor John L. Routt, November 17, 1891, *Reports of the Office of the Governor*, John L. Routt Papers, State Archives, Colorado.

[13] *Second, Third, Fourth, and Fifth Biennial Reports of the State Inspector of Coal Mines of the State of Colorado*, 1885-92.

[14] *Sixth Biennial Report of the State Inspector of Coal Mines of the State of Colorado*, 1893-94.

[15] For data on Colorado coal monopolies, see Chapter 3.

[16] *Executive Records*, VIII (July 6, 1893), 308-10.

[17] U. S. Bureau of the Census, *Historical Statistics*, pp. 91-92.

[18] *Greeley Sun*, June 2, 1894.

[19] *Ibid.*

[20] Almont Lindsey, *The Pullman Strike*, Phoenix, ed. (Chicago: University of Chicago Press, 1964), pp. 168, 246-48; *Report of Brigadier-General A. M. McCook to Adjutant General of the United States* (Washington, D. C.: Government Printing Office, 1894), pp. 136-39, quoted in Fuller, "History of the People's Party in Colorado," p. 273.

[21] Fuller, "History of the People's Party in Colorado," p. 275.

[22]Lindsey, Pullman Strike, p. 262.

[23]Fuller, "History of the People's Party in Colorado," p. 276.

[24]Waite essay on "The Commonweal Army," Waite Papers, no date, Box 11.

[25]From an untitled Waite essay on the money question, Waite Papers, no date, Box 11. See also the pertinent material on Coxey's March in the Jacob S. Coxey Papers, Ohio Historical Society, Columbus, Ohio.

[26]Waite to Senator William Stewart of Nevada, November 7, 1895, Waite Papers.

[27]Vernon H. Jensen, Heritage of Conflict: Labor Relations in the Nonferrous Metals Industry up to 1930 (Ithaca, N. Y.: Cornell University Press, 1950), pp. 30, 57. The present writer is indebted to Jensen for much of the factual material on the 1894 Cripple Creek strike.

[28]Ibid., p. 40.

[29]Ibid., p. 41; John R. Commons, et al, History of Labor in the United States (New York: Macmillan Co., 1935), IV, 174.

[30]Jensen, Heritage of Conflict, pp. 42-44; Commons, History of Labor, IV, 174.

[31]Charles W. Henderson, Mining in Colorado, A History of Discovery, Development, and Production (Washington, D. C.: Government Printing Office, 1926), p. 56.

[32]Herbert C. Brayer, "History of Colorado Railroads," in Leroy R. Hafen, ed., Colorado and Its People (New York: Lewis Historical Publishing Co., 1948), II, 673-74.

[33]Jensen, Heritage of Conflict, p. 41.

[34]Greeley Sun, June 2, 1894.

[35]Biennial Report of the Adjutant General of Colorado, 1893-94, p. 41.

[36]Fuller, "History of the People's Party in Colorado," p. 257.

37Waite essay, "Cripple Creek Difficulties," Waite Papers, no date, Box 11.

38Jensen, _Heritage of Conflict_, p. 41.

39_Greeley Sun_, June 2, 1894.

40_Pueblo Chieftain_, May 29, 1894.

41_Pueblo Chieftain_, June 4, 1894.

42_Denver Republican_, May 31, 1894.

43_Denver Republican_, June 4, 1894.

44_Denver Republican_, May 31, 1894.

45_Colorado Springs Weekly Gazette_, May 31, 1894.

46_Castle Rock Journal_, June 6, 1894.

47_Leadville Herald Democrat_, June 2, 1894.

48Jensen, _Heritage of Conflict_, p. 47.

49Executive Records, IX (June 4, 1894), 77-78.

50_Greeley Sun_, June 9, 1894; Fuller, "History of the People's Party in Colorado," p. 265; Commons, _History of Labor_, IV, 176.

51Jensen, _Heritage of Conflict_, p. 49, and _Report of the Adjutant General of Colorado_, 1893-94 (Denver: State Printing Office, 1894), pp. 44-45.

52Executive Records, IX (June 7, 1894), 80.

53Jensen, _Heritage of Conflict_, p. 50; Commons, _History of Labor_, IV, 177.

54Executive Records, IX (June 8, 1894), 80.

55_Ibid_.

56Jensen, _Heritage of Conflict_, pp. 50-52.

57Jensen, _Heritage of Conflict_, p. 52; Commons, _History of Labor_, IV, 178.

58For a more detailed though rather flippant account of the Tarsney episode, see Marshall Sprague,

Money Mountain: The Story of Cripple Creek Gold (Boston: Little, Brown & Co., 1953).

[59]Waite to the Honorable John Campbell, District Judge, El Paso County, June 25, 1894, Waite Papers.

[60]M. L. Parr of Aspen Assembly, No. 2726, K. of L. to Waite, June 28, 1894; William H. Joyce, Secretary, Lake County Miners' Assembly, No. 2625, K. of L. to Waite, June 28, 1894, Waite Papers.

[61]Letter of eight anonymous miners in jail in Colorado Springs to Waite, October 4, 1894, Waite Papers.

[62]Report of the Attorney General of Colorado, 1893-94, pp. 10-11.

[63]W. H. Harvey to Waite, June 9, 1894, Waite Papers.

[64]Frank Wolfe, Financial Secretary, Free Coinage Miners Union, Altman, Colorado, to Waite, August 8, 1894, Waite Papers.

[65]Foner, History of the Labor Movement, II, 323.

[66]As an example, see R. G. Dill, The Political Campaigns of Colorado (Denver: Arapahoe Publishing Co., 1895), pp. 245-51.

[67]Commons, History of Labor, IV, 178.

[68]Waite to Donnelly, December 11, 1894, Donnelly Papers.

[69]Ibid.

[70]From political advertisement, Waite Papers.

[71]William Haywood, The Autobiography of "Big Bill" Haywood (New York: International Publishers, 1929), p. 64.

[72]James Hogan, Director, American Railway Union, Ogeden, Utah, to Waite, November 11, 1894, Waite Papers.

[1]Eleanor Flexner, Century of Struggle, The Woman's Rights Movement in the United States (Cambridge: Belknap Press of Harvard University Press, 1959), pp. 52, 193.

[2]Alice Felt Tyler, Freedom's Ferment (Minneapolis: University of Minnesota Press, 1944), pp. 429-35.

[3]Ibid., p. 426.

[4]Flexner, Century of Struggle, pp. 18-22, 37-40, 127-30, 186-92.

[5]Ibid., pp. 193-202.

[6]Ibid., p. 132.

[7]Ibid., p. 194.

[8]Denver Tribune-Republican, February 23, 1885; John R. Morris, "The Early Setting," in Harry Seligson and George E. Bardwell, Labor-Management Relations in Colorado (Denver: Sage Books, 1961), p. 80.

[9]National American Woman Suffrage Association, Victory: How Women Won It (New York: H. W. Wilson Company, 1940), pp. 73-74.

[10]Flexner, Century of Struggle, p. 160.

[11]National American Woman Suffrage Association, Victory: How Women Won It, p. 73.

[12]Joseph G. Brown, History of Equal Suffrage in Colorado, 1868-1898 (Denver: News Job Printing Co., 1898), p. 5.

[13]Ibid., pp. 9-10.

[14]Ibid., p. 13.

[15]Elizabeth Cady Stanton, et. al., History of Woman Suffrage, 1848-1900, IV (Indianapolis: Hollenbeck Press, 1902), 510.

[16]Billie Barnes Jensen, "The Woman Suffrage Movement in Colorado" (unpublished M. A. thesis, University of Colorado, 1959), p. 62.

[17]Bureau of Labor Statistics of Colorado, First Biennial Report, 1888, p. 20 and appendix; John R. Morris, "The Early Setting," pp. 81-82.

[18]Aspen Times, October 20, 1887.

[19]Aspen Union Era, April 14, 1892.

[20]Stanton, History of Woman Suffrage, IV, 509.

[21]Denver Republican, April 18, 1892.

[22]Denver Republican, May 15, 1892.

[23]Davis H. Waite, "Women Suffrage in Practice," North American Review, CLVIII (June, 1894), 740.

[24]Denver Republican, July 28, 1892.

[25]Ibid., July 29, 1892.

[26]Quitman Brown to Waite, December 15, 1892, Waite Papers.

[27]Ibid., December 22, 1892, Waite Papers.

[28]Sallie Mortimer, Denver, to Waite, December 18, 1892, Waite Papers.

[29]Inaugural Address of Governor Davis H. Waite, 1893.

[30]Rocky Mountain News, January 11, 1893.

[31]Letter Press Books, IX (April 17, 1893), 189.

[32]Brown, History of Equal Suffrage in Colorado, p. 18; Waite, "Woman Suffrage in Practice," p. 740.

[33]Brown, History of Equal Suffrage in Colorado, pp. 23-24.

[34]Executive Records, VIII (December 2, 1893), 394-95.

[35]Stanton, History of Woman Suffrage, IV, 518.

[36]Helen M. Reynolds, Denver, to Waite, December 19, 1893, Waite Papers.

[37] Women's Christian Temperance Union to Waite, January 2, 1894, Waite Papers.

[38] Waite, "Woman Suffrage in Practice," pp. 737-41.

[39] Waite Speeches, 1894, Waite Papers, no title, Box 11.

[40] Ibid.

[41] Brown, History of Equal Suffrage in Colorado, pp. 30-36.

[42] Fuller, "History of the People's Party in Colorado," p. 305.

[43] Waite to Ignatius Donnelly, December 11, 1894, Donnelly Papers.

[44] Idaho Springs News, November 9, 1894.

[45] Mrs. Phila Bliven, Durango, Colorado, to Waite, November 9, 1894, Waite Papers.

[46] Hicks, The Populist Revolt, p. 337.

[47] Brown, History of Equal Suffrage in Colorado, p. 27.

[48] Eugene V. Debs to Waite, December 11, 1896, Waite Papers.

[49] Ignatius Donnelly to Waite, December 7, 1894, Waite Papers.

[50] Mrs. Elizabeth S. Crannell of Albany, New York, to Waite, December 14, 1897, Waite Papers.

[51] Mrs. Alice W. Faulkner, Denver, to Waite, February 7, 1899, Waite Papers.

[52] Stanton, History of Woman Suffrage, IV, 522-523, 526; Brown, History of Equal Suffrage in Colorado, p. 44.

[53] Stanton, History of Woman Suffrage, IV, 522-28; Brown, History of Equal Suffrage, pp. 30-44.

[54] Inaugural Address of Governor Davis H. Waite, p. 17.

[55]Ibid.

[56]Report of the Attorney General of Colorado, 1893-94, p. 15.

[57]Arthur M. Schlesinger, The Rise of the City (New York: The Macmillan Co., 1933), p. 363.

[58]Chicago Times, January 25, 1895.

[59]Report of State Board of Pardons, State of Colorado, 1893-94, p. 98; Biennial Report of the Colorado State Penitentiary, 1891-92, pp. 127-28; Biennial Report of the Colorado State Penitentiary, 1895-96, pp. 58-60. The pardons report covered the governor's term while the penitentiary reports dated from December 1, causing some possible discrepancy.

[60]Aspen Union Era, March 17, 1892.

[61]Colorado State Business Directory, 1892, p. 651.

[62]Waite to Mrs. W. O. Taylor, Townsend, Mass., November 1, 1895, Waite Papers.

[63]Session Laws of Colorado, 1893, quoted in Fuller, "History of the People's Party in Colorado," p. 147.

[64]Fuller, "History of the People's Party in Colorado," p. 223.

[65]Waite article in Georgetown Courier, December 8, 1894.

[66]Women's Christian Temperance Union, Denver, to Waite, April 24, 1894, Waite Papers.

[67]Aspen Times, June 28, 1888.

[68]Aspen Union Era, April 14, 1892.

[69]Aspen Union Era, November 26, 1891.

[70]Waite Speeches, Waite Papers, no title, no date, Box 11.

[71]Aspen Union Era, March 31, 1892.

[72]S. H. Allen, Associate Justice of the Supreme Court of Kansas, to Waite, July 31, 1894, Waite Papers.

[73]Waite to E. D. Benson, Seattle, May 27, 1895, Waite Papers.

[74]Hicks, The Populist Revolt, pp. 186-88.

[75]Aspen Union Era, January 28, 1892, reprint of article by Davis H. Waite in the National Economist (Washington, D. C., January, 1892).

[76]Waite Speeches, Waite Papers, no title, no date, Box 11.

[77]Ibid.

[78]Aspen Union Era, March 24, 1892.

Chapter IX

[1]Waite to Fred A. Truesdall, Recording Secretary, Washington Camp No. 15, Patriotic Sons of America, May 19, 1894, Letter Press Books, X, 130.

[2]Aspen Union Era, November 19, 1891.

[3]Waite Speeches, Waite Papers, no title, no date, Box 11.

[4]Ibid.

[5]With regard to Populist leaders, there is evidence to support Waite's contention. Ignatius Donnelly was reared as a Roman Catholic, but revolted against the Church. See Martin Ridge, Ignatius Donnelly, p. 401. Henry Demarest Lloyd's father was a Dutch Reformed Church minister, but the younger Lloyd grew tired of ceremony and dogma and felt that the Church was too impractical and lacked a sense of justice. See Caro Lloyd, Henry Demarest Lloyd, I, 116-118. Tom Watson attended revival meetings, but is said to have had a typical deist's feeling of suspicion and hostility towards clergymen. See C. Vann Woodward, Tom Watson, p. 41. Eugene Debs and Clarence Darrow were other examples Waite might have mentioned. On the other hand, James B. Weaver was a Methodist. See Fred E. Haynes, James Baird Weaver (Iowa City, Iowa: The State Historical Society of Iowa, 1919), p. 113. Senator James H. Kyle of South Dakota was a Congregational minister. See John D. Hicks, The Populist

<u>Revolt</u>, p. 181. Probably many of the midwestern and southern Populist leaders were religious traditionalists.

[6]Waite speech on religion and politics, pp. 2-4, Waite Papers, no title, no date, Box 11.

[7]<u>Ibid</u>., pp. 5-6.

[8]<u>Ibid</u>., pp. 11-13, 16-17.

[9]Waite to Fred A. Truesdall, May 19, 1894, Letter Press Books, X, 130.

[10]<u>Aspen</u> <u>Union</u> <u>Era</u>, March 3, 1892.

[11]Waite to C. T. Beatty, National Secretary of the A. P. A., April 24, 1895, Waite Papers.

[12]Jasper W. Johnson, Aspen, to Waite, August 13, 1894, Waite Papers; Donald L. Kinzer, <u>An Episode in Anti-Catholicism: The American Protective Association</u> (Seattle: University of Washington Press, 1964), p. 156.

[13]C. T. Beatty, A. P. A., Detroit, to Waite, March 6, 1895,[1896], Waite Papers.

[14]It is generally acknowledged that the A. P. A. was active inside the Republican Party in each state where it had organized strength. There were a few local exceptions. The Populists, on the other hand, did not welcome A. P. A. members. See Kinzer, <u>An Episode in Anti-Catholicism</u>, pp. 140-41.

[15]Waite to Beatty, April 24, 1895, Waite Papers.

[16]Paul Van Dervoort, Omaha, to Waite, April 3, 1895, Waite Papers.

[17]Van Dervoort to Waite, June 8, 1895, Waite Papers.

[18]Mrs. Semper, Denver, to Waite, July 31, 1895, Waite Papers.

[19]Robert L. Perkin, <u>The First Hundred Years</u> (New York: Doubleday & Co., 1959), p. 389.

[20] Resolution from Fred A. Truesdell, Recording Secretary, Patriotic Order Sons of America, Washington Camp No. 15, to Waite, May 11, 1894, Waite Papers.

[21] Waite to Truesdell, May 19, 1894, Letter Press Books, X, 129-30.

[22] Oscar Handlin, "American Views of the Jew at the Opening of the Twentieth Century," Publications of the American Jewish Historical Society, XL (June, 1951), 324-44.

[23] Carey McWilliams, A Mask for Privilege: Anti-Semitism in America (Boston: Little, Brown and Co., 1948).

[24] Peter Viereck, The Unadjusted Man: A New Hero for Americans (Boston: Beacon Press, 1956), pp. 201-04.

[25] Richard Hofstadter, The Age of Reform (New York: Vintage Books, 1960), p. 80.

[26] Walter T. K. Nugent, The Tolerant Populists (Chicago: University of Chicago Press, 1963), pp. 180, 231.

[27] Norman Pollack, "Handlin on Anti-Semitism: A Critique of 'American Views of the Jew'," Journal of American History, LI (December, 1964), 391-403.

[28] Waite to Stewart, November 7, 1895, Waite Papers.

[29] Waite speech on "The People's Party," 1894, Waite Papers.

[30] Waite speech, "Mission of the Populist Party," Waite Papers.

[31] Nugent, The Tolerant Populists, pp. 114-15.

[32] Waite to Donnelly, December 19, 1893, Donnelly Papers.

[33] Waite Speeches, Waite Papers, no title, no date, Box 11.

[34] Jack Abramowitz, "The Negro in the Populist Movement," The Journal of Negro History, XXXVIII (July, 1953), 288.

[35]Ibid., p. 264.

[36]U. S. Bureau of the Census, Eleventh Census of the United States: 1890 Population, I, 478, 541.

[37]Denver Republican, August 24, 1892.

[38]Denver Republican, August 30, 1893.

[39]John W. Dickinson to Waite, August 16, 1894, Waite Papers.

[40]Waite Speeches, Waite Papers, no title, no date, Box 11.

[41]Davis H. Waite, "Woman Suffrage in Practice," North American Review, CLVIII (June, 1894), 737.

[42]The Reverend John J. Smallwood, Claremont, Va., to Waite, November 14, 1894, Waite Papers.

[43]Viereck, The Unadjusted Man, p. 203.

[44]Woodward, Tom Watson, p. 222.

[45]Eugene V. Debs, et. al., Debs: His Life, Writings, and Speeches (Chicago: Charles H. Kerr and Co., 1908), p. 44.

[46]Caro Lloyd, Henry Demarest Lloyd, II, 268-69.

[47]See Dee Brown, Bury My Heart at Wounded Knee (New York: Bantam Books, 1972), Chapters 4 and 16.

[48]Waite to President Cleveland, May 9, 1893, Letter Press Books, IX, 332-35.

[49]Waite to Secretary of Interior Smith, November 17, 1893, Executive Records, VIII, 386.

[50]Aspen Union Era, March 3, 1892.

[51]Aspen Union Era, February 18, 1892.

[52]Waite Speeches, Waite Papers, no title, no date, Box 11.

[53]Waite Speeches, Waite Papers, no title, no date, Box 11.

[54]Waite to Donnelly, December 11, 1894, Donnelly Papers.

[55]Waite to Secretary of State W. L. Gresham, Washington, D. C., August 8, 1893, Executive Records, VIII, 334-36.

[56]See Salvator J. LaGumina, ed., Wop! A Documentary History of Anti-Italian Discrimination in the United States (San Francisco: Straight Arrow Books, 1973), especially pp. 222-23.

[57]Waite speech, "Mission of the Populist Party," p. 17, Waite Papers.

[58]Donnelly to Waite, October 7, 1895, Waite Papers; Waite to Donnelly, November 2, 1895, Donnelly Papers.

[59]Waite speech, "International Conference," p. 5, Waite Papers.

[60]Ibid., pp. 4-5.

[61]Ibid., p. 5.

[62]Waite to Diaz, March 9, 1894, Waite Papers.

[63]Waite to the Boston Daily Traveller in answer to an inquiry on the Nicaragua Canal, March 26, 1894, Waite Papers. Inaugural Address of Governor Davis H. Waite, 1893.

[64]Davis H. Waite, "Extension of our National Boundaries," Waite's Magazine, I (October 1, 1898), 32.

[65]Speech on the Philippines by John P. Altgeld, John Peter Altgeld Collection, Springfield, Illinois.

[66]Ridge, Ignatius Donnelly, pp. 381-82; Caro Lloyd, Henry Demarest Lloyd, II, 130-34; Ginger, The Bending Cross, pp. 202-03; Woodward, Tom Watson, pp. 334-35; Haynes, Weaver, p. 386.

Chapter X

[1]Waite speech, "The People's Party: Its Past, Present, and Future," Waite Papers.

[2]Ibid.

[3]Aspen Union Era, April 14, 1892.

[4]Aspen Union Era, June 23, 1892.

[5]Aspen Union Era, June 30, 1892.

[6]Ibid.

[7]Foner, History of the Labor Movement, II, 327-28; Buckner, "Silver Mining Interests in Silver Politics, 1876-1896" (unpublished M. A. thesis, University of Colorado, 1947), pp. 9-10, 63-65.

[8]Hicks, The Populist Revolt, pp. 318-19.

[9]Daniel Feins, "Labor's Role in the Populist Movement, 1890-1896" (unpublished M. A. thesis, Columbia University, 1939), pp. 24-25.

[10]Woodward, Tom Watson, p. 280; Buckner, "Silver Mining Interests in Silver Politics," p. 44.

[11]Waite to Donnelly, December 19, 1893, Donnelly Papers.

[12]Waite to Donnelly, November 16, 1893, Donnelly Papers. Waite spoke ardently of the need for union of the South and the West, and remarked that he had sent his views to Benjamin Tillman, Thomas E. Watson, and others in the South.

[13]Thomas E. Watson to Waite, November 25, and December 4, 1893, Waite Papers.

[14] Senator James Kyle of South Dakota to Waite, October 24, 1893, Waite Papers.

[15]James B. Weaver to Waite, February 26, 1894, Waite Papers.

[16]Herman E. Taubeneck to Waite, January 20, March 6, and March 7, 1894, Waite Papers.

[17]John W. Breidenthal to Waite, February 13, 1894; H. L. Loucks to Waite, February 15, 1894, Waite Papers.

[18]Daniel M. Feins, "Labor's Role in the Populist Movement, 1890-1896," p. 77; Foner, *History of the Labor Movement*, II, 315-19.

[19]Feins, "Labor's Role in the Populist Movement," pp. 24-25.

[20]George F. Washburn, Boston, to Waite, December 22, 1894, Waite Papers.

[21]Waite to Robert Schilling, December 17, 1894, Waite Papers.

[22]*Ibid.*

[23]Paul Van Dervoort, Omaha, to Waite, December 15, 1894, Waite Papers.

[24]Feins, "Labor's Role in the Populist Movement," p. 69.

[25]Foner, *History of the Labor Movement*, II, 329.

[26]*St. Louis Labor*, January 5, 1895, quoted in Foner, *History of the Labor Movement*, II, 329-30.

[27]Waite to Donnelly, December 11, 1894, Donnelly Papers.

[28]Pollack, *The Populist Response to Industrial America*, pp. 63-64.

[29]Foner, *History of the Labor Movement*, II, 326, 331-32.

[30]*National Watchman*, February, 1895, quoted in Foner, *History of the Labor Movement*, II, 331.

[31]Herman E. Taubeneck to W. S. Morgan, January 10, 1895, Waite Papers.

[32]Taubeneck to Waite, January 29, 1895, Waite Papers.

[33]Taubeneck to Waite, April 29, 1895, Waite Papers.

[34]Waite to Donnelly, April 22, 1895, Donnelly Papers.

[35]W. S. Morgan to Waite, September 13, 1895, Waite Papers.

[36]H. L. Loucks to Waite, September 20, 1895, Waite Papers.

[37]George Washburn to Waite, October 2, 1895, Waite Papers.

[38]W. S. Morgan to Waite, September 15, 1895, Waite Papers.

[39]Waite to John Peter Altgeld, November 25, 1895, Waite Papers.

[40]William Jennings Bryan to Waite, December 2, 1895, Waite Papers.

[41]Feins, "Labor's Role in the Populist Movement," p. 72; W. S. Morgan to Waite, January 12, 1896, Waite Papers.

[42]Ralph Beaumont to Waite, January 19, 1896, Waite Papers.

[43]Edwin Isaac Burdick to Waite, January 31, 1896, Waite Papers.

[44]Benjamin P. Tillman to Waite, January 9, 1896, Waite Papers.

[45]Waite to Tillman, March 23, 1896, Waite Papers.

[46]Richard Bland was a Missouri Congressman interested in silver, and co-author of the Bland-Allison Act of 1878.

[47]Waite to Tillman, March 23, 1896, Waite Papers.

[48]Tillman to Waite, April 6, 1896, Waite Papers.

[49]H. G. Clark, Populist State Chairman, Greeley, to Waite, April 19, 1896, Waite Papers.

[50]Ibid.

[51]Paul Van Dervoort to Waite, April 28, and April 30, 1896, Waite Papers.

[52]Taubeneck to Donnelly, May 15, 1896, Waite Papers.

[53]Waite to the Populist Party Central Committee of Arapahoe County, May 7, 1896, Waite Papers.

[54]Waite to Donnelly, July 12, 1896, Donnelly Papers.

[55]Waite to the publisher of The Arena, November 21, 1896, Waite Papers.

[56]Davis H. Waite to Celia and May Waite, July 7, 1896, Waite Papers.

[57]Waite to The Arena, November 21, 1896, Waite Papers.

[58]Watson to Waite, October 13, 1896, Waite Papers.

[59]Watson to Waite, November 8, 1896, Waite Papers.

[60]Altgeld to Waite, November 23, 1896, Waite Papers.

[61]Waite to Bryan, late 1896, Waite Papers.

[62]Waite speech on Populist Party factionalism, 1897, Waite Papers.

[63]Davis H. Waite to Celia Waite, October 24, 1897, Waite Papers.

Appendix A

[1]Hicks, The Populist Revolt, pp. 291-99.

[2]Ibid., p. 291.

[3]Ibid., p. 292.

[4]Ibid., p. 293.

[5]Ibid., p. 294.

[6]Ibid.

[7]Ibid., p. 297.

Appendix B

[1] Solomon Landman and Benjamin Efron, Story Without End: An Informal History of the Jewish People (New York: Henry Holt and Co., 1949), p. 204.

[2] Ibid., p. 210.

[3] See, for example, Max L. Margolis and Alexander Marx, A History of the Jewish People (Philadelphia: The Jewish Publication Society of America, 1927); Cecil Rotte, A History of the Jews (New York: Schocken Books, Rev. ed., 1970); James Parkes, Antisemitism (Chicago: Quadrangle Books, 1963); Sigmund Livingston, Must Men Hate? (New York and London: Harper & Bros., 1944); Landman and Efron, Story Without End; and McWilliams, A Mask for Privilege.

[4] McWilliams, A Mask for Privilege, preface XIII.

[5] Ibid., p. 7.

[6] See G. William Domhoff, The Higher Circles: The Governing Class in America (New York: Vintage Books, 1971); Ferdinand Lundberg, The Rich and the Super-Rich (New York: Lyle Stuart, Inc., 1968); Victor Perlo, The Empire of High Finance (New York: International Publishers, 1957).

BIBLIOGRAPHY

This work, which was originally my doctoral dissertation, was based on materials available to 1965. The heart of the work stems from primary materials, especially the Waite Papers. While there have been alterations, there has been no real change in substance. However, many of the more pertinent books and some of the articles and theses appearing since then have been included.

Manuscripts

Davis Hanson Waite Papers. The Waite Papers are on file in fourteen boxes in the Colorado State Archives and Public Records, Denver, Colorado. These papers consist of his correspondence and some of his speeches from 1891-99. Also included is some printed material related to his administration and his reform endeavors. The papers came into the possession of the Colorado State Archives in 1959, and were in an unsorted state when the writer researched them. A number of the speeches and speech fragments, mainly in Waite's own handwriting, are untitled and undated. An approximate estimate of the date could sometimes be ascertained by the contents of the speech. The speeches cover the period from 1892 to 1897. The correspondence is contained in boxes 1-10 and in two large scrapbooks. The writer arranged the correspondence chronologically, excluding the scrapbook letters. The speeches are contained in box 11 and the same two scrapbooks. The papers are on microfilm (box 14). Records of the Waite administration are also on file in the Colorado State Archives.

John Peter Altgeld Collection. Illinois State Historical Society, Springfield, Illinois.

John C. Bell Papers. University of Colorado, Boulder, Colorado.

William Jennings Bryan Collection. State Archives of Nebraska, Lincoln, Nebraska.

Jacob S. Coxey, Sr. Papers. Ohio Historical Society, Columbus, Ohio.

Ignatius Donnelly Papers. Minnesota Historical Society, St. Paul, Minnesota.

John L. Routt Papers. Colorado State Archives and Public Records, Denver, Colorado.

James Baird Weaver Papers. State Archives of Iowa, Des Moines, Iowa.

Documents

United States

U. S. Bureau of the Census. Eleventh Census of the United States: 1890. Population, Part I.

U. S. Bureau of the Census. Historical Statistics of the United States, Colonial Times to 1957. 1960.

U. S. Commissioner of Labor. A Report on the Labor Disturbances in the State of Colorado from 1880 to 1904, Inclusive, with Correspondence Relating Thereto. 1906.

State of Colorado

Abstract of Votes Cast for State Officers at the General Elections cf the Years 1892-1900, Inclusive.

Agricultural Statistics of the State of Colorado for 1892 and 1893.

Annual Message of Governor Davis H. Waite, January 4, 1895.

Biennial Report — Commissioner of Bureau of Labor Statistics — State of Colorado, 1891-1892.

Biennial Report of the Adjutant General of the State of Colorado, 1893-1894.

Biennial Report of the Colorado State Penitentiary,
    1891-1892.

Biennial Report — Railroad Commissioner — State of
    Colorado, 1891-1892.

Biennial Report of the State Inspector of Coal Mines
    of the State of Colorado, 1885-1894.

Biennial Report of the State Penitentiary of Colorado,
    1895-1896.

Bureau of Immigration and Statistics. The Natural
    Resources and Industrial Development and Condition
    of Colorado, 1889.

Bureau of Labor Statistics Report, Colorado, 1893-1894.

Bureau of Labor Statistics of Colorado, Seventh Bien-
    nial Report, 1900.

Colorado State Business Directory, 1892.

Correspondence of Contending Attorneys in Re Gov. Waite
    and the Denver Fire and Police Board Controversy
    over Appointments and Calling out of the Militia,
    1894.

Evidence Taken Before the Special Railroad Committee
    of the House of Representatives of Colorado, 1885.

Executive Records. Vols. VIII and IX.

Executive Telegrams, 1893-1894.

House Journals, 1893-1894.

Inaugural Address of Governor Davis H. Waite to the
    Ninth General Assembly of the State of Colorado,
    January 10, 1893.

Letter Press Books, Vols. VIII, IX, and X.

Manuscripts Relating to the Removal of State Inspector
    of Coal Mines John McNeil.

Manuscripts Relating to the State Board of Pardons.

Message of Governor Davis H. Waite to the Special
    Session of the Ninth General Assembly of Colorado,

January 10, 1894.

Miscellaneous Correspondence, Petitions, and Papers of the Waite Administration, 1893-1895.

Ninth Biennial Report of the Superintendent of Public Instruction of the State of Colorado, 1893-1894.

Opinions of the (Colorado) Supreme Court, 1893-1894.

Proclamation for Extra Session of State Legislature of Colorado by Governor Davis H. Waite, December 27, 1893.

Report of the Attorney General of Colorado, 1893-1894.

Report of the Railroad Commissioner of Colorado, 1885.

Report of the State Board of Land Commissioners of Colorado, 1893-1894.

Report of the State Board of Pardons, State of Colorado, 1893-1896.

Senate Journals, 1893-1894.

Session Laws of Colorado, 1893-1894.

Testimony in Re Investigation of State Industrial School at Golden, 1890-1894.

University of Colorado Pamphlets (P-2). Congressional Speeches on the free silver issue during the 1890's.

Unpublished Theses and Dissertations

Atchison, Carla Joan. "Nativism in Colorado Politics: The American Protective Association and the Ku Klux Klan." M. A. thesis, University of Colorado, 1972.

Besser, Virgil Myrtle. "The Administration of Governor Waite and the Populist Party in Colorado, 1893 to 1895." M. A. thesis, University of Colorado, 1924.

Buckner, Philip F. "Silver Mining Interests in Silver Politics, 1876-96." M. A. thesis, Columbia University, 1954.

Dawson, Lois L. "The Populist Movement in Colorado." M. A. thesis, University of Denver, 1930.

Day, Frank E., Jr. "The Populist Congressmen from Colorado, 1893-1895." M. A. thesis, University of Colorado, 1947.

Feins, Daniel M. "Labor's Role in the Populist Movement, 1890-1896." M. A. thesis, Columbia University, 1939.

Flower, Edward. "Anti-Semitism in the Free Silver and Populist Movements and the Election of 1896." M. A. thesis, Columbia University, 1952.

Fox, Leonard Peter. "Origins and Early Development of Populism in Colorado." Ph.D. dissertation, University of Pennsylvania, 1916.

Fuller, Leon W. "History of the People's Party in Colorado." Ph.D. dissertation, University of Wisconsin, 1933.

Griffiths, David B. "Populism in the Far West, 1890-1900." Ph.D. dissertation, University of Washington, 1967.

Hensel, Donald Wayne. "A History of the Colorado Constitution in the Nineteenth Century." Ph.D. dissertation, University of Colorado, 1957.

Jensen, Billie Barnes. "The Woman Suffrage Movement in Colorado." M. A. thesis, University of Colorado, 1959.

Kountze, Harold, Jr. "Davis H. Waite and the People's Party in Colorado." M. A. thesis, Yale University, 1944.

Lonsdale, David L. "The Movement for an Eight-Hour Law in Colorado, 1893-1913." Ph.D. dissertation, University of Colorado, 1963.

Rudolph, Gerald E. "The Chinese in Colorado, 1869-1911." M. A. thesis, University of Denver, 1964.

Thompson, George. "The History of Penal Institutions in the Rocky Mountain West." Ph.D. dissertation, University of Colorado, 1965.

Newspapers

Akron Pioneer Press (Akron, Colo.), 1892.

Aspen Times (Aspen, Colo.), 1887-1894.

Aspen Union Era (Aspen, Colo.), August 13, 1891-August 4, 1892.

Castle Rock Journal (Castle Rock, Colo.), 1894.

Cheyenne Wells Gazette (Cheyenne Wells, Colo.), 1888-1892.

Chicago Times (Chicago, Ill.), 1894-1895.

Colorado Springs Weekly Gazette (Colo. Springs, Colo.), 1894.

Colorado Sun (Denver, Colo.), 1892-1894.

Delta Independent (Delta, Colo.), 1894.

Denver Republican (Denver, Colo.), 1892-1896.

Denver Times (Denver, Colo.), 1892.

El Moro Monitor (El Moro, Colo.), 1893.

Georgetown Courier (Georgetown, Colo.), 1888-1900.

Greeley Sun (Greeley, Colo.), 1894.

Gunnison Tribune (Gunnison, Colo.), 1891-1894.

Idaho Springs News (Idaho Springs, Colo.), 1892-1894.

Lake City Times (Lake City, Colo.), 1894.

Leadville Herald-Democrat (Leadville, Colo.), 1892-1896.

New York Times (New York, N. Y.), 1892-1896.

Pueblo Chieftain (Pueblo, Colo.), 1892-1894.

Rocky Ford Enterprise (Rocky Ford, Colo.), 1893-1894.

Rocky Mountain News (Denver, Colo.), 1892-1896.

Trinidad Evening Chronicle (Trinidad, Colo.), 1892-1894.

Articles and Periodicals

Abramowitz, Jack. "The Negro in the Populist Movement,"
   The Journal of Negro History, XXXVIII, No. 3
   (July, 1953), 257-89.

Bicha, Karel D. "Jerry Simpson: Populist Without
   Principles," The Journal of American History,
   LIV (September, 1967), 291-306.

Bird, Leah M. "Minor Political Parties in Colorado,"
   Colorado Magazine, XIX (November, 1942), 208-13.

Cannon, Helen. "First Ladies of Colorado: Celia O.
   Crane Waite," Colorado Magazine, XLVI (Spring,
   1969), 120-30.

Destler, Chester McArthur. "Western Radicalism, 1865-
   1901: Concepts and Origins," Mississippi Valley
   Historical Review, XXXI (December, 1944), 335-68.

Dubofsky, Melvyn. "The Origins of Western Working
   Class Radicalism, 1890-1905," Labor History, VII
   (1966), 131-54.

Durden, Robert F. "The 'Cow-Bird' Grounded: The Populist Nomination of Bryan and Tom Watson in 1896,"
   Mississippi Valley Historical Review, L (December,
   1963), 397-424.

Ewing, John B. "Joseph R. Buchanan, 'The Riproarer of
   the Rockies,'" Colorado Magazine, XI (May, 1934),
   116-19.

Faberty, Wm. B. "Regional Minorities and the Woman
   Suffrage Struggle," Colorado Magazine, XXXIII
   (July, 1956), 212-17.

Farmer, Hallie. "The Economic Background of Frontier
   Populism," Mississippi Valley Historical Review,
   X (March, 1924), 406-27.

Ferkiss, Victor C. "Populist Influences on American
   Fascism," The Western Political Quarterly, X
   (June, 1957), 350-73.

Fuller, Leon W. "A Populist Newspaper of the Nineties," Colorado Magazine, IX (May, 1932), 81-87.

_____. "Colorado's Revolt Against Capitalism," Mississippi Valley Historical Review, XXI (February, 1934), 343-61.

_____. "Governor Waite and His Silver Panacea," Colorado Magazine, X (March, 1933), 41-47.

Griffiths, David B. "Far Western Populism: The Case of Utah, 1893-1900," Utah Historical Quarterly, XXXVII (Fall, 1969).

_____. "Far Western Populist Thought: A Comparative Study of John R. Rogers and Davis H. Waite," Pacific Northwest Quarterly, LX (October, 1969).

_____. "Populism in Wyoming," Annals of Wyoming, XL (April, 1968), 56-67.

Handlin, Oscar. "American Views of the Jew at the Opening of the Twentieth Century," Publications of the American Jewish Historical Society, XL (1951).

Hicks, John D. "The Sub-Treasury: A Forgotten Plan for the Relief of Agriculture," Mississippi Valley Historical Review, XV (December, 1928), 355-73.

_____. "The Political Career of Ignatius Donnelly," Mississippi Valley Historical Review, VIII, Nos. 1-2 (June-September, 1921), 80-132.

Jensen, Billie Barnes. "Let the Women Vote," Colorado Magazine, XLI (Winter, 1964), 13-25.

Larson, Robert W. "Students, Populists, and a Sense of History: An Essay," Colorado Magazine, XLVII (Winter, 1971), 43-48.

Lloyd, Henry D. "The Populists at St. Louis," Review of Reviews, XIV, No. 3 (September, 1896), 298-303.

McCarthy, G. Michael. "Colorado's Populist Leadership," Colorado Magazine, XLVII (Winter, 1971), 30-42.

McClung, Quantrille D. "Governors of Colorado: Davis Hanson Waite," Colorado Genealogist, XXI (October, 1960), 101-09.

_____. "The Governors of Colorado — Their Ancestries and Interests," Colorado Magazine, XXIII (May, 1946), 97-105.

McMurray, Donald L. "The Industrial Armies and the Commonweal," Mississippi Valley Historical Review, X (December, 1923), 215-52.

McVey, Frank. "The Populist Movement," Economic Studies, I (August, 1896), 133-209.

Nixon, Herman C. "The Cleavage Within the Farmers' Alliance Movement," Mississippi Valley Historical Review, XV (June, 1928), 22-34.

Pollack, Norman. "Fear of Man: Populism, Authoritarianism and the Historian," Agricultural History, XXXIX (April, 1965), 59-67.

_____. "Handlin on Anti-Semitism: A Critique of 'American Views of the Jew,'" The Journal of American History, LI (December, 1964), 391-403.

_____. "Ignatius Donnelly on Human Rights: A Study of Two Novels," Mid-America, XLVII (1965).

_____. "Hofstadter on Populism: A Critique of 'The Age of Reform,'" Journal of Southern History, XXVI (November, 1960), 478-500.

_____. "The Myth of Populist Anti-Semitism," American Historical Review, LXVIII (October, 1962), 76-80.

"Populist Factions, 1900," Review of Reviews, XXI, No. 6 (June, 1900), 647-49.

Saunders, Robert. "Southern Populists and the Negro, 1893-1895," Journal of Negro History, LIV (July, 1969), 240-61.

Spence, Clark C. "Colorado's Terrible Mine: A Study in British Investment," Colorado Magazine, XXIV (January, 1957), 48-61.

Suggs, George G., Jr. "Catalyst for Industrial Change: The WFM, 1893-1903," Colorado Magazine, XLV (Fall, 1968), 322-39.

Tischendorf, Alfred P. "British Investments in Colorado Mines," Colorado Magazine, XXX (October, 1953), 241-46.

Turner, James. "Understanding the Populists," The Journal of American History, LXVII (September, 1980), 354-73.

Waite, Davis Hanson, "Are the Silver States Ruined?" North American Review, CLVIII (January, 1894), 24-29.

_____. "Woman Suffrage in Practice," North American Review, CLVIII, No. 451 (June, 1894), 737-41.

_____. "Extension of Our National Boundaries," Waite's Magazine, I, No. 1 (October, 1898).

_____. "The War of the Gamblers," Waite's Magazine, I, No. 1 (October, 1898).

Waite's Magazine, I, No. 1 (October, 1898).

Walker, Francis A. "The Relation of Changes in the Volume of the Currency to Prosperity," Economic Studies, I (April, 1896), 25-45.

Warren, Sidney. "Ignatius Donnelly and the Populists," Current History, XXVIII (June, 1955), 336-42.

Watson, Thomas E. "Why I Am Still a Populist," Review of Reviews, XXXVIII, No. 3 (September, 1908), 303-06.

Wells, Merle W. "The Western Federation of Miners," Journal of the West, XII (1973), 18-35.

Welty, Richard C. "The Greenback Party in Colorado," Colorado Magazine, XXVIII (October, 1951), 301-11.

Warner, Jane. "The Press and the Populists," Colorado Magazine, XLVII (Winter, 1970), 44-61.

Woodward, C. Vann. "The Populist Heritage and the Intellectual," American Scholar, XXIX (Winter, 1959-1960), 55-72.

Wortman, Roy E. "Denver's Anti-Chinese Riot, 1880," Colorado Magazine, XLII (Fall, 1965), 276-91.

Books

Abbott, Carl. _Colorado: A History of the Centennial State_. Boulder: Colorado Associated University Press, 1976.

Aptheker, Herbert (ed.). _A Documentary History of the Negro People in the United States_. Vol. II. New York: The Citadel Press, 1951.

Argersinger, Peter H. _Populism and Politics: William Afred Peffer and the People's Party_. Lexington: University Press of Kentucky, 1974.

Arnett, Alex Mathews. _The Populist Movement in Georgia_. New York: Longmans, Green & Co., 1922.

Athearn, Robert G. _High Country Empire_. New York: McGraw-Hill Co., 1960.

_____. _Rebel of the Rockies: A History of the Denver and Rio Grande Western Railroad_. New Haven: Yale University Press, 1962.

_____. _The Coloradans_. Albuquerque: University of New Mexico Press, 1976.

_____. _Union Pacific Country_. Chicago: Rand McNally & Co., 1971.

Baker, James H., and Hafen, Leroy R. _History of Colorado_. Vol. III. Denver: Linderman Co., Inc., 1927.

Bancroft, Caroline. _Famous Aspen_. Boulder, Colorado: Johnson Publishing Co., 1960.

Barker, Charles Albro. _Henry George_. New York: Oxford University Press, 1955.

Barnard, Harry. _Eagle Forgotten, The Life of John Peter Altgeld_. Indianapolis and New York: Bobbs-Merrill Co., 1938.

Barrett, Don C. _The Greenbacks and Resumption of Specie Payments, 1862-1879_. Cambridge, Mass.: Harvard University Press, 1931.

Beals, Carleton. Porfirio Diaz, Dictator of Mexico.
    Philadelphia and London: J. B. Lippincott Co.,
    1932.

_____. The Great Revolt and Its Leaders: The
    History of Popular American Uprisings in the
    1890's. New York: Abelard-Schuman, Ltd., 1968.

Bell, Daniel (ed.). The New American Right. New York:
    Criterion Books, 1955.

Bell, John C. The Pilgrim and the Pioneer. Lincoln,
    Neb.: The International Publishing Assn., 1906.

Bellamy, Edward. Looking Backward. New York: Modern
    Library, 1951.

Bicha, Karel D. Western Populism: Studies in an
    Ambivalent Conservatism. Lawrence, Kansas:
    Coronado, 1976.

Blawis, Patricia Bell. Tijerina and the Land Grants:
    Mexican Americans in Struggle for Their Heritage.
    New York: International Publishers, 1971.

Boyer, Richard O., and Morais, Herbert M. Labor's
    Untold Story. New York: Cameron Associates,
    1955.

Brodhead, Michael J. Persevering Populist: The Life
    of Frank O. Doster. Reno, Nevada: University of
    Nevada Press, 1969.

Brown, Dee. Bury My Heart at Wounded Knee: An Indian
    History of the American West. New York: Bantam
    Books, Inc., 1972. (First published in 1971,
    New York: Holt, Rinehart and Winston, Inc.)

Brown, Joseph G. The History of Equal Suffrage in
    Colorado, 1868-1898. Denver: News Job Printing
    Co., 1898.

Brown, Ronald C. Hard-Rock Miners: The Intermountain
    West, 1860-1920. College Station: Texas A. & M.
    University Press, 1979.

Bryan, William Jennings, and Bryan, Mary Baird. The
    Memoirs of William Jennings Bryan. Philadelphia:
    The John C. Winston Co., 1925.

Buchanan, Joseph R. The Story of a Labor Agitator. New York: The Outlook Company, 1903.

Buck, Solon J. The Agrarian Crusade. New Haven: Yale University Press, 1920.

_____. The Granger Movement. Cambridge, Mass.: Harvard University Press, 1913.

Campbell, E. G. The Reorganization of the American Railroad System, 1893-1900. New York: Columbia Press, 1938.

Carstensen, Vernon (ed.). Farmer Discontent, 1865-1900. New York: John Wiley & Sons, Inc., 1974.

Clanton, O. Gene. Kansas Populism: Ideas and Men. Lawrence: University of Kansas Press, 1969.

Clinch, Thomas A. Urban Populism and Free Silver in Montana: A Narrative of Ideology in Political Action. Helena: University of Montana Press, 1970.

Coletta, Paolo E. William Jennings Bryan, I: Political Evangelist, 1860-1908. Lincoln: University of Nebraska Press, 1964.

Commager, Henry Steele. The American Mind. New Haven: Yale University Press, 1950.

Commons, John R. History of Labor in the United States. 4 Vols. New York: Macmillan Co., 1918-1935.

Cooper, Peter. Ideas for a Science of Good Government. New York: Trow's Printing & Bookbinding Co., 1883.

Copeland, Vince. Southern Populism and Black Labor. New York: World View Publishers, 1973.

Cowing, Cedric B. Populists, Plungers, and Progressives: A Social History of Stock and Commodity Speculation, 1890-1936. Princeton: Princeton University Press, 1965.

Curti, Merle. The Growth of American Thought. 2nd ed. New York: Harper, 1951.

David, Henry. The History of the Haymarket Affair. New York: Farrar & Rinehart, Inc., 1936.

205

Debs, Eugene V., and Others. Debs: His Life, Writings and Speeches. Chicago: Charles H. Kerr & Co., 1908.

_____. Writings and Speeches of Eugene V. Debs. New York: Hermitage Press, Inc., 1948.

DeSantis, Vincent P. The Shaping of Modern America: 1877-1916. St. Louis: Forum Press, 1977.

Destler, Chester McArthur. American Radicalism, 1865-1901. New London: Connecticut College, 1946.

_____. Henry Demarest Lloyd and the Empire of Reform. Philadelphia: University of Pennsylvania Press, 1963.

Dewey, David Rich. Financial History of the United States. New York: Longmans, Green & Co., 1918.

Dill, R. G. The Political Campaigns of Colorado. Denver: The Arapahoe Publishing Co., 1895.

Donnelly, Ignatius. (Walter Rideout, ed.). Caesar's Column. Cambridge, Mass.: Harvard University Press, 1960.

_____. Doctor Huguet. Chicago: F. J. Schulte & Co., 1891.

Dorsett, Lyle W. The Queen City: A History of Denver. Boulder, Colo.: Pruett Publishing Co., 1977.

Dulles, Foster Rhea. Labor in America. New York: Thomas Y. Crowell Co., 1949.

Dunning, N. A. (ed.). The Farmers' Alliance History and Agricultural Digest. Washington, D. C.: Alliance Publishing Co., 1891.

Durden, Robert F. The Climax of Populism: The Election of 1896. Lexington: University of Kentucky Press, 1965.

Ellis, Elmer. Henry Moore Teller, Defender of the West. Caldwell, Idaho: The Caxton Printers, Ltd., 1941.

Evans, Eldon Cobb. A History of the Australian Ballot System in the United States. Chicago: University of Chicago Press, 1917.

Falzone, Vincent J. Terence Powderly: Middle Class Reformer. Washington, D. C.: University Press of America, 1978.

Faulkner, Harold U., and Starr, Mark. Labor in America. New York: Harper & Brothers, 1949.

Faulkner, Harold U. Politics, Reform, and Expansion, 1890-1900. New York: Harper & Brothers, 1959.

Feitz, Leland. Cripple Creek Railroads. Denver: The Golden Bell Press, 1968.

Fine, Nathan. Labor and Farmer Parties in the United States, 1828-1928. New York: Rand School of Social Science, 1928.

Fite, Gilbert C. The Farmers' Frontier, 1865-1900. New York: Holt, Rinehart, and Winston, 1966.

Flexner, Eleanor. Century of Struggle: The Woman's Rights Movement in the United States. Cambridge, Mass.: Belknap Press of Harvard University Press, 1959.

Foner, Philip S., and Chamberlin, Brewster (eds.). Friedrich A. Sorge's Labor Movement in the United States. Westpoint, Conn.: Greenwood Press, 1977.

Foner, Philip S. History of the Labor Movement in the United States. Vols. I and II. New York: International Publishers, 1947 and 1955.

Fowler, Gene. Timber Line. New York: Ballantine Books, 1974. First published in 1933.

Franklin, John Hope. From Slavery to Freedom, A History of Negro Americans. 4th ed., revised. New York: Alfred A. Knopf, Inc., 1974.

Fritz, Percy Stanley. Colorado The Centennial State. New York: Prentice-Hall, Inc., 1941.

Gaither, Gerald H. Blacks and the Populist Revolt: Ballots and Bigotry in the "New South." Montgomery: University of Alabama Press, 1977.

Garraty, John A. The New Commonwealth, 1877-1890. New York: Harper & Row, 1968.

George, Henry. Progress and Poverty. New York: Robert Schalkenbach Foundation, 1953.

Ginger, Ray. Altgeld's America, The Lincoln Ideal Versus Changing Realities. New York: Funk & Wagnalls Co., 1958.

_____. The Bending Cross. New Brunswick: Rutgers University Press, 1949.

Glad, Paul W. McKinley, Bryan, and the People. Philadelphia and New York: J. B. Lippincott Co., 1964.

Glass, Mary Ellen. Silver and Politics in Nevada: 1892-1902. Reno: University of Nevada Press, 1969.

Goldberg, Harvey (ed.). American Radicals: Some Problems and Personalities. New York: Monthly Review Press, 1957.

Gompers, Samuel. Seventy Years of Life and Labor. Vols. I and II. New York: E. P. Dutton & Co., 1925.

Goodwyn, Lawrence. Democratic Promise: The Populist Movement in America. New York: Oxford University Press, 1976.

Green, James R. Grass-Roots Socialism in the Southwest, 1895-1943. Baton Rouge: Louisiana State University Press, 1978.

Greever, William S. The Bonanza West: The Story of the Western Mining Rushes, 1848-1900. Norman: University of Oklahoma Press, 1963.

Gronlund, Laurence. The Cooperative Commonwealth. Boston: Lee & Shepard Publishers, 1893.

Hafen, Leroy R. (ed.) Colorado and Its People. Vols. I and II. New York: Lewis Historical Publishing Co., 1948.

Hafen, Leroy R., and Hafen, Ann. The Colorado Story. Denver: The Old West Publishing Co., 1953.

Hair, William Ivy. Bourbonism and Agrarian Protest: Louisiana Politics, 1877-1900. Baton Rouge: Louisiana State University Press, 1969.

208

Hall, Frank. History of the State of Colorado. Four
    Vols. Chicago: Blakely Printing Co., 1889-1895.

Handlin, Oscar. Adventure in Freedom — Three Hundred
    Years of Jewish Life in America. New York:
    McGraw-Hill Book Co., 1954.

Handlin, Oscar, and Mary F. Danger in Discord.
    Origins of Anti-Semitism in the United States.
    New York and Chicago: Anti-Defamation League of
    B'nai B'rith, 1948.

Harvey, George. Henry Clay Frick — The Man. New York:
    Scribner, 1928.

Harvey, W. H. A Tale of Two Nations. Chicago: Coin
    Publishing Co., 1894.

_____. Coin's Financial School. Chicago: Coin
    Publishing Co., 1894.

_____. Coin's Financial School Up to Date. Chicago:
    Coin Publishing Co., 1895.

_____. The Patriots of America. Chicago: Coin
    Publishing Co., 1895.

Haynes, Fred Emory. James Baird Weaver. Iowa City:
    The State Historical Society of Iowa, 1919.

_____. Third Party Movements Since the Civil War,
    With Special Reference to Iowa. Iowa City: The
    State Historical Society of Iowa, 1916.

Hayter, Earl W. The Troubled Farmer, 1850-1900: Rural
    Adjustment to Industrialism. De Kalb: Northern
    Illinois University Press, 1968.

Haywood, William D. Bill Haywood's Book, the Auto-
    biography of William D. Haywood. New York:
    International Publishers, 1929.

Henderson, Charles W. Mining in Colorado — A History
    of Discovery, Development, and Production.
    Washington, D. C.: Government Printing Office,
    1926.

Hesseltine, William B. The Rise and Fall of Third
    Parties from Anti-Masonry to Wallace. Washington,
    D. C.: Public Affairs Press, 1948.

Hibben, Paxton. The Peerless Leader: William Jennings
    Bryan. New York: Farrar and Rinehart, Inc.,
    1929.

Hicks, John D. The Populist Revolt. Minneapolis:
    University of Minnesota Press, 1931.

Hofstadter, Richard. The Age of Reform. New York:
    Vintage Books, 1960. (First published in 1955:
    New York, Alfred A. Knopf.)

_____. The American Political Tradition and the
    Men Who Made It. New York: Alfred A. Knopf, 1948.

_____. Anti-Intellectualism in American Life. New
    York: Alfred A. Knopf, 1963.

Holbrook, Stewart H. The Story of American Railroads.
    New York: Crown Publishers, 1947.

_____. The Rocky Mountain Revolution. New York:
    Henry Holt & Co., 1956.

Hymowitz, Carol, and Weissman, Michaele. A History of
    Women in America. New York: Bantam Books, Inc.,
    1978.

Jelset, Christ. Money and Money Reforms. Chicago:
    Charles H. Kerr and Co., 1947.

Jensen, Vernon H. Heritage of Conflict: Labor Rela-
    tions in the Nonferrous Metals Industry Up to
    1930. Ithaca, N. Y.: Cornell University Press,
    1950.

Jones, Stanley L. The Presidential Election of 1896.
    Madison: University of Wisconsin Press, 1964.

Jones, Maldwyn Allen. American Immigration. Chicago:
    University of Chicago Press, 1960. .

Johnson, Oakley C. Marxism in United States History
    Before the Russian Revolution (1876-1917). New
    York: Humanities Press, 1974.

Josephson, Matthew. The Politicos 1865-1896. New
    York: Harcourt, Brace & Co., 1934.

_____. The Robber Barons. New York: Harcourt,
    Brace, & Co., 1934.

Karsner, David. *Silver Dollar: The Story of the Tabors*. New York: Crown Publishers, 1932.

Kinzer, Donald L. *An Episode in Anti-Catholicism: The American Protective Association*. Seattle: University of Washington Press, 1964.

Kipnis, Ira. *The American Socialist Movement: 1897-1912*. New York: Monthly Review Press, 1972. (First published in 1952: New York, Columbia University Press.)

Kuhn, Henry, and Johnson, Olive M. *The Socialist Labor Party During Four Decades, 1890-1930*. New York: New York Labor News Co., 1931.

LaGumina, Salvatore J. (ed.) *"WOP!" — A Documentary History of Anti-Italian Discrimination in the United States*. San Francisco: Straight Arrow Books, 1973.

Landman, Solomon, and Efron, Benjamin. *Story Without End: An Informal History of the Jewish People*. New York: Henry Holt & Co., 1949.

Larrabee, William. *The Railroad Question*. 10th ed. Chicago: Schulte Publishing Co., 1898.

Larson, Robert W. *New Mexico Populism: A Study of Radical Protest in a Western Territory*. Boulder: Colorado Associated University Press, 1974.

Lavender, David. *The Rockies*. New York: Harper and Row, 1968.

Lee, Mabel Barbee. *Cripple Creek Days*. Garden City, N. Y.: Doubleday & Co., 1958.

Leech, Margaret. *In the Days of McKinley*. New York: Harper & Brothers, 1959.

Lindsey, Almont. *The Pullman Strike*. Phoenix, ed. Chicago: University of Chicago Press, 1964.

Lingenfelter, Richard E. *The Hardrock Miners: A History of the Mining Labor Movement in the American West, 1864-1893*. Berkeley: University of California Press, 1974.

211

Lloyd, Caro. Henry Demarest Lloyd. 2 Vols. New York:
G. P. Putnam's Sons, 1912.

Lloyd, Henry Demarest. Lords of Industry. New York
and London: G. P. Putnam's Sons, 1910.

_____. Wealth Against Commonwealth. New York and
London: Harper & Brothers, 1902.

Logan, Rayford W. The Betrayal of the Negro from
Rutherford B. Hayes to Woodrow Wilson. New York:
Collier Books, 1965. (First published in 1954 as
The Negro in American Life and Thought: The Nadir,
1877-1901. New York: Macmillan Co.)

Lundberg, Ferdinand. America's Sixty Families. New
York: Citadel Press, 1960. (First published in
1937: New York, Vanguard Press.)

Mandel, Bernard. Samuel Gompers: A Biography. Yellow
Springs: Antioch Press, 1963.

Marshall, James. Santa Fe: The Railroad That Built
an Empire. New York: Random House, 1945.

Martin, Roscoe C. The People's Party in Texas. Austin:
University of Texas Press, 1970. (First published
in 1933 as University of Texas Bulletin No. 3308.)

McMath, Jr., Robert C. Populist Vanguard: A History
of the Southern Farmers' Alliance. Chapel Hill:
University of North Carolina Press, 1975.

McWilliams, Carey. A Mask for Privilege: Anti-
Semitism in America. Boston: Little, Brown &
Co., 1948.

_____. North from Mexico: The Spanish-Speaking
People of the United States. Philadelphia and
New York: J. B. Lippincott Co., 1949.

Merrill, Horace Samuel. Bourbon Leader: Grover Cleveland and the Democratic Party. Boston: Little,
Brown and Co., 1957.

Mitchell, Wesley C. A History of the Greenbacks.
Chicago: University of Chicago Press, 1903.

Morgan, Arthur E. Edward Bellamy. New York: Columbia
University Press, 1944.

Morgan, H. Wayne. From Hayes to McKinley: National Party Politics, 1877-1896. Syracuse, N. Y.: Syracuse University Press, 1969.

_____. William McKinley and His America. Syracuse: N. Y.: Syracuse University Press, 1963.

Morgan, W. Scott. History of the Wheel and Alliance, and the Impending Revolution. Fort Scott, Kansas: J. H. Rice & Sons, 1889.

Myers, Gustavus. History of Bigotry in the United States. Ed. with addenda by Henry M. Christman. New York: Capricorn Books, 1960.

_____. History of the Great American Fortunes. New York: Random House, Inc., 1936.

National American Woman Suffrage Association. Victory: How Women Won It. New York: H. W. Wilson, Co., 1940.

Nevins, Allan. Grover Cleveland: A Study in Courage. New York: Dodd, Mead, 1932.

Noblin, Stuart. Leonidas LaFayette Polk: Agrarian Crusader. Chapel Hill: University of North Carolina Press, 1949.

Norden, D. Sven. Rich Harvest: A History of the Grange, 1867-1900. Jackson: University Press of Mississippi, 1974.

Nugent, Walter T. K. From Centennial to World War: American Society, 1876-1917. Indianapolis: Bobbs-Merrill, 1977.

_____. Money and American Society, 1865-1880. New York: Free Press, 1968.

_____. The Tolerant Populists. Chicago: University of Chicago Press, 1963.

Osgood, Ernest S. The Day of the Cattleman. Phoenix ed. Chicago: University of Chicago Press, 1957.

Palmer, Bruce. "Man Over Money": The Southern Populist Critique of American Capitalism. Chapel Hill: University of North Carolina Press, 1980.

213

Parrington, Vernon Louis. Main Currents in American Thought. New York: Harcourt, Brace & Co., 1927.

Parsons, Stanley B. The Populist Context: Rural Versus Urban Power on a Great Plains Frontier. Westport, Conn.: Greenwood Press, 1973.

Paul, Rodman W. Mining Frontiers of the Far West, 1848-1880. New York: Holt, Rinehart & Winston, 1963.

Peffer, William A. The Farmer's Side. New York: D. Appleton & Co., 1891.

Perkin, Robert L. The First Hundred Years. Garden City, N. Y.: Doubleday & Co., 1959.

Petersen, Arnold. Daniel DeLeon, Social Architect. Vols. I and II. New York: New York Labor News Co., 1941.

Peterson, Merrill D. The Jefferson Image in the American Mind. New York: Oxford University Press, 1962.

Pollack, Norman (ed.). The Populist Mind. Indianapolis and New York: Bobbs-Merrill Co., 1967.

Pollack, Norman. The Populist Response to Industrial America. Cambridge, Mass.: Harvard University Press, 1962.

Quint, Howard H. The Forging of American Socialism: Origins of the Modern Movement. Columbia: University of South Carolina Press, 1953.

Rayback, Joseph G. A History of American Labor. New York: Macmillan Co., 1959.

Reeve, Carl. The Life and Times of Daniel DeLeon. New York: Humanities Press, 1972.

Ridge, Martin. Ignatius Donnelly: The Portrait of a Politician. Chicago: University of Chicago Press, 1962.

Riegel, Robert E. The Story of the Western Railroads. New York: Macmillan Co., 1926.

Robbins, Roy M. Our Landed Heritage: The Public Domain 1776-1936. Lincoln: University of Nebraska Press, 1962.

Rochester, Anna. The Populist Movement in the United
    States. New York: International Publishers,
    1943.

Seligson, Harry, and Bardwell, George E. Labor-
    Management Relations in Colorado. Denver: Sage
    Books, 1961.

Shannon, Fred A. American Farmers' Movements. Anvil
    ed. Princeton, N. J.: D. Van Nostrand Co., Inc.,
    1957.

_____. The Farmer's Last Frontier: Agriculture,
    1860-1897. Vol. V of The Economic History of the
    United States. New York: Farrar & Rinehart, Inc.,
    1945.

Simkins, Francis B. Pitchfork Ben Tillman, South
    Carolinian. Baton Rouge: Louisiana State Univer-
    sity Press, 1944.

Smiley, Jerome C. History of Denver. Denver: Denver
    Times, 1901.

Smith, Duane A. Horace Tabor: His Life and the Legend.
    Boulder: Colorado Associated University Press,
    1973.

_____. Rocky Mountain Mining Camps: The Urban
    Frontier. Bloomington: Indiana University Press,
    967.

Sprague, Marshall. Colorado: A Bicentennial History.
    New York: W. W. Norton & Co., 1976.

_____. Money Mountain: The Story of Cripple Creek
    Gold. Boston: Little, Brown & Co., 1953.

Stanton, Elizabeth Cady, Anthony, Susan B., and Gage,
    Matilda Joslyn. History of Woman Suffrage, 1848-
    1900. Vol. III, Rochester, N. Y.: Charles Mann
    Printing Co., 1886. Vol. IV, Indianapolis: Hol-
    lenbeck Press, 1902.

Stedman, Murray S., Jr., and Stedman, Susan W.
    Discontent at the Polls: A Study of Farmer and
    Labor Parties, 1827-1948. New York: Columbia
    University Press, 1950.

215

Steinel, Alwin T. History of Agriculture in Colorado, 1858-1926. Fort Collins, Colo.: State Agricultural College, 1926.

Stone, Wilbur Fisk. History of Colorado. Vol. I. Chicago: The S. J. Clarke Publishing Co., 1918.

Taft, Philip. Organized Labor in American History. New York: Harper & Row, 1964.

Taylor, Ralph C. Colorado South of the Border. Denver: Sage Books, 1963.

Tindall, George B. (ed.) A Populist Reader: Selections from the Works of American Populist Leaders. New York: Harper & Row, 1966.

Tyler, Alice Felt. Freedom's Ferment. Minneapolis: University of Minnesota Press, 1944.

Ubbelohde, Carl W., Benson, Maxine, and Smith, Duane A. A Colorado History. Boulder, Colo.: Pruett Publishing Co., 1976.

Viereck, Peter. The Unadjusted Man: A New Hero for Americans: Reflections of the Distinction Between Conforming and Conserving. Boston: Beacon Press, 1956.

Ware, Norman J. The Labor Movement in the United States, 1860-1895. New York: D. Appleton & Co., 1929.

Watson, Thomas E. The Life and Times of Thomas Jefferson. New York: D. Appleton & Co., 1903.

Weaver, James B. A Call to Action. Des Moines: Iowa Printing Co., 1892.

Webb, Walter Prescott. The Great Plains. Boston: Ginn & Co., 1931.

Weinstein, Allen. Prelude to Populism — Origins of the Silver Issue, 1867-1878. New Haven: Yale University Press, 1970.

Williams, William Appleman. The Contours of American History. Cleveland and New York: The World Publishing Co., 1961.

Wisner, Edward. Cash vs. Coin, An Answer to "Coin's
     Financial School". Chicago: Charles N. Kerr &
     Co., 1895.

Woodward, C. Vann. Origins of the New South. Baton
     Rouge: Louisiana State University Press, 1951.

_____. The Strange Career of Jim Crow. New York:
     Oxford University Press, 1955.

_____. Tom Watson, Agrarian Rebel. New York:
     Rinehart & Co., 1938.

Wright, James E. The Politics of Populism: Dissent
     in Colorado. New Haven: Yale University Press,
     1974.

Wu, Cheng-Tsu (ed.). "CHINK" — A Documentary History
     of Anti-Chinese Prejudice in America. New York:
     World Publishing Co., 1972.

Youngdale, James M. Populism: A Psychohistorical
     Perspective. New York: Kennikat Press, 1975.

217

INDEX

220

Faulkner, Harold U., 44

Felker, William B., 60

Field, James G., 4, 12, 134, 142

Fish, A. C., 19

Flanders, L. H., 19

Florence and Cripple Creek Railroad, 84

Ford, Henry, 122

Fort Collins Courier, 14

Foster, Benjamin F., 124

Franklin, Benjamin, 47

Fremont, John C., 8

French Revolution, 155

Frick, Henry Clay, 74

Frost, Albert, 19-20

Gambling, 108-10

Garner, William, 64

George, Henry, 27, 69-71

Gompers, Samuel, 93, 139

Goodwyn, Lawrence, 154

Goodykoontz, Floyd M., 19

Gordon, F. G. R., 51

Grange, 1, 3-4, 58

"Granger" laws, 58

Great Britain, 70, 129-30

Great Western Sugar Co., 45

Greeley, Horace, 7

Greeley Sun, 84-85

Greenback Party (Greenback - Labor Party), 11, 25-26

Greenbackism, 1, 3-4, 11, 24-29

Gresham, Walter Q., 134

Gresham's law, 27

Hagerman, J. J., 45, 86-88

Hamill, W. A., 60-61

Handlin, Oscar, 122-23, 157

Harper's Weekly, 33

Harris, Arthur C., 19

Harris, W. A., 4

Harrison, Benjamin, 74, 75, 151

Harvey, William H. "Coin," 28, 91

Hearst, George F., 135

Heartz, Evangeline, 106

Heath, J. T., 100

Hicks, John D., 151-53

Hill, Nathaniel P., 45

Hindman, Matilda, 98

Hofstadter, Richard, 122-23, 157

227

228

ABOUT THE AUTHOR

Dr. John R. Morris has been a professor of history at Eastern New Mexico University in Portales since 1967. A native of Colorado, he attended public schools in Trinidad, Colorado, and earned the B. A. and Ph.D. degrees from the University of Colorado and the M. A. degree from the University of Chicago. He has taught at Western State in Colorado, Kearney State in Nebraska, Mesa College in Arizona, Northeastern State in Oklahoma, and the University of Dayton. The author of several book reviews and articles dealing with Davis H. Waite, Colorado labor history, baseball history, and contemporary issues, he is currently engaged in a study of the Western labor leader Joseph Buchanan. His main teaching interests are the Populist-Progressive era and U. S. social and intellectual history, but he has taught a variety of courses in U. S. history as well as courses in English, Asian, and African history. His wife, Mary Lee, is a catalog librarian and an instructor in library science at Eastern New Mexico University.